Male Art Form

by

artist
stephen **moody**

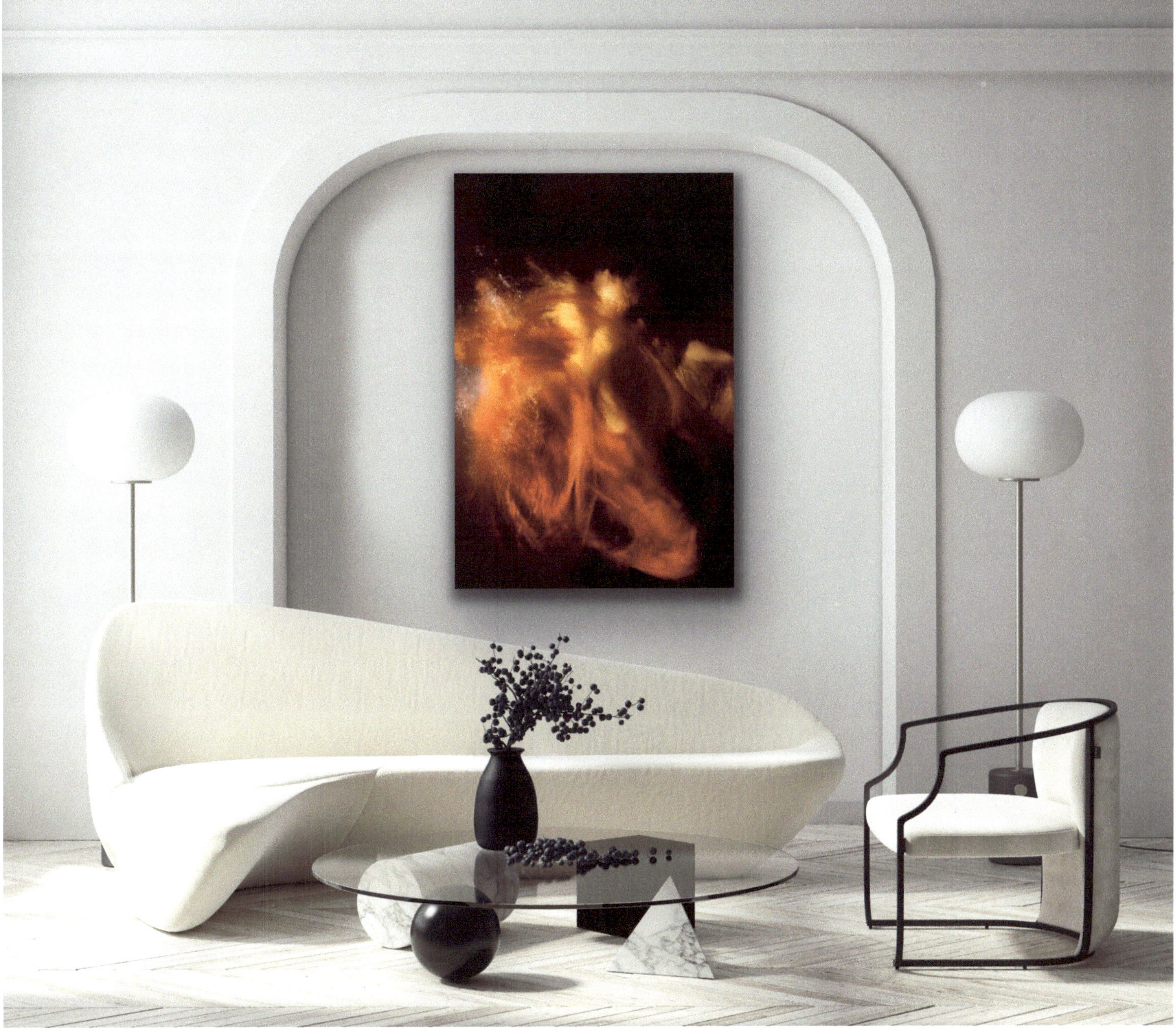

Moody's artwork doesn't hang on your wall, it lives in your room.

ISBN-: 979-8-9884697-1-1

Cover Design & Artwork by: Stephen Moody
Publisher: Stephen Moody Ltd.
Library of Congress
Control Number:
Printed in the United States of America

For Mia, My Muse, My Inspiration.

A big 'Thank You' to Edgar Tomines for all of the countless hours in the pool modeling for this book.

Foreword

As I sit here, penning these words that carry the weight of my artistic journey, I am humbled by the boundless imagination of those who have witnessed my creations. Overwhelmed by the myriad interpretations and the kaleidoscope of emotions that my artwork evokes; I am reminded of the extraordinary power of art to transcend the boundaries of perception.

Within the pages of this book, I invite you to explore a world that defies definition—a world where imagery possesses the chameleon-like ability to transcend the confines of a mere frame. They are not meant to hang passively on a wall, but rather to breathe life into the spaces they inhabit, dancing and shifting with the light that bathes them throughout the day. Each person who beholds them will witness a unique story, discover hidden nuances, and embark on a personal voyage of self-discovery.

From the tender age of six, when my father placed that Kodak 126 Instamatic camera in my hands, I embarked on a lifelong odyssey through the realm of visual storytelling. Innocently, I wasted countless rolls of film, capturing everything my eyes could behold. Little did I know that this seemingly playful endeavor would unfold into a profound calling, shaping my destiny.

Photography became an inseparable part of my being. Guided by the wisdom and support of local professionals, I delved into the depths of this art form, transforming a humble family bathroom into my very own darkroom - a sanctuary where the alchemy of creation unfolded. Through the lens, I captured the raw energy of local rock bands and the essence of corporate entities, giving voice to their stories with every click.

In my twenties, I journeyed further into uncharted territories, opening a boudoir studio in the heart of Salt Lake City. Provocatively and intimately, I immortalized the beauty and sensuality of countless women, preserving their essence for themselves and sometimes for their loved ones. Yet, even amidst this creative exploration, I sensed a yearning for something more—a longing to transcend boundaries, to unlock the true depth of my artistic vision.

It was at a state fair, surrounded by captivating images of nudes immersed in the depths of a pool, that destiny's hand reached out to guide me. In my mind's eye, I saw the elusive essence of what I wanted to create—an artistic masterpiece that would transcend the boundaries of the ordinary. But I lacked the pool that would birth my next phase of artistic evolution.

As fate would have it, the Universe led me to the enchanting landscapes of Scottsdale, Arizona, in the early 2000's. Here, amidst the sun-kissed canvas of the desert, I embarked on a tireless exploration of underwater photography, tirelessly experimenting with different cameras and housings, seeking to extract a unique vision that defied replication. Yet, it eluded me like a distant mirage shimmering on the horizon.

It was during this period of seeking that a serendipitous encounter with an Australian shaman unfolded, forever altering the trajectory of my artistic path. In the sacred space of her wisdom, she offered to unblock the creative reservoir that lay buried deep within me. Together, we e mbarked on a transformative journey, weaving the threads of ancient wisdom and contemporary artistry.

Through three intense sessions, the shaman unraveled the knots that had restrained my artistic potential. The last session left me exhausted, but as I surrendered to sleep, I could feel the invisible barriers crumbling, paving the way for the revelation that awaited me at the dawn of a new day.

With the first light, I awoke with a clarity that resonated deep within my being. Akin to an artist possessed, I roused my girlfriend from her slumber and whispered, "It's time. I know how to do it." In that moment, we plunged into the watery depths, where the realm of my envisioned imagery unfolded before our very eyes.

Gratitude wells within me as I reflect upon the incredible individuals who have graced my lens throughout the years, sharing their vulnerability and strength. I am indebted to the first gallery in Old Town Scottsdale that dared to showcase my work back in 2003—an act of faith that would forever alter the course of my artistic destiny. Opening night, where three large canvases found new homes, heralded a sign from the Universe, propelling me forward on this extraordinary path.

And now, dear reader, as you embark on the journey within these pages, I invite you to immerse yourself in the provocative, sensual, and abstract world that unfolds before you. Through the interplay of movement, color, and vibration, I strive to evoke emotions that transcend the mundane, to stir something deep within your soul.

Within these chapters, you will encounter three distinct realms—Abstract, Angels & Demons, and l'Homme—each an invitation to delve into the rich tapestry of the male art form. From the intangible forms of the abstract to the celestial dance of angels and demons, and finally, to the celebration of masculine strength and beauty, my art seeks to intertwine reality and dreamscape, inviting you to discover the extraordinary in the ordinary.

As you journey through these captivating images, I urge you to abandon preconceived notions and surrender to the allure of the unknown. Allow the vibrations of art to awaken dormant emotions within you, to kindle the fires of imagination, and to reveal the depths of the male art form in all its boldness and vulnerability.

Embrace the beauty that lies in the contours of defined muscles—the eight-pack, the hard pecs, the tight butt, the deep 'V' that adorns the upper body, the energetic arms, and the masculine legs. But know that these images are merely a gateway to a realm that extends far beyond physicality—a realm that resonates with the pulsating energy of life itself.

In this book, I offer you a glimpse into the enigmatic world I have traversed, where perception shapeshifts, and art lives and breathes within the spaces we occupy. May these pages ignite a fire within your soul, a fire that will forever illuminate your journey through the intricate tapestry of life.

Welcome, dear reader, to the evocative masterpiece that is "Male Art Form" — the coffee-table book that seeks to awaken your senses and inspire your spirit.

- Stephen Moody

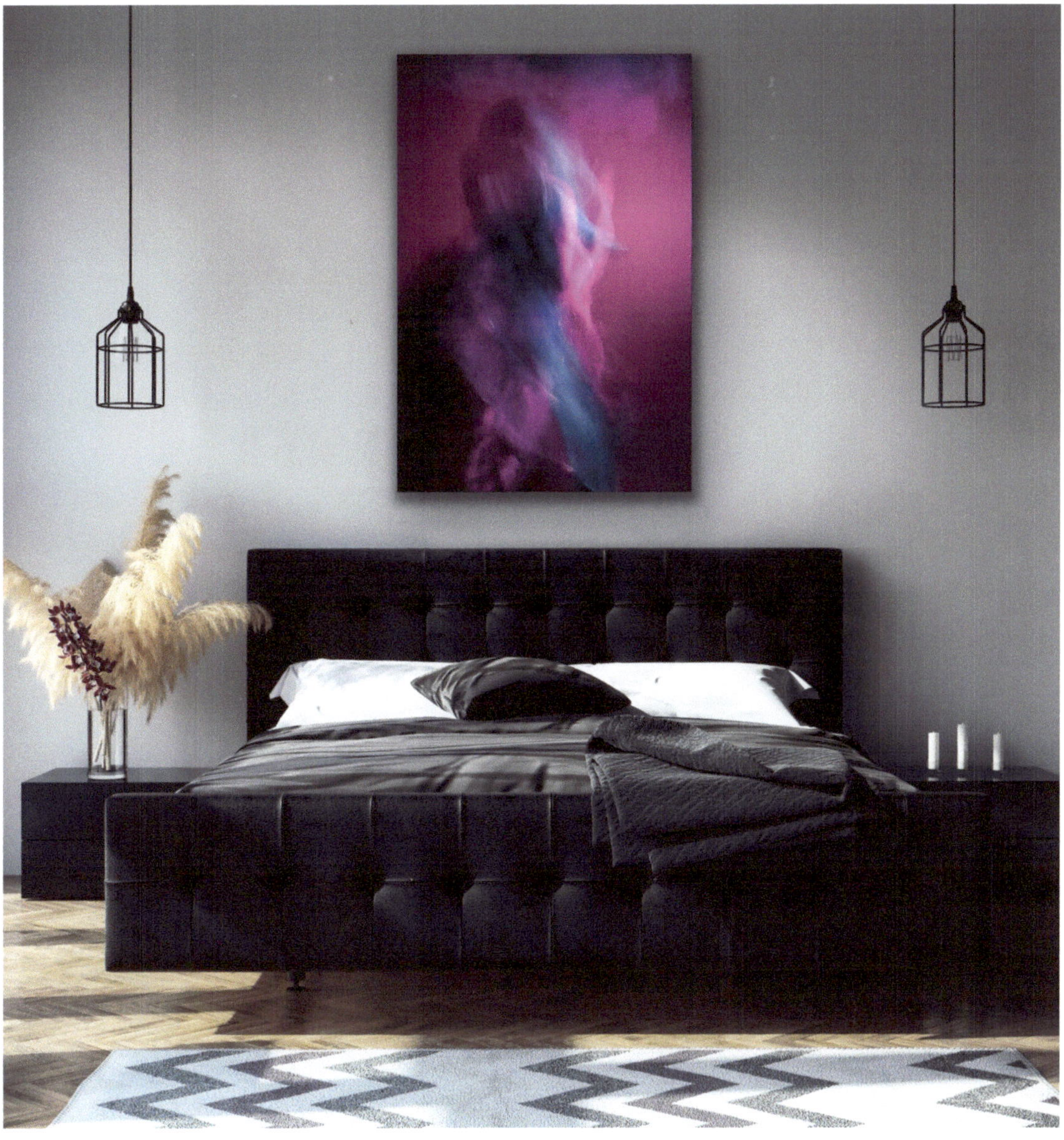

Abstract

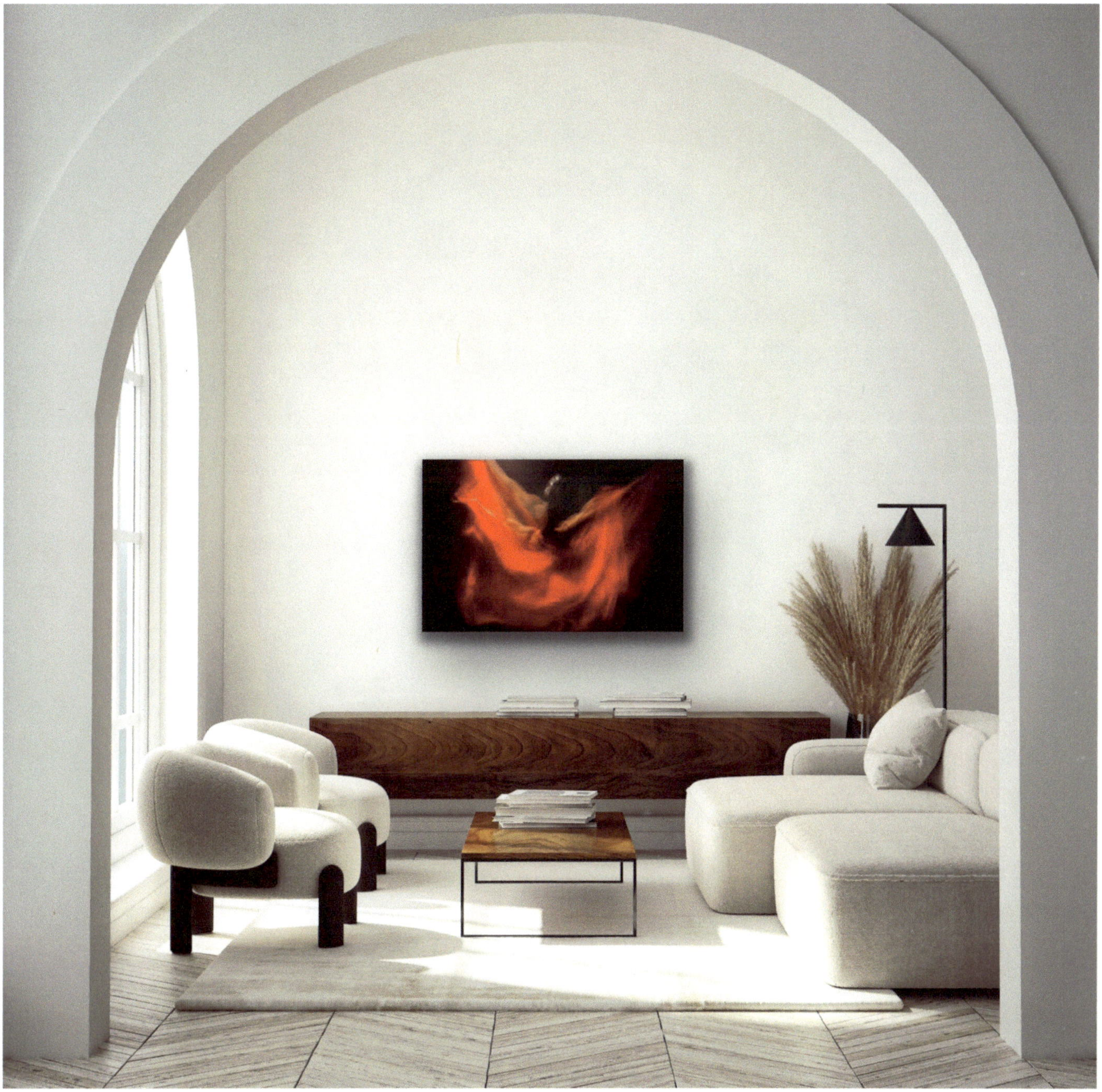

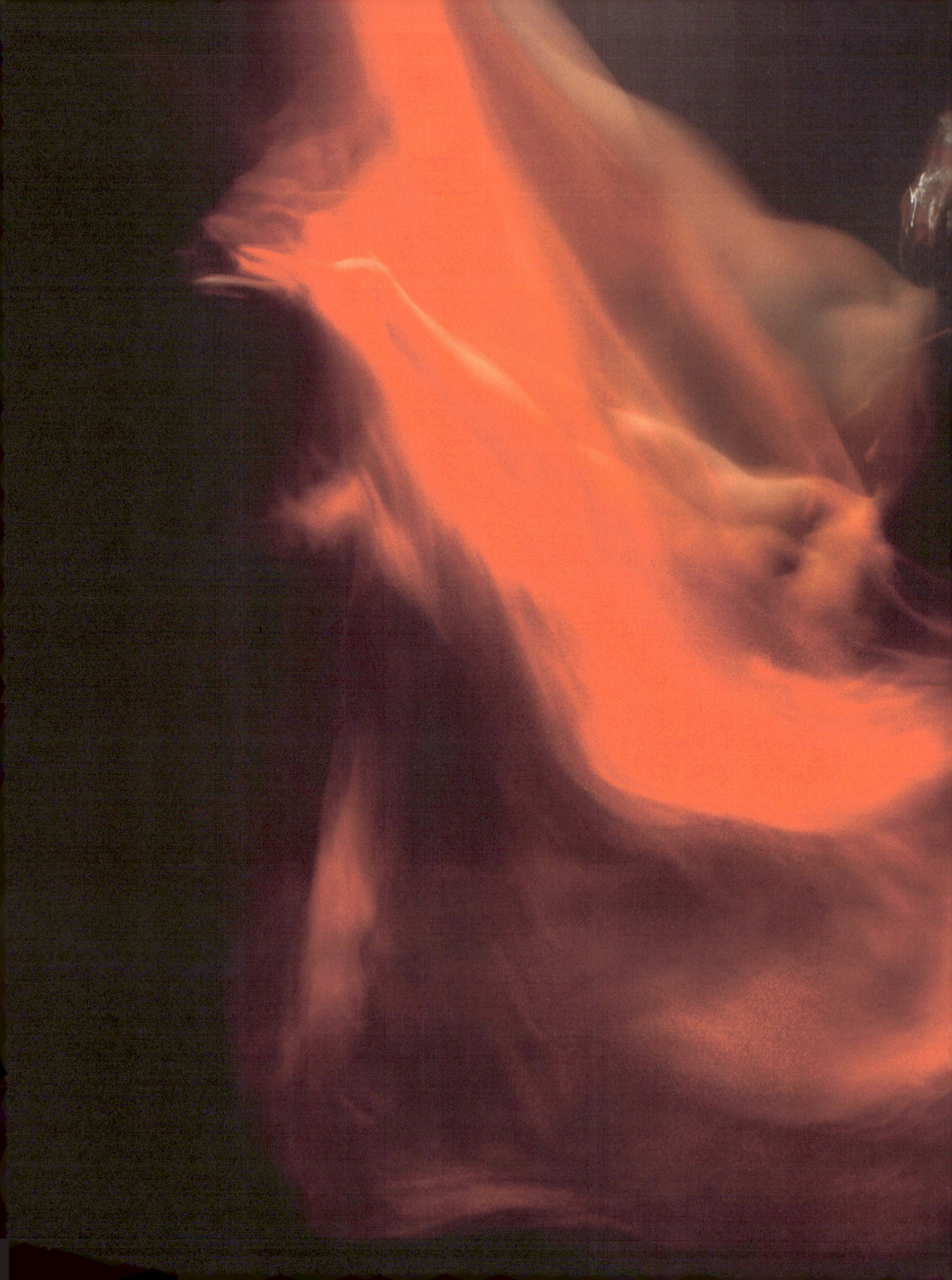

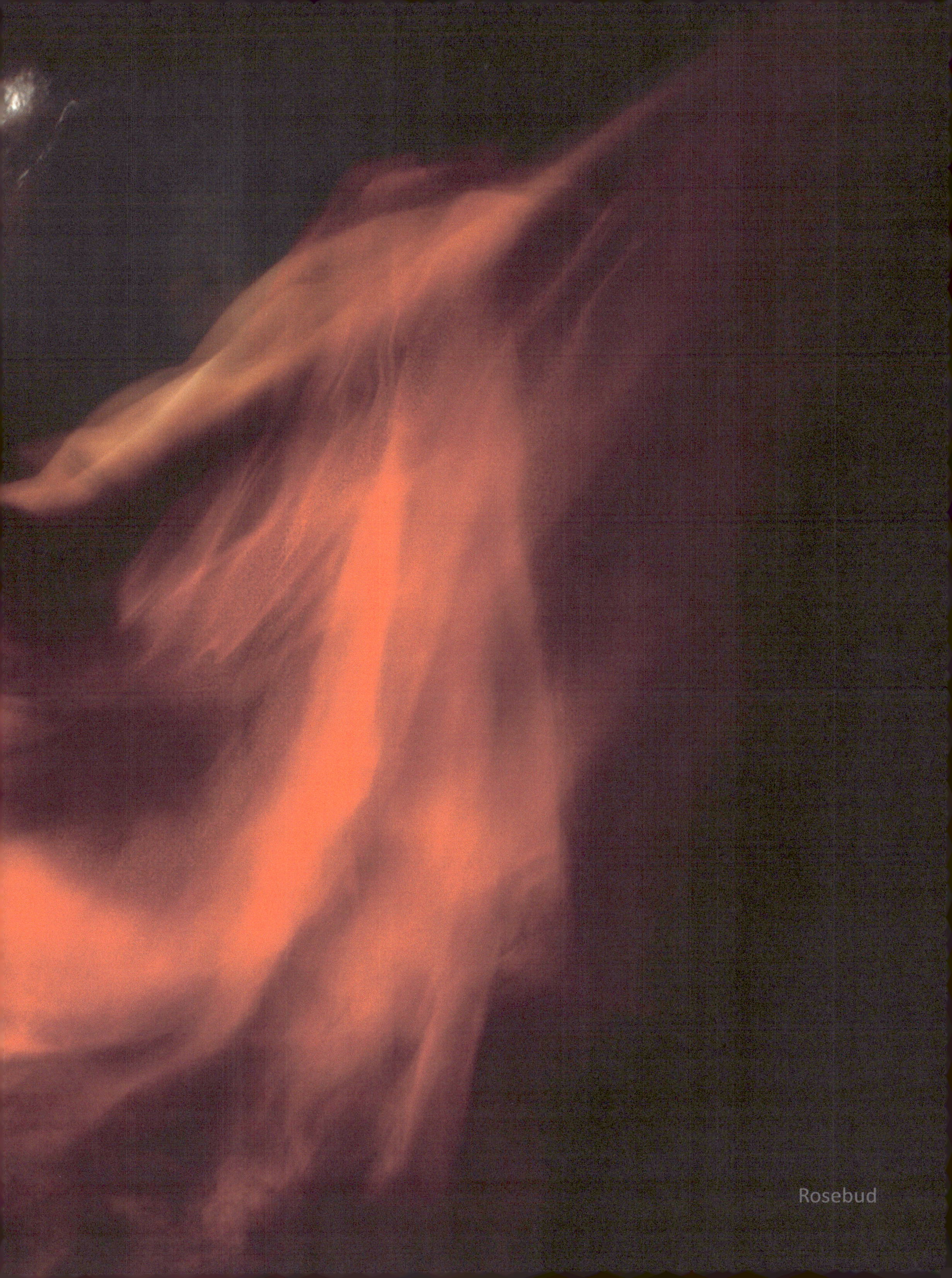

Rosebud

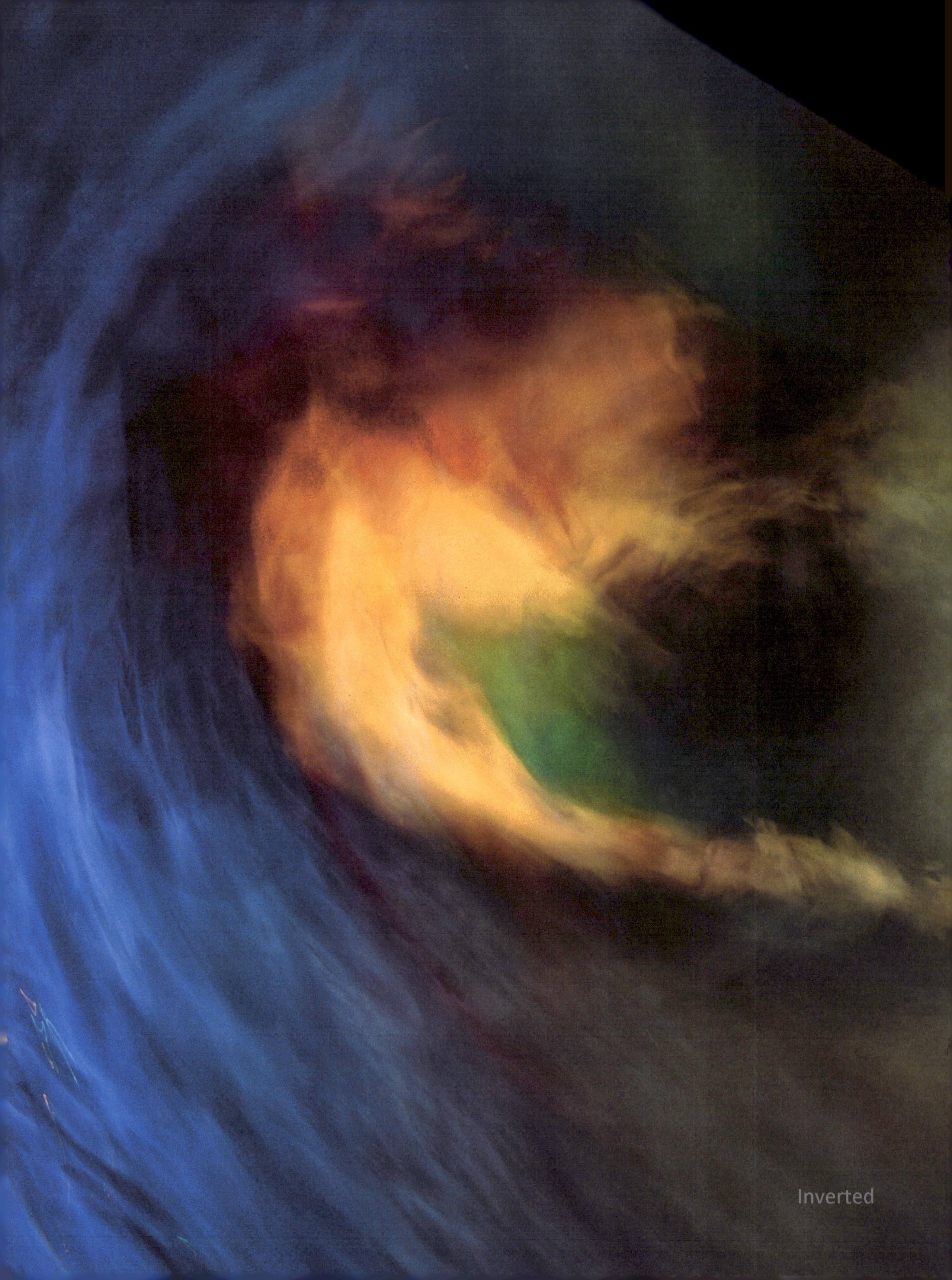

Inverted

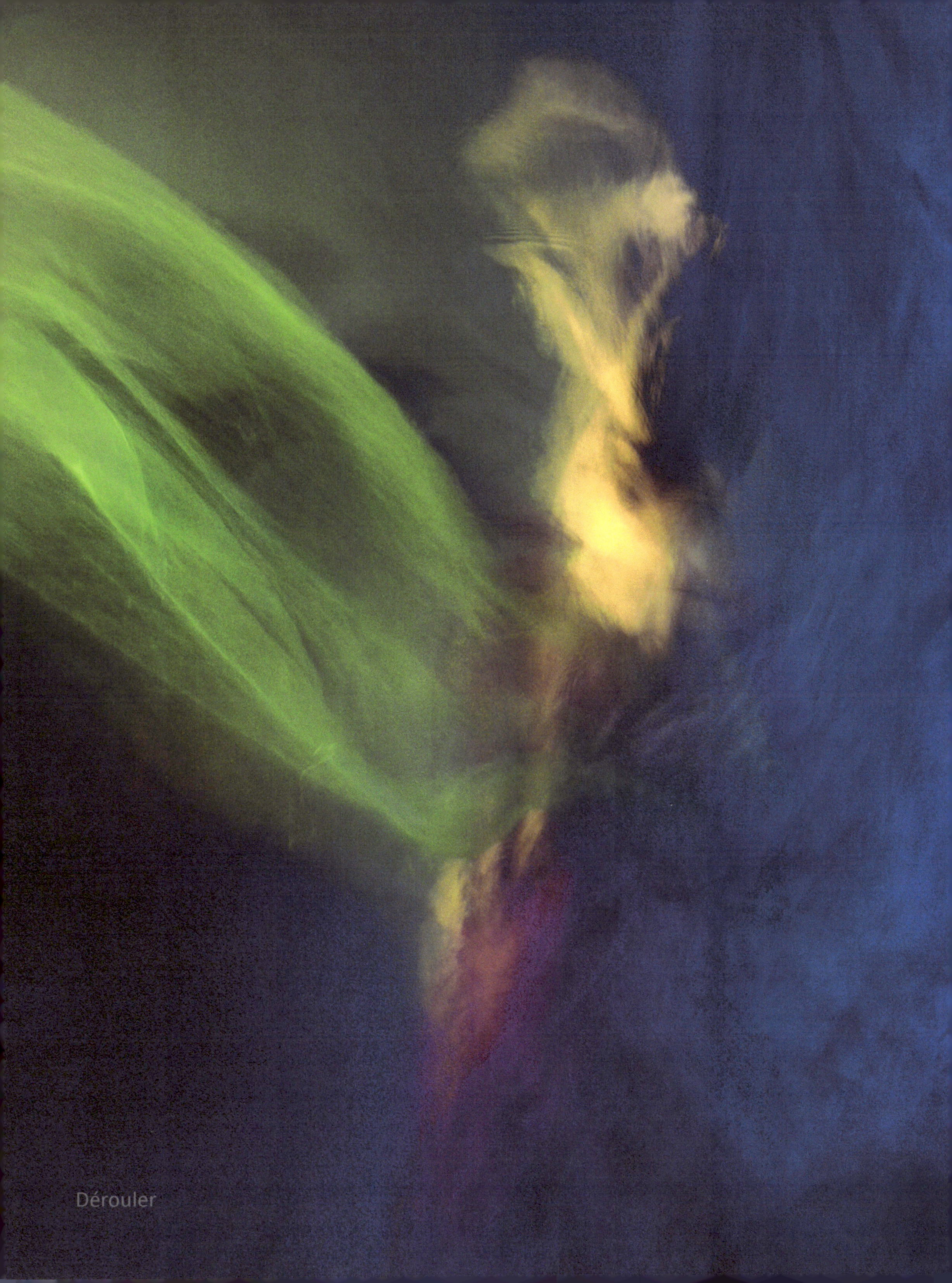

Dérouler

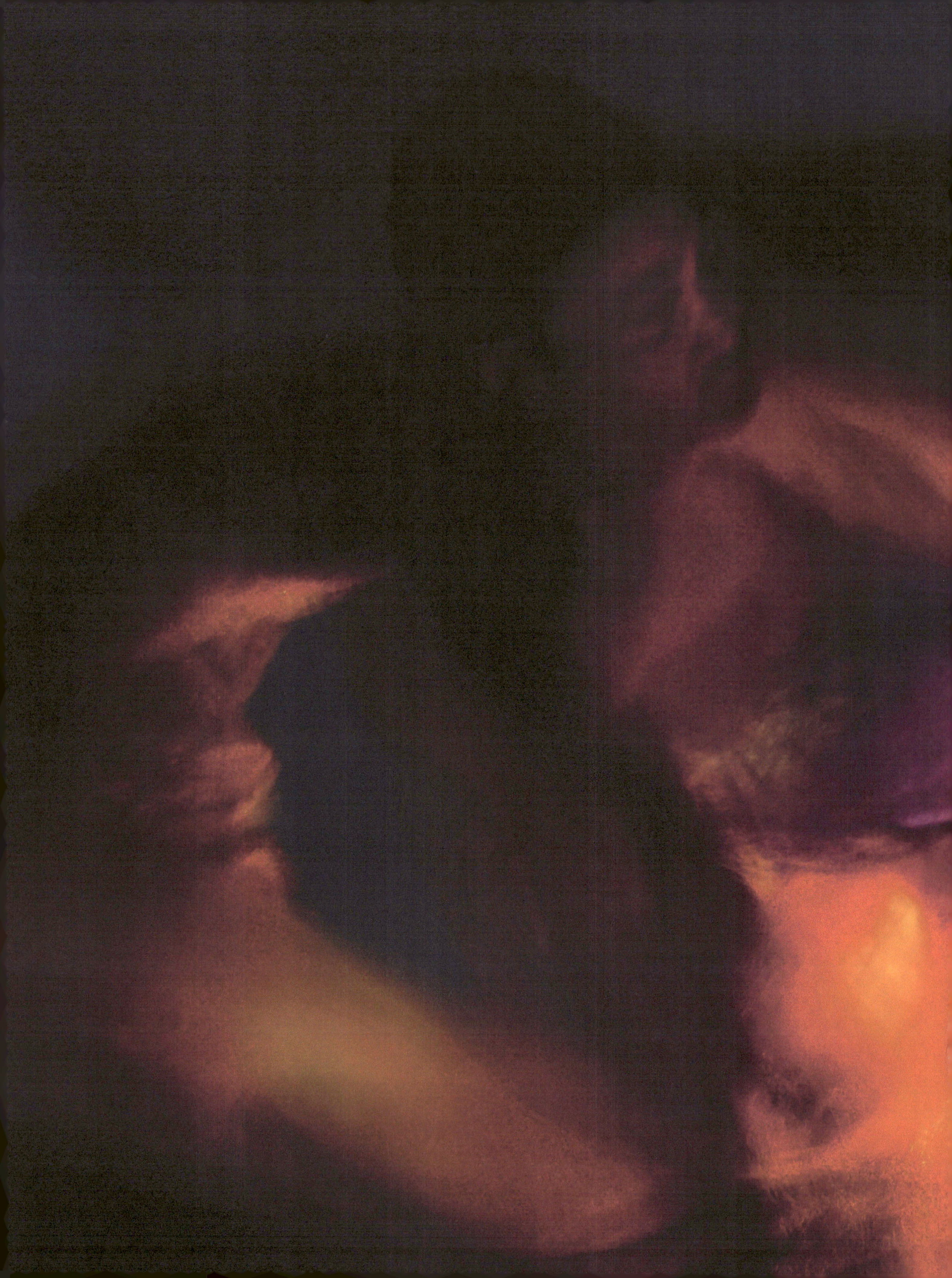

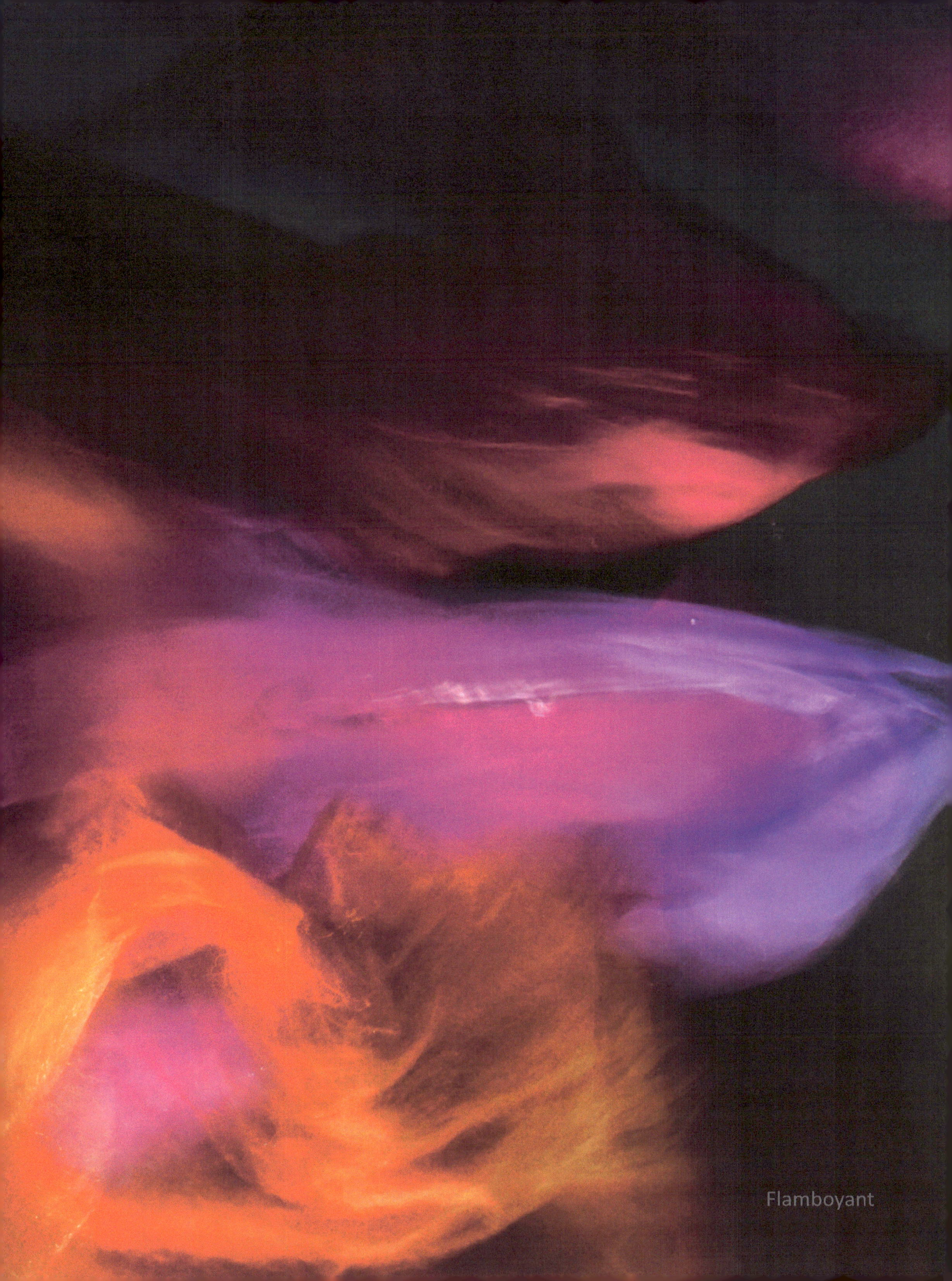

Flamboyant

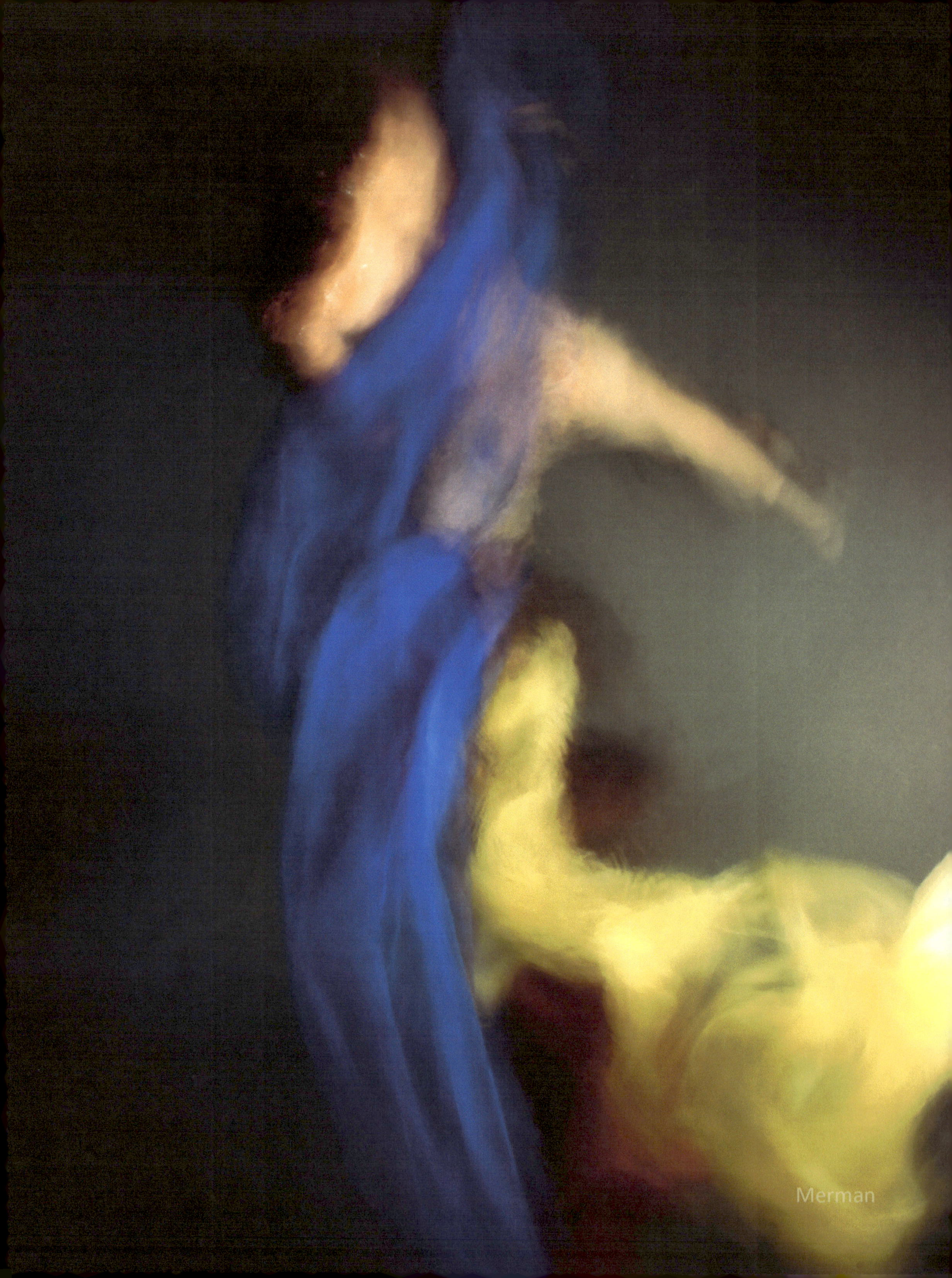
Merman

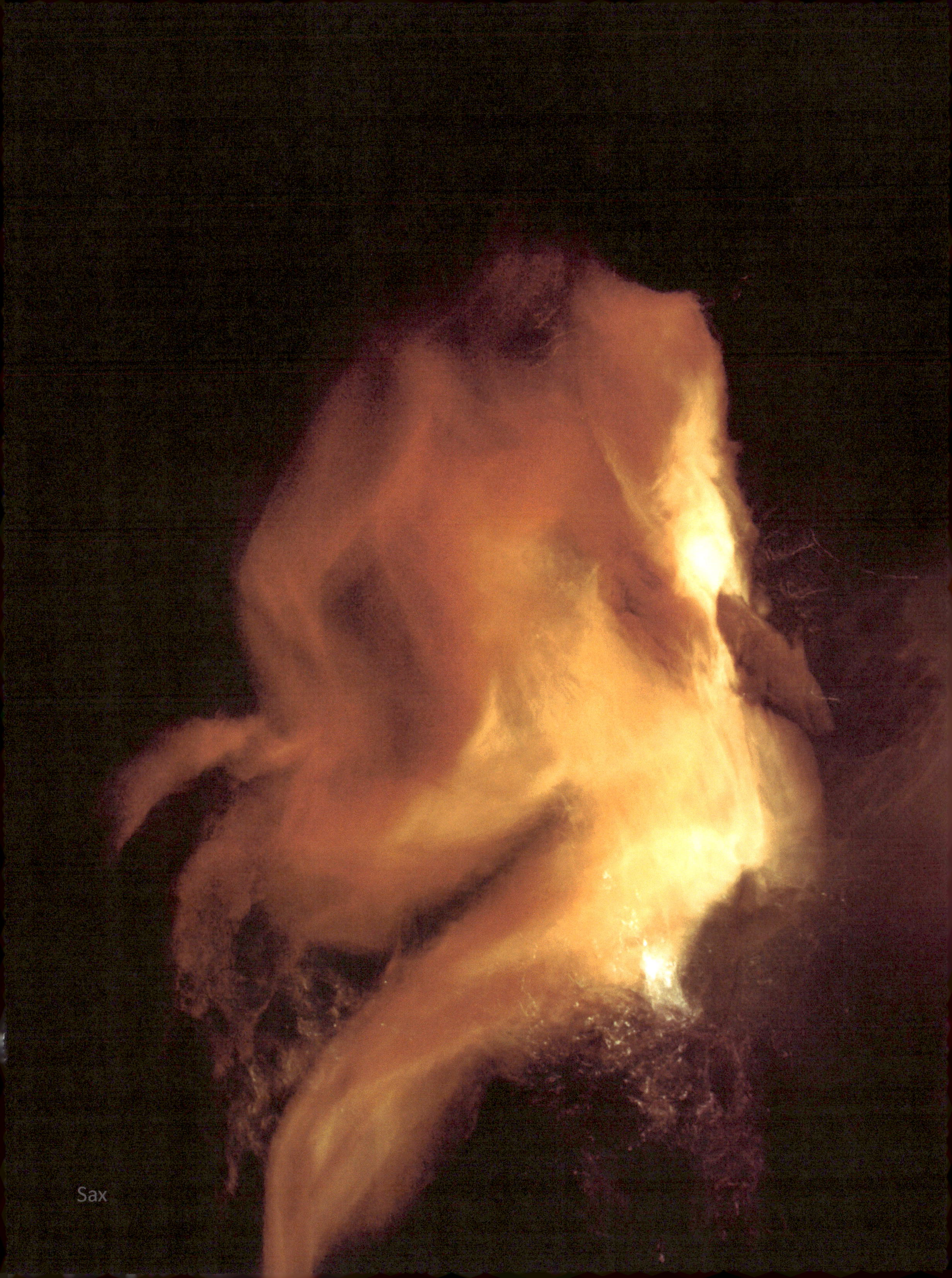

Sax

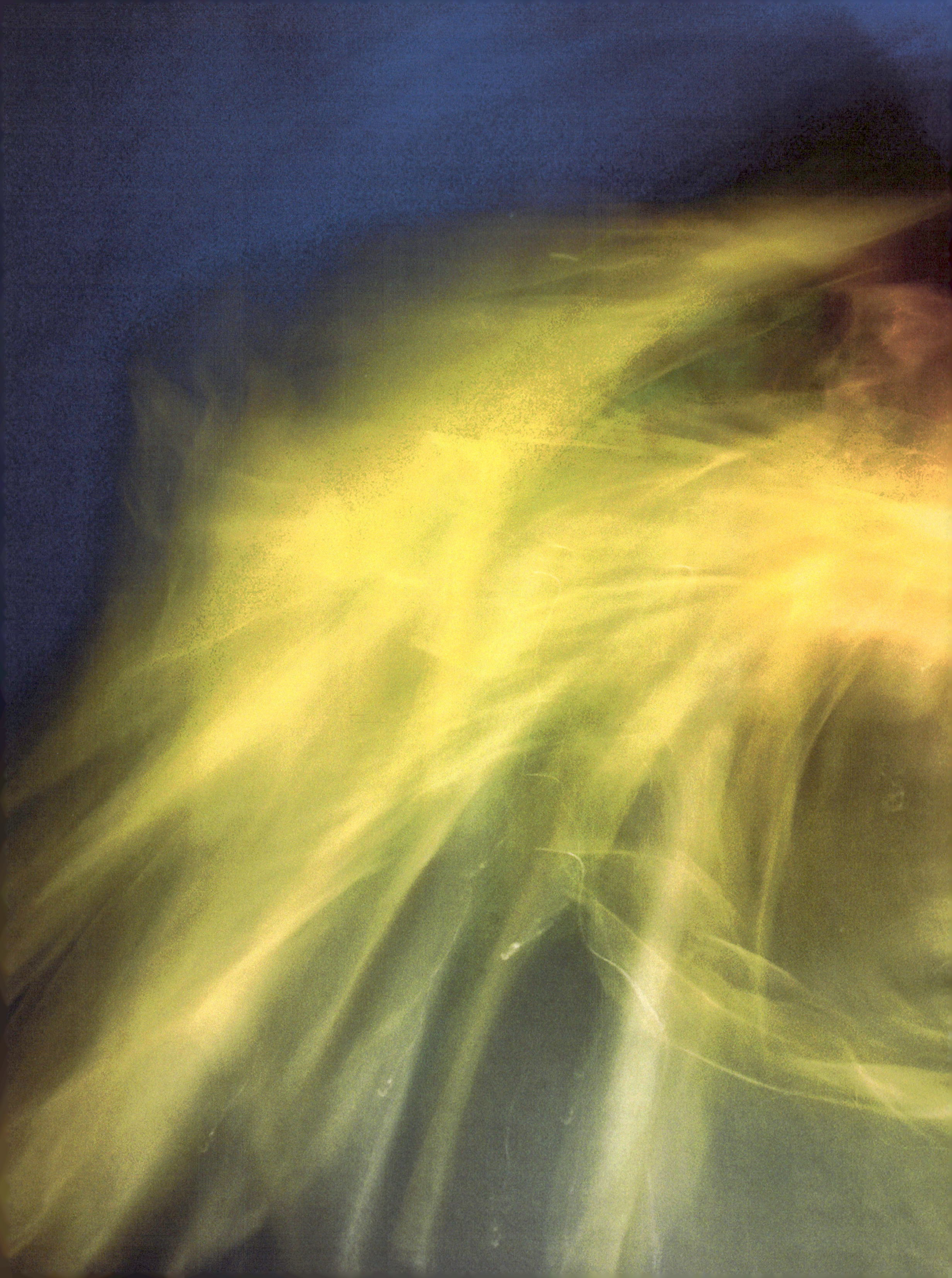

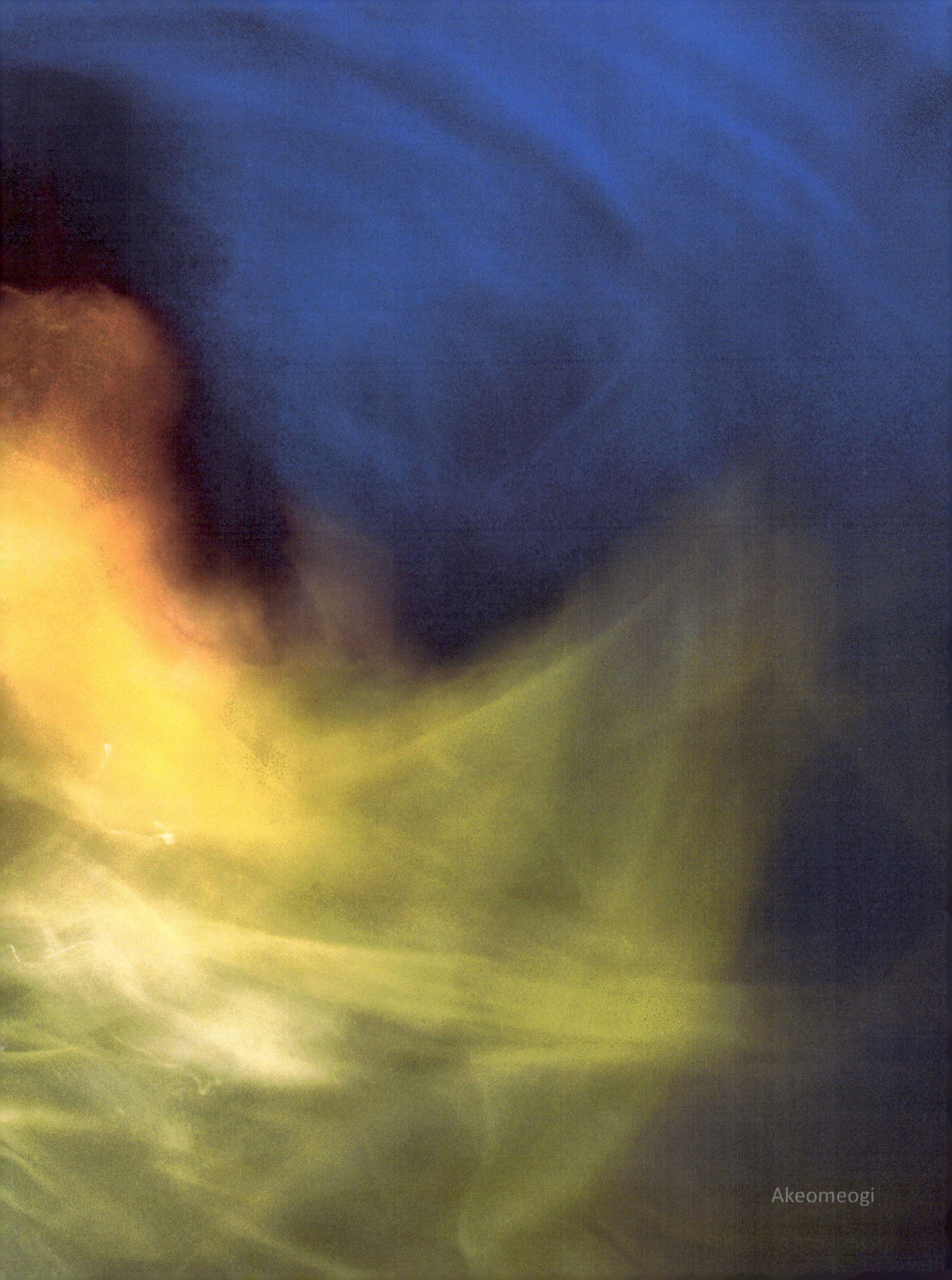
Akeomeogi

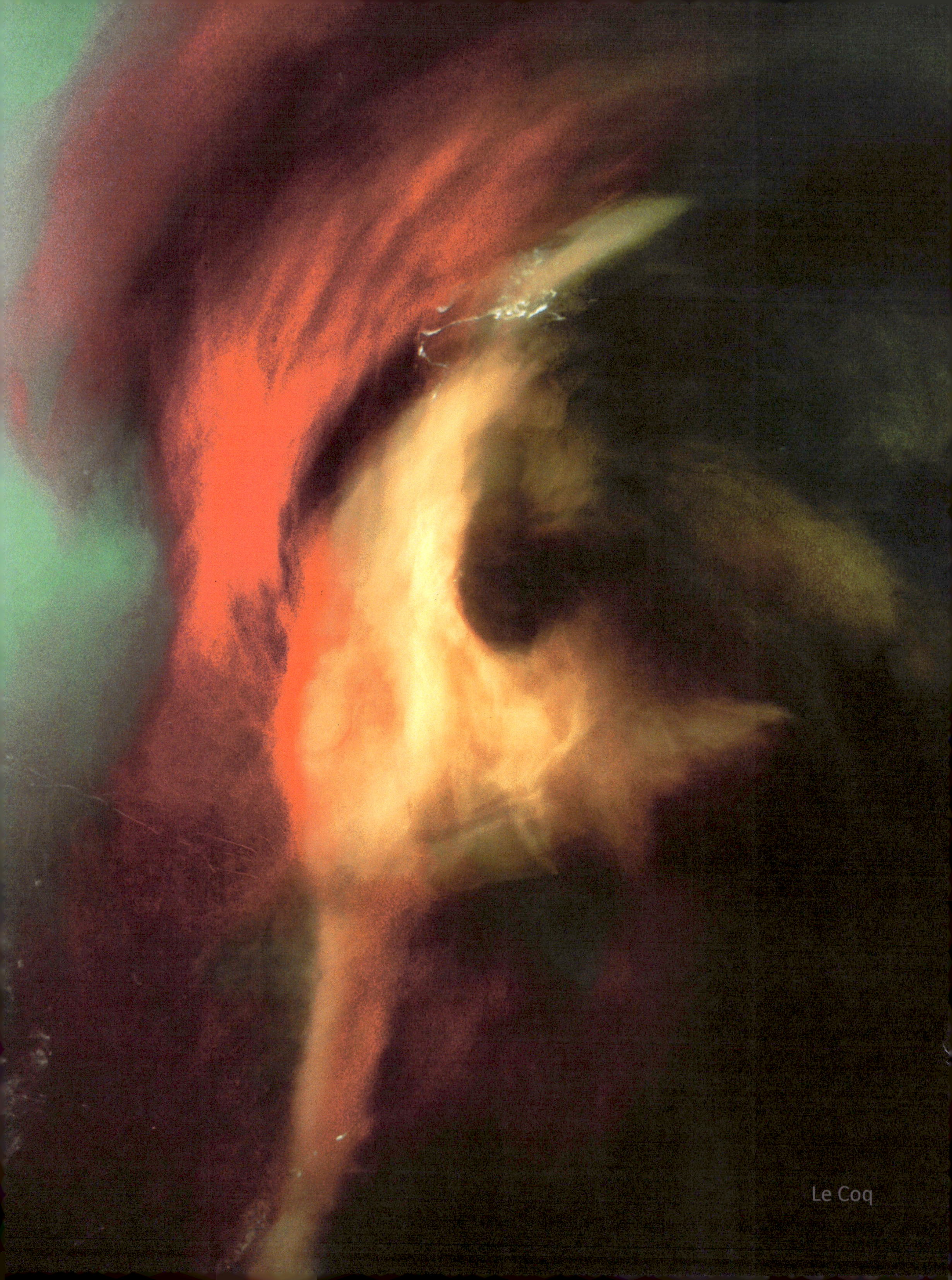

Le Coq

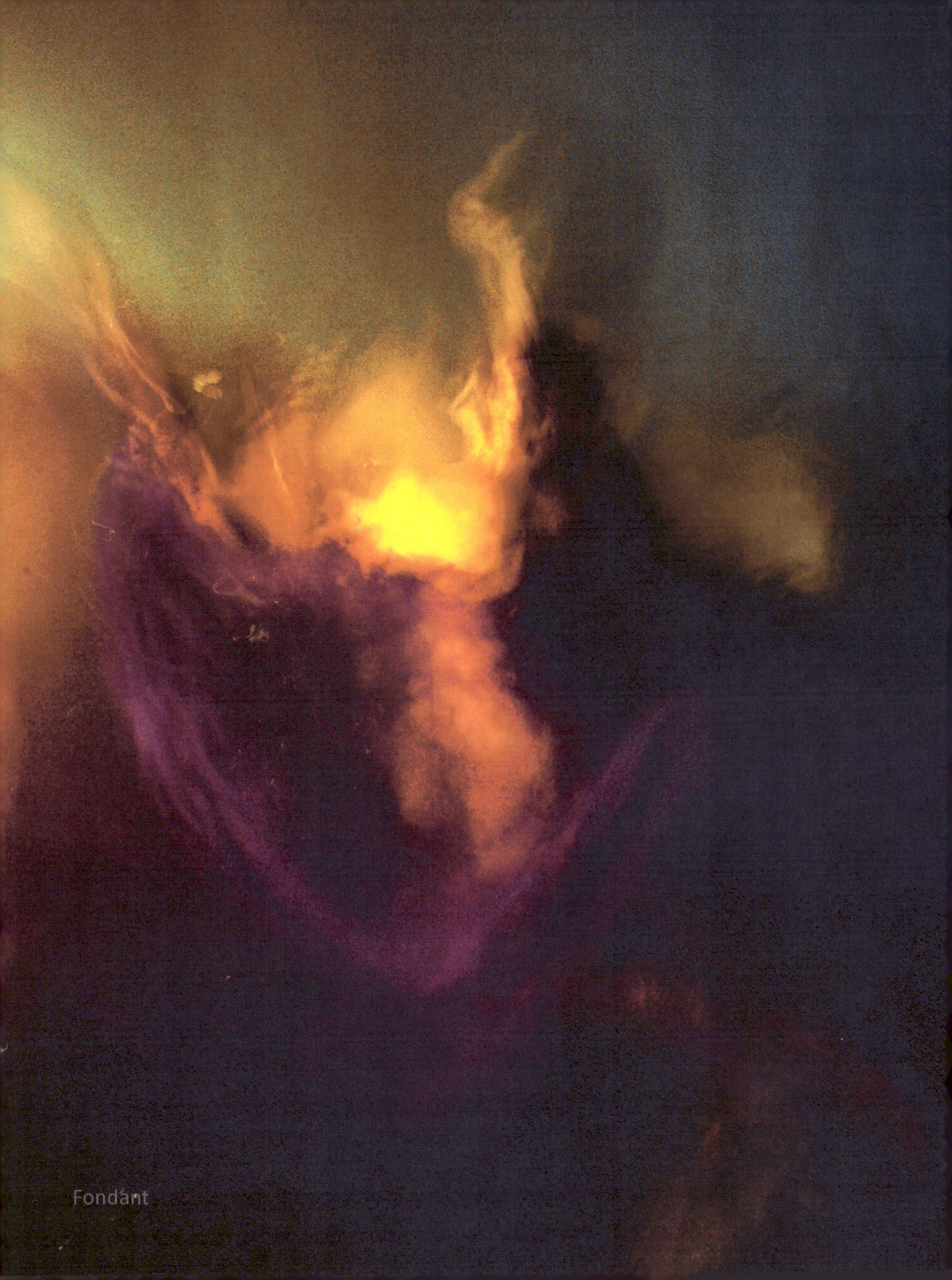

Fondant

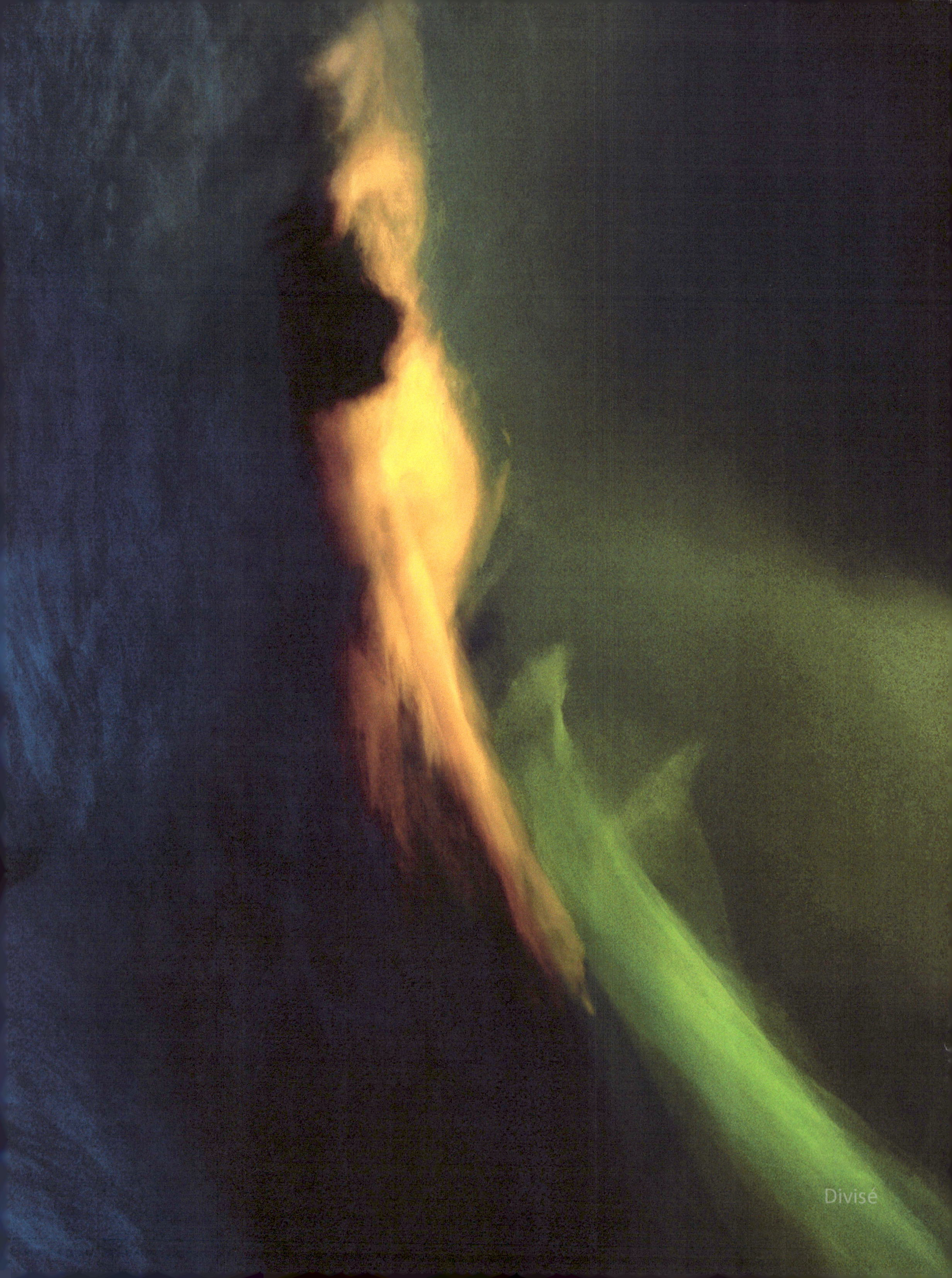
Divisé

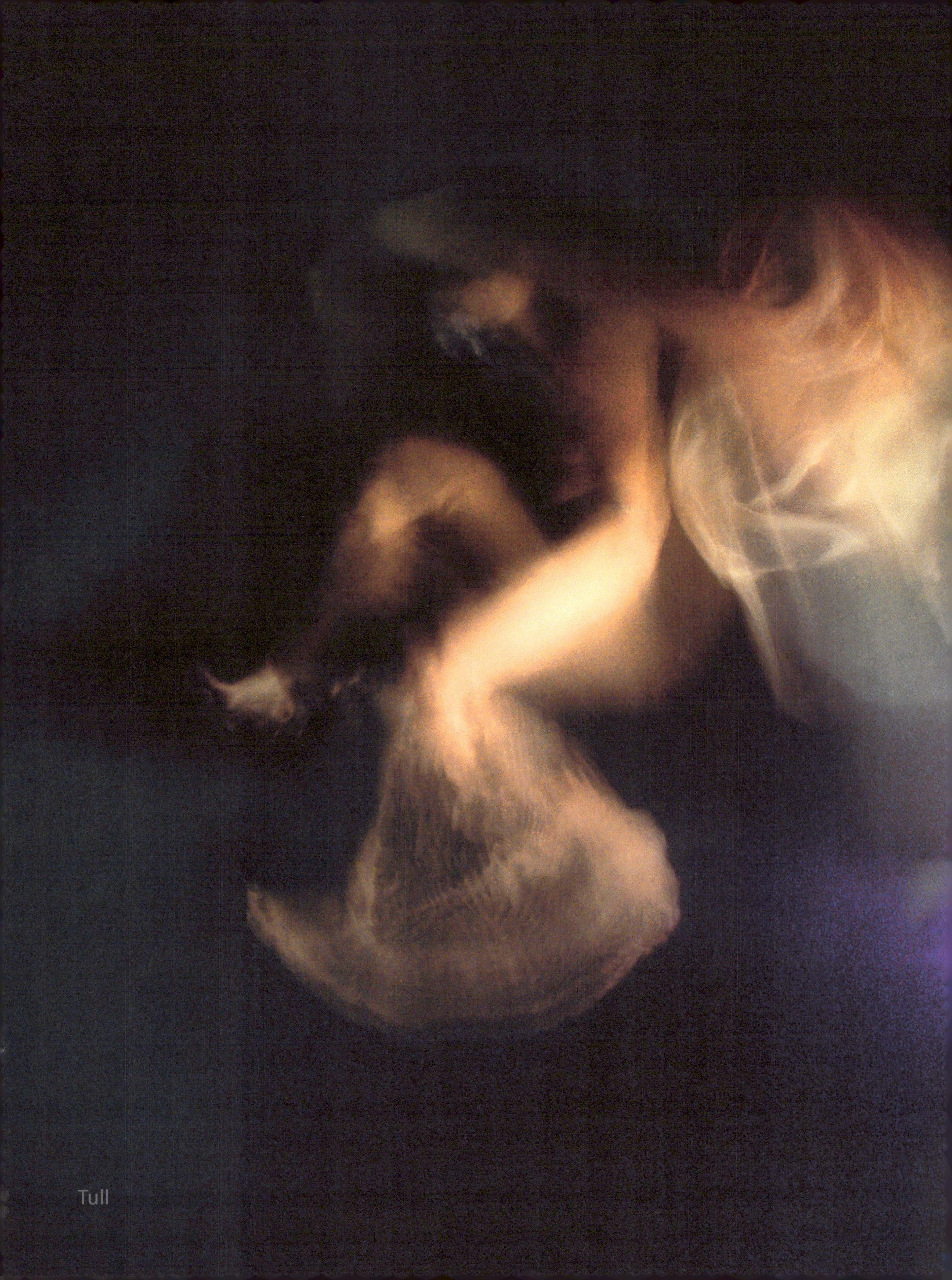

Tull

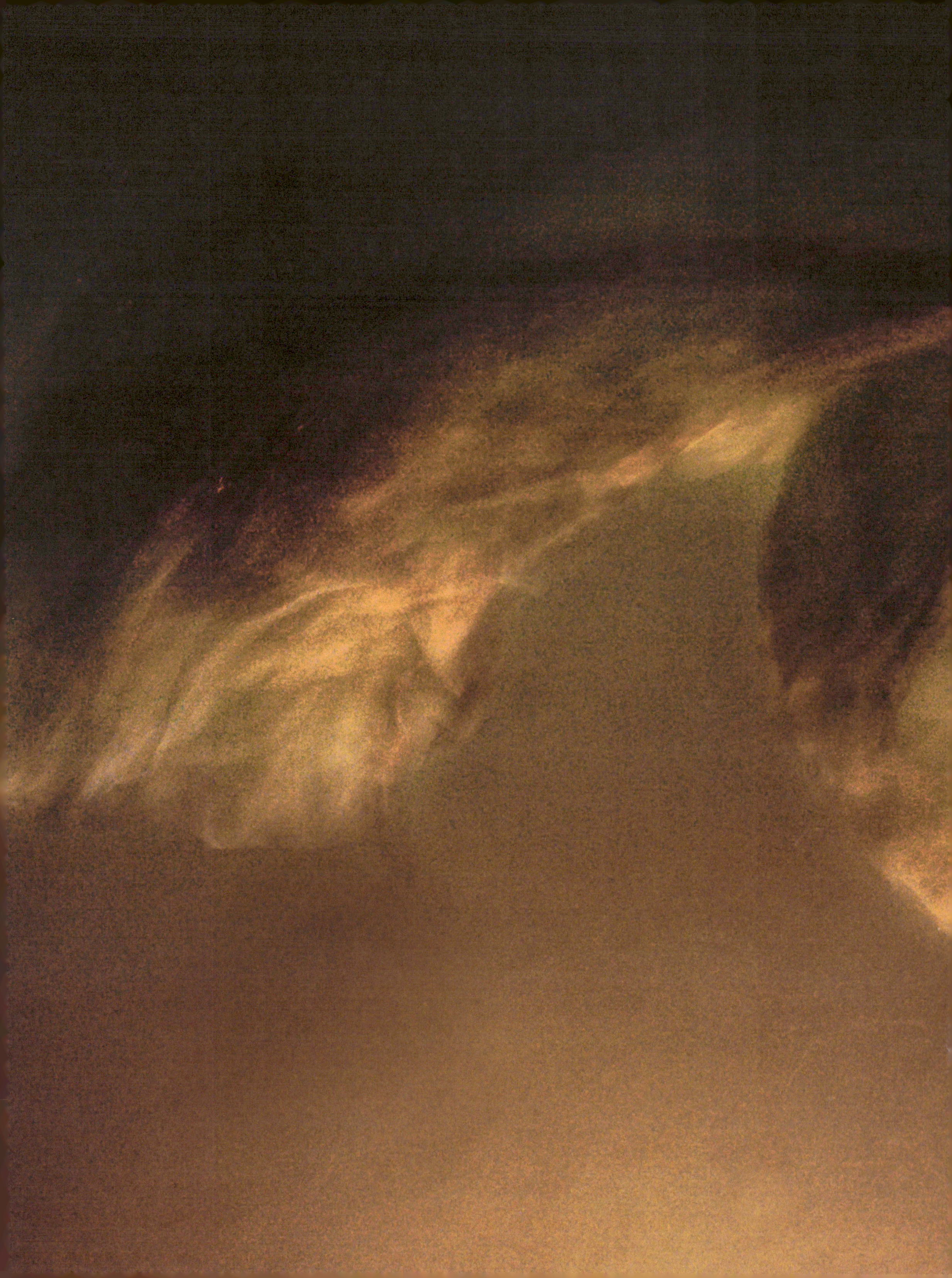

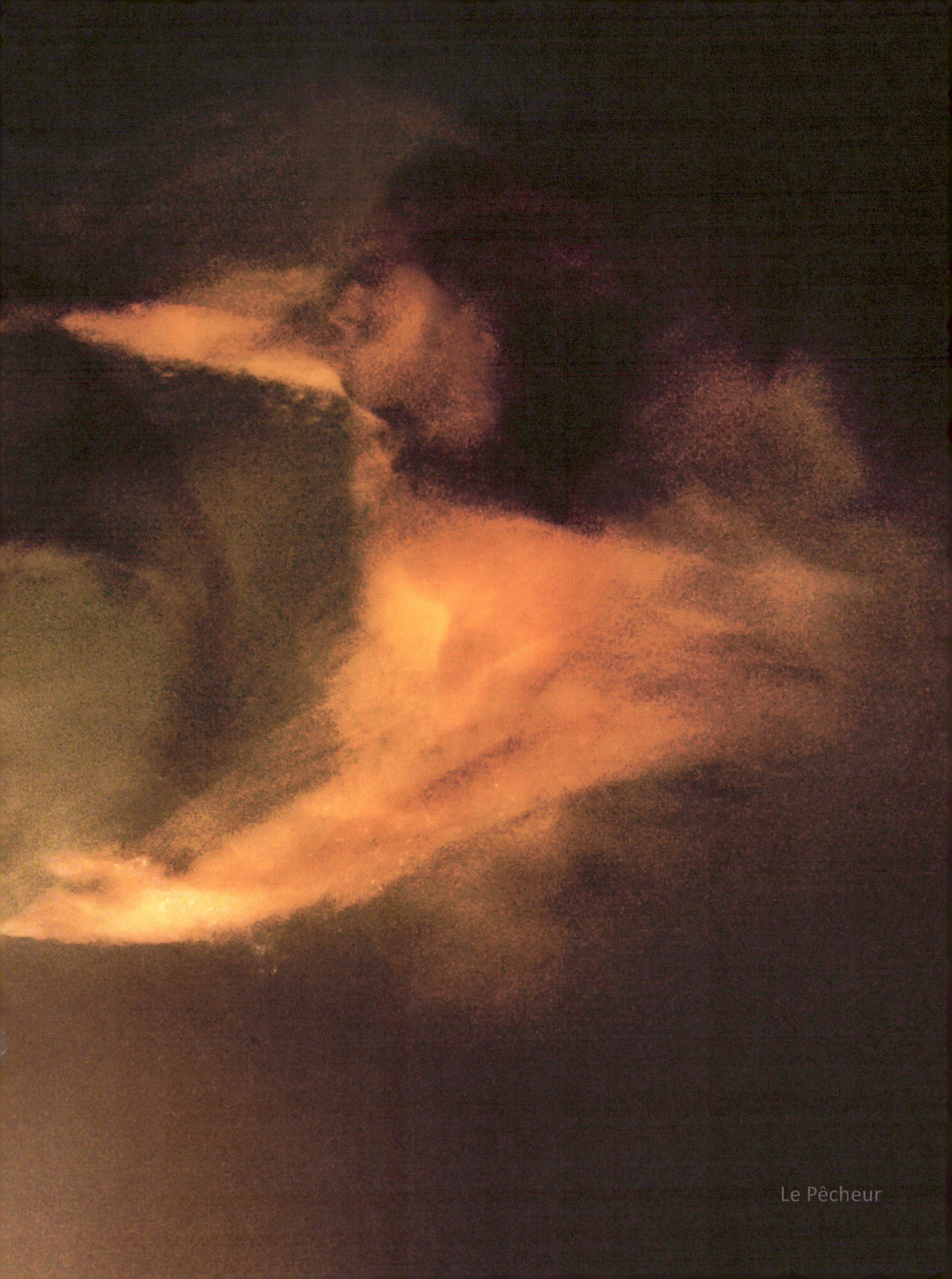

Le Pêcheur

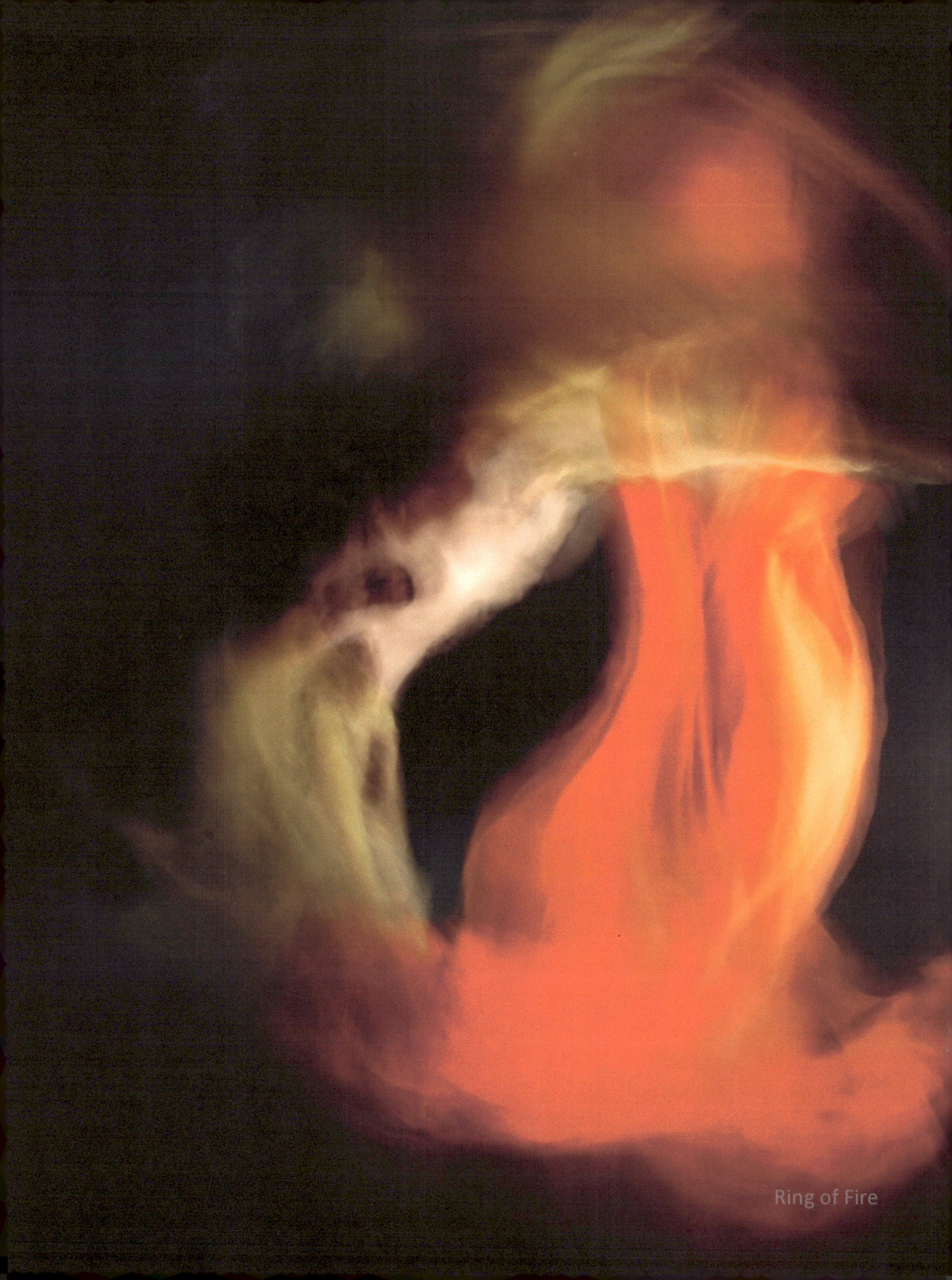

Ring of Fire

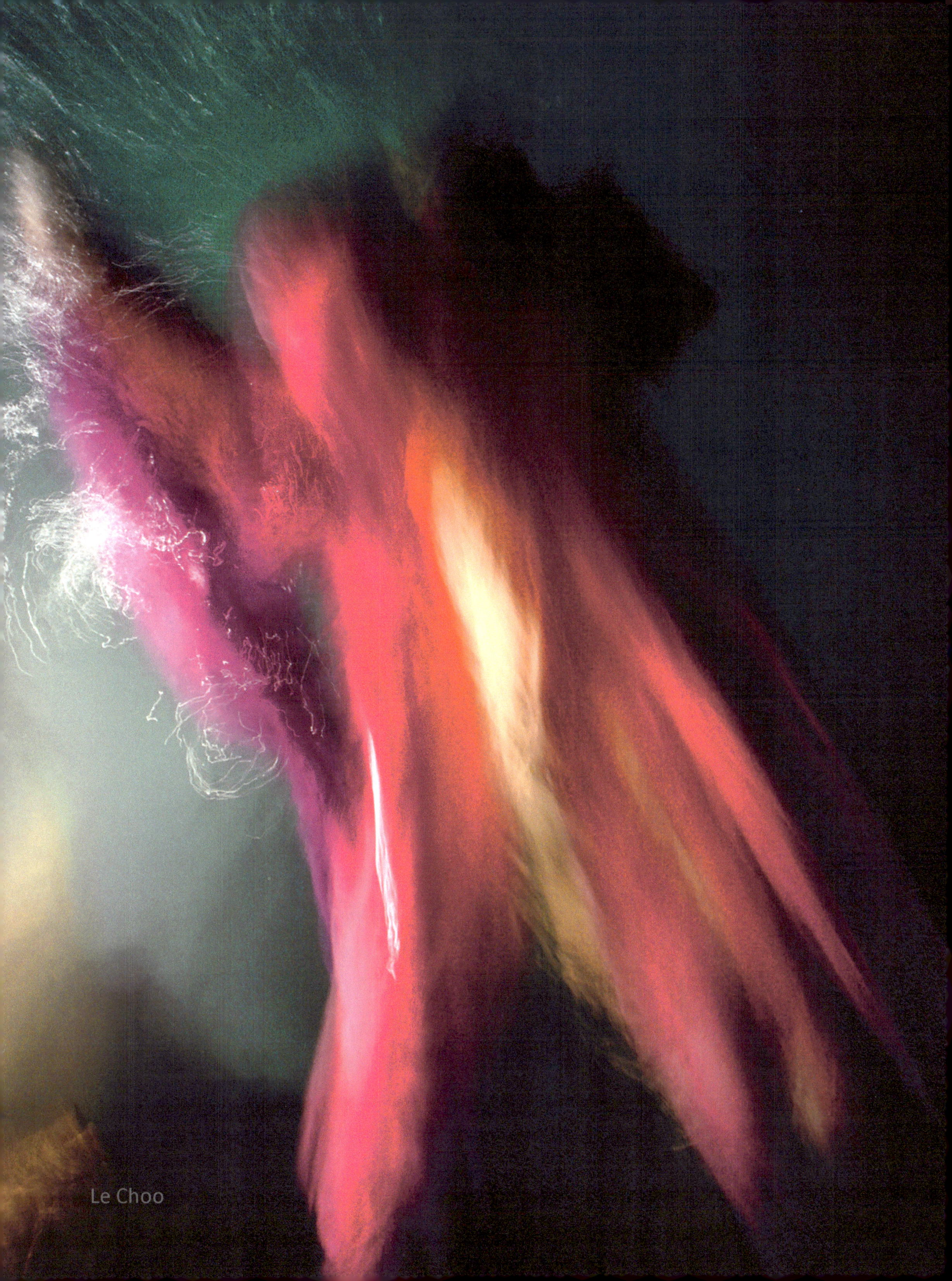
Le Choo

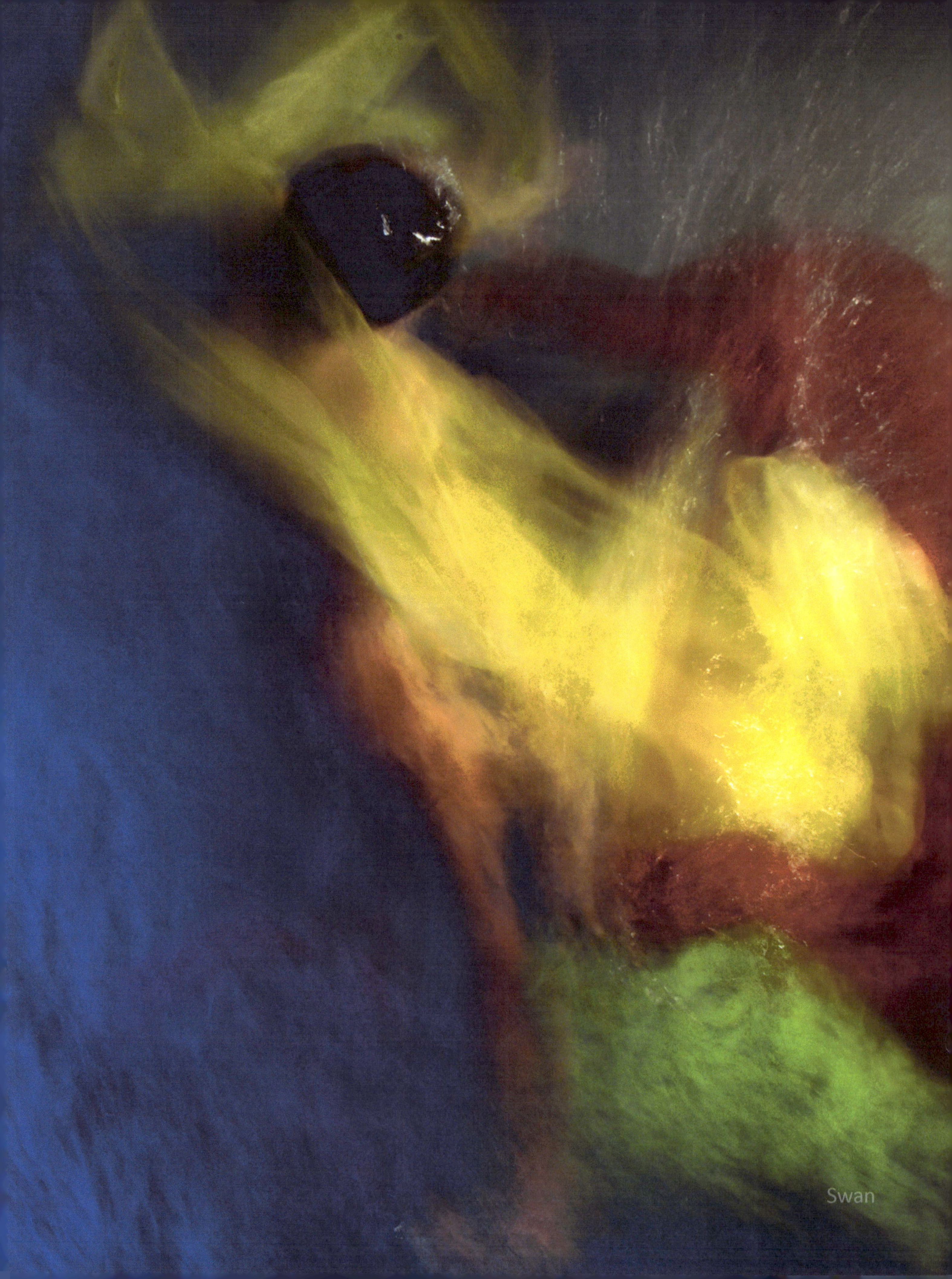
Swan

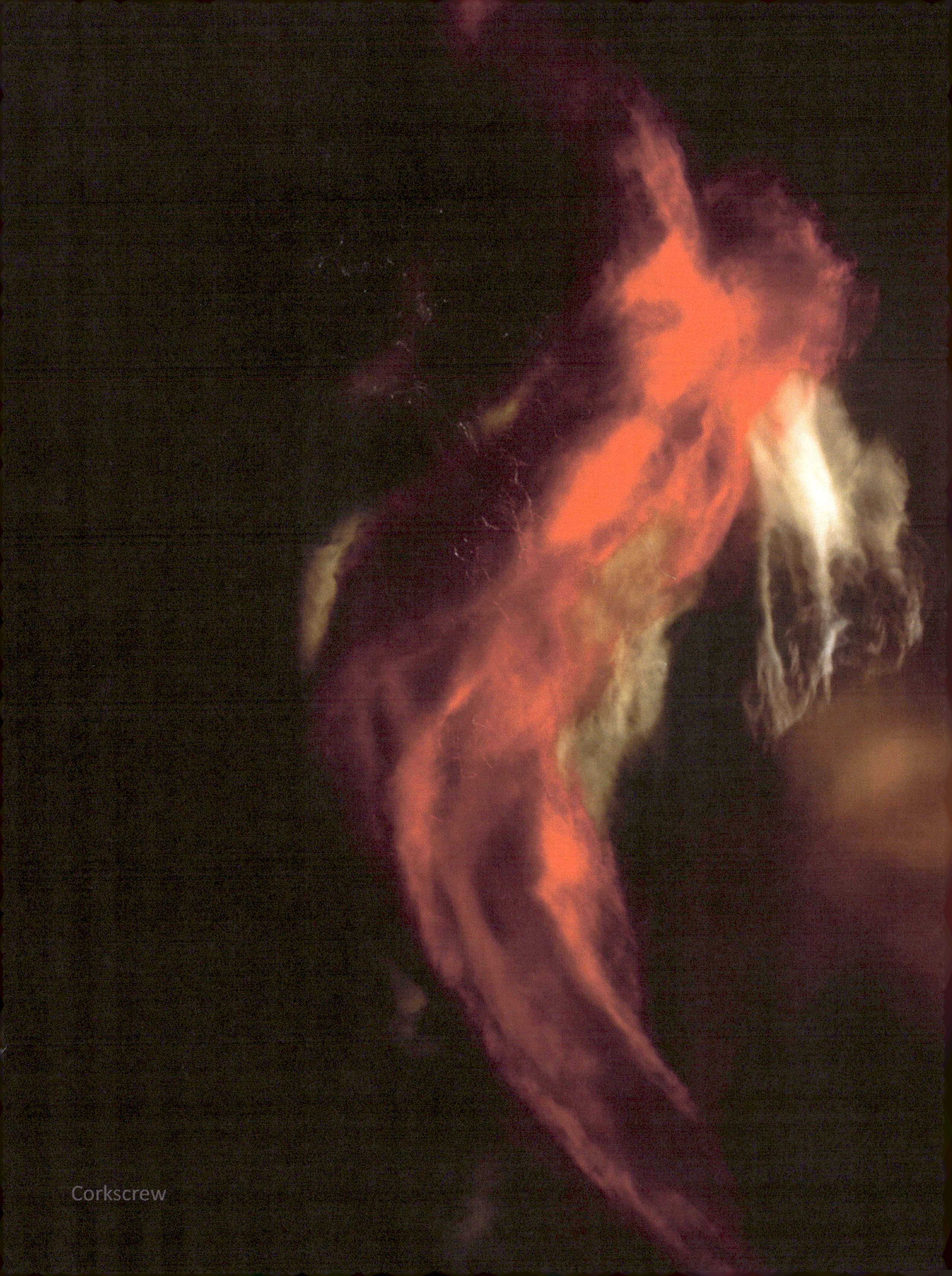

Corkscrew

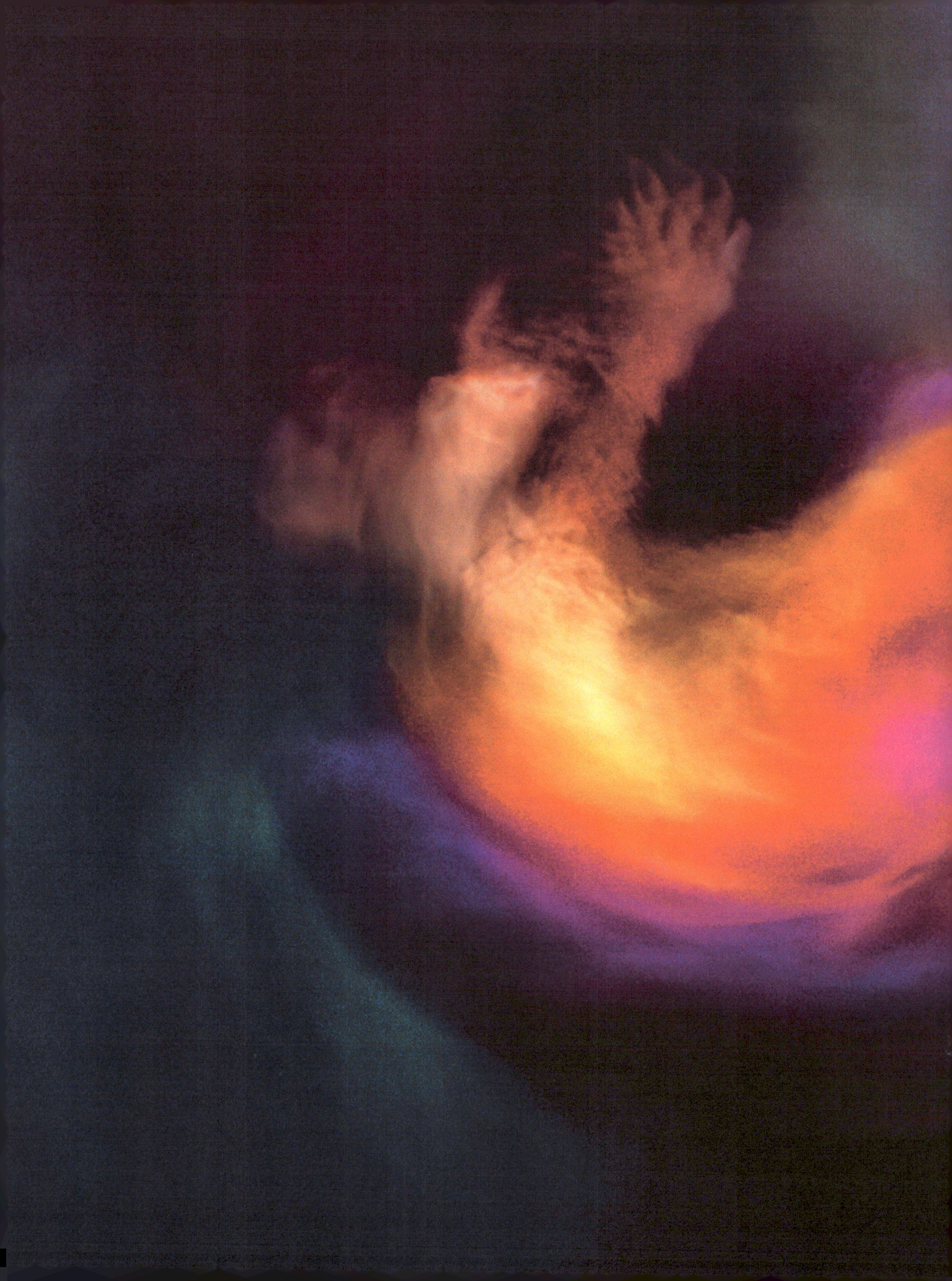

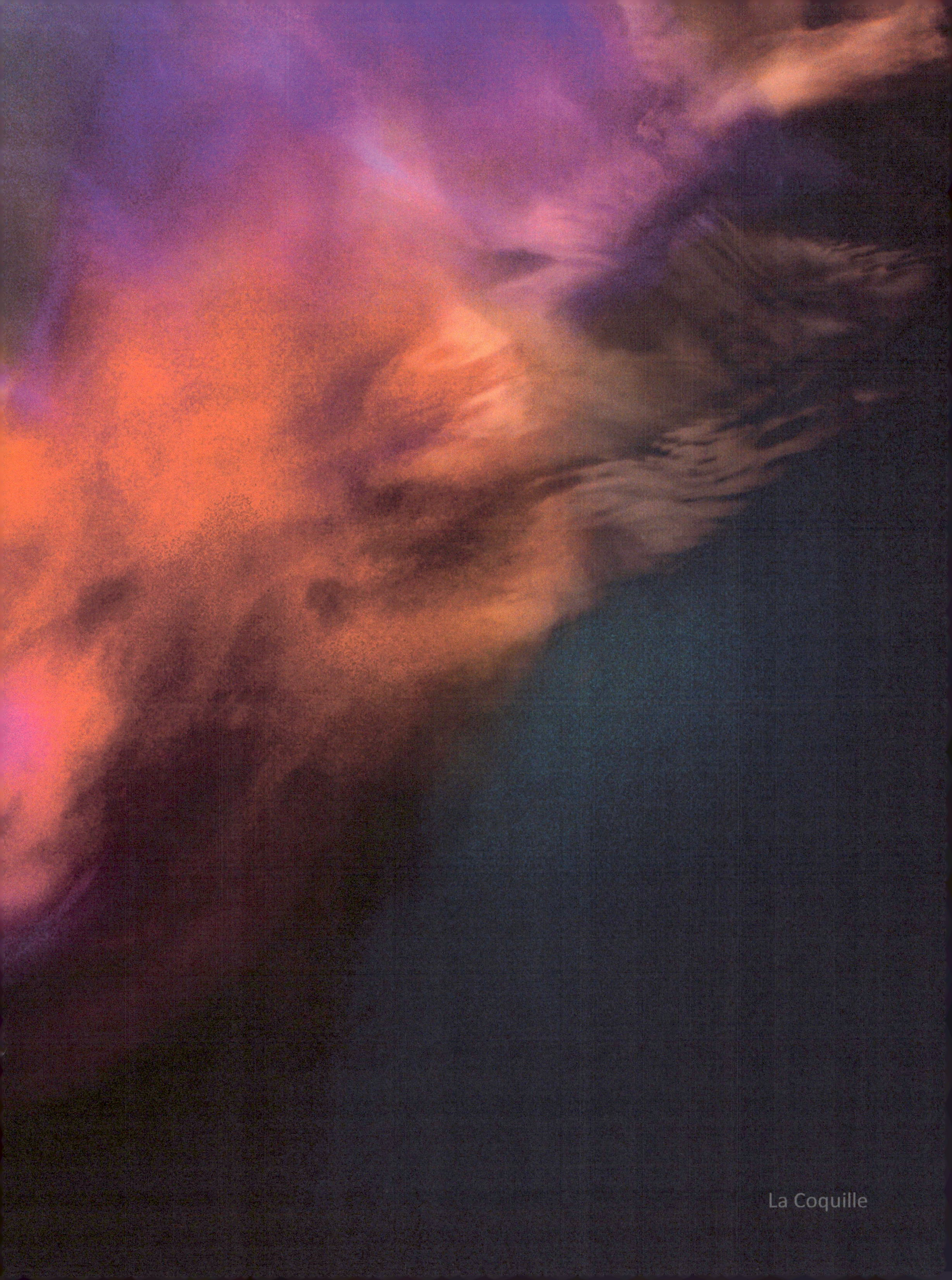

La Coquille

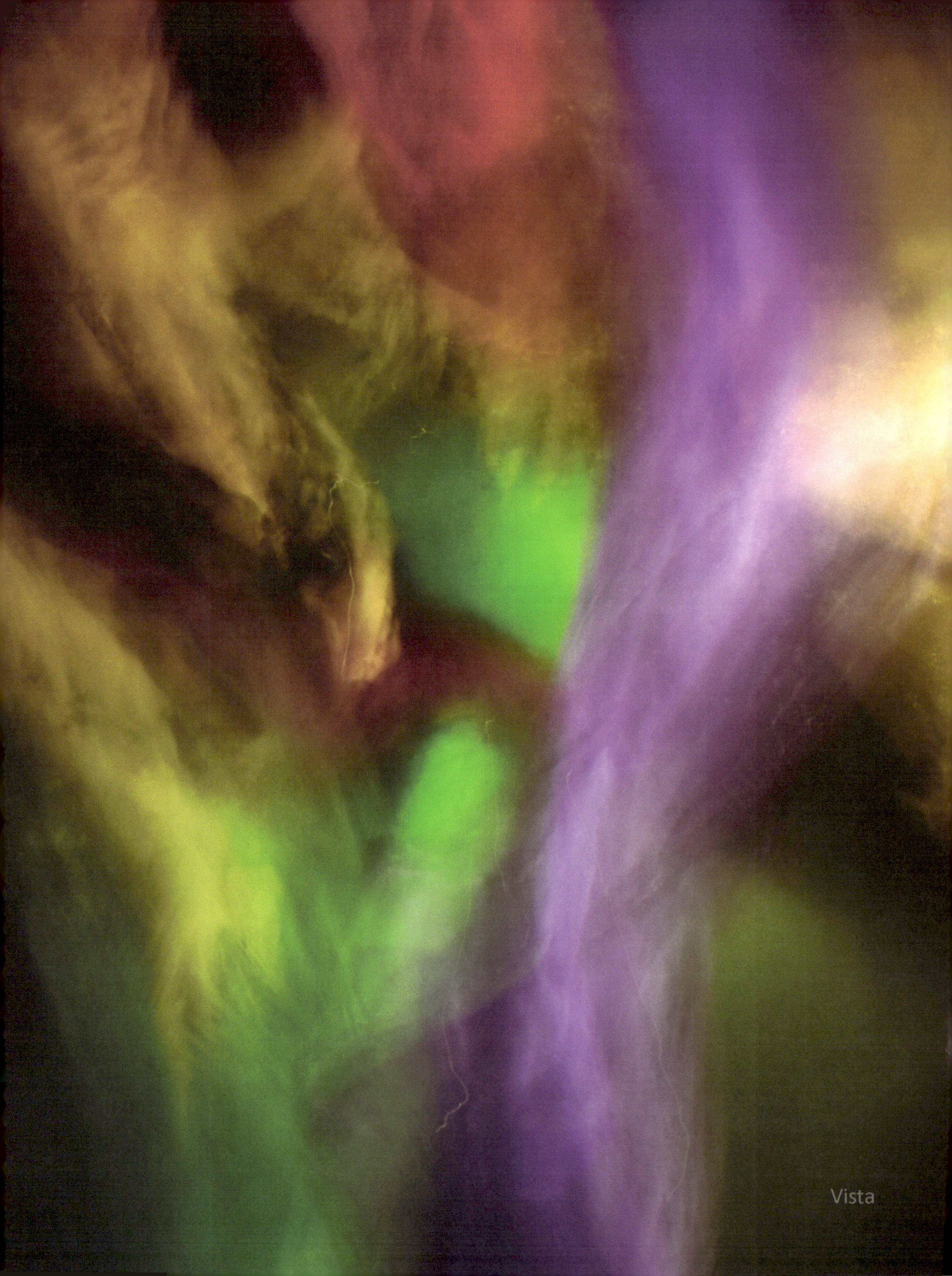

Vista

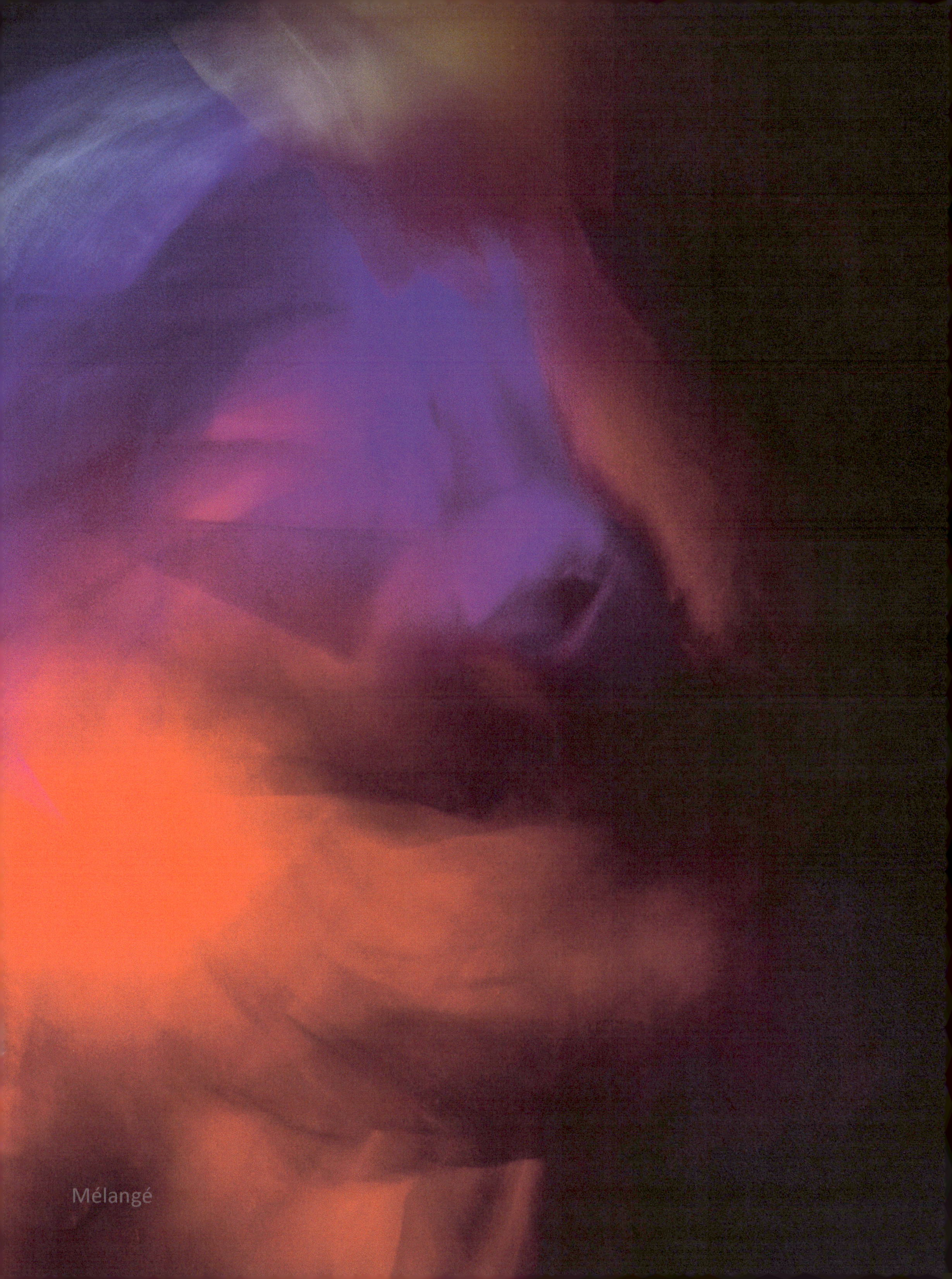
Mélangé

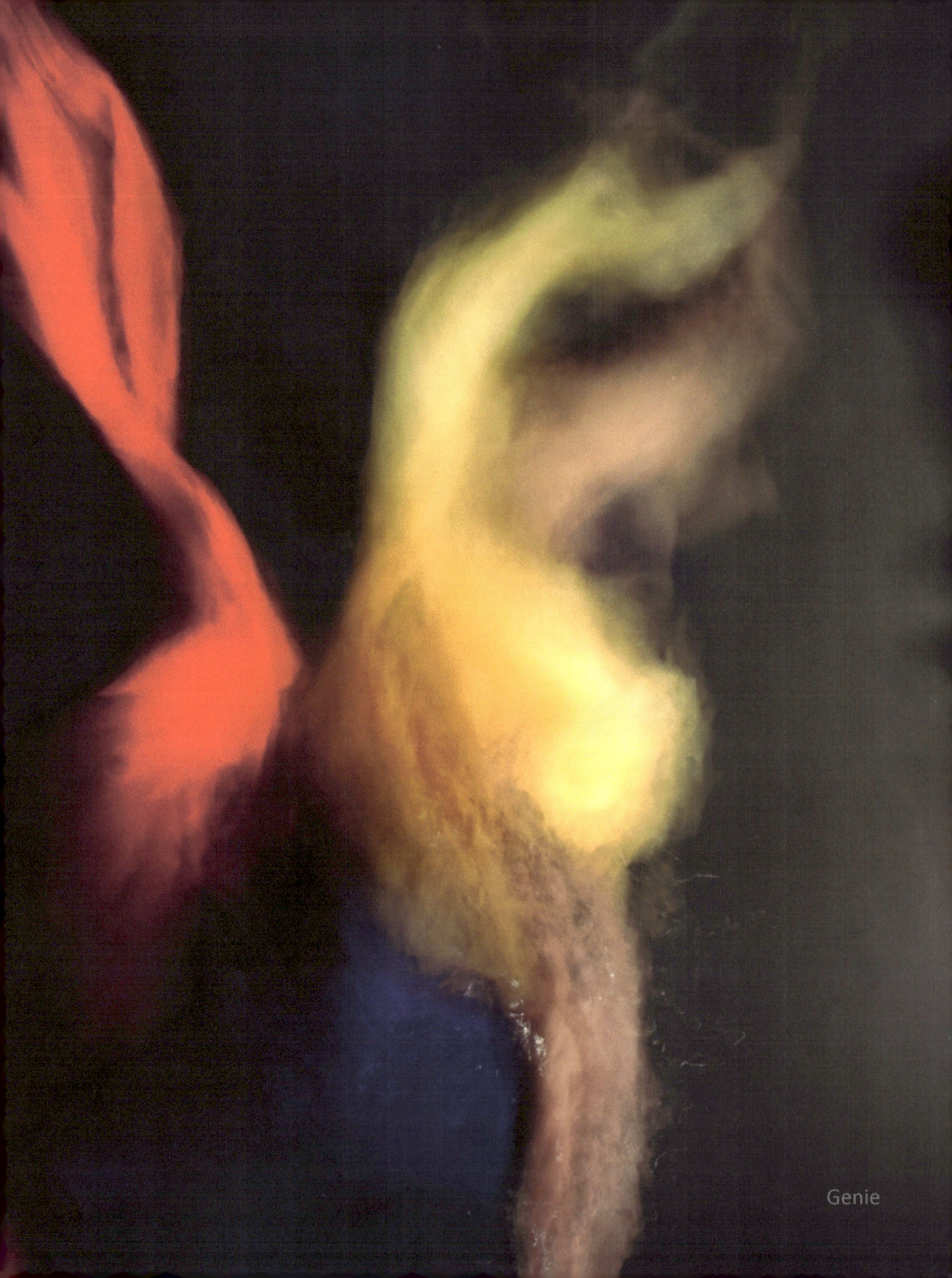

Genie

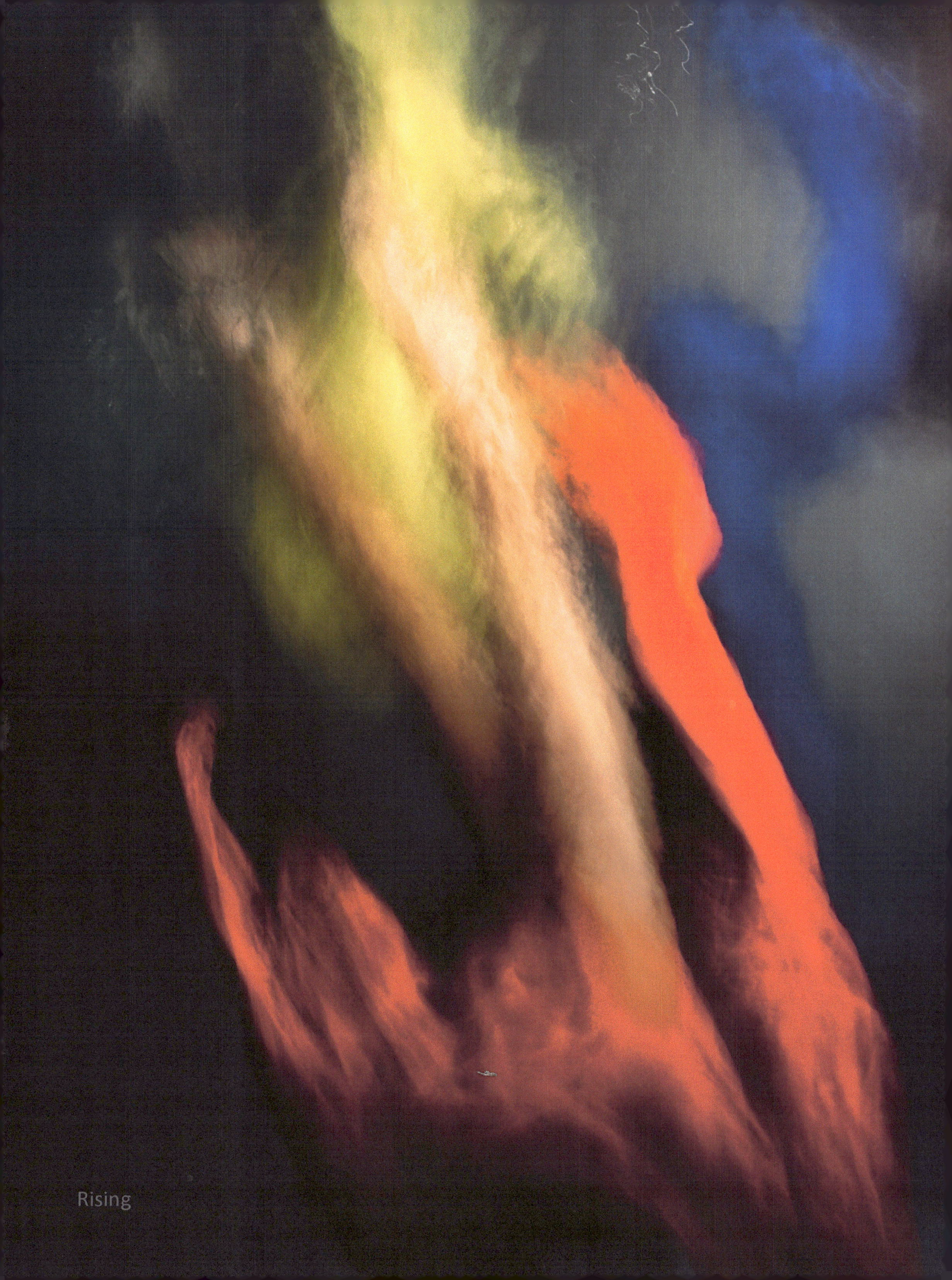

Rising

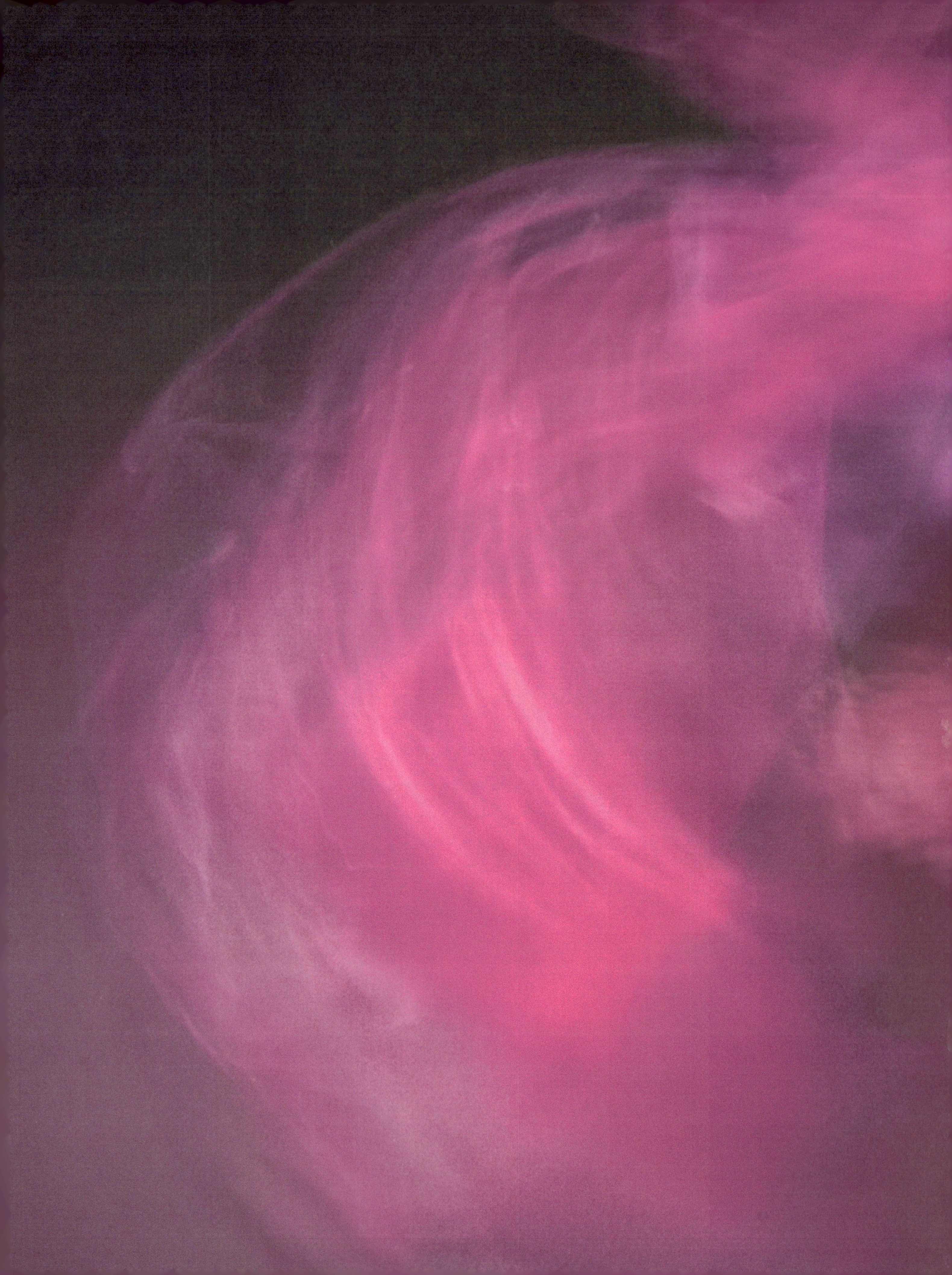

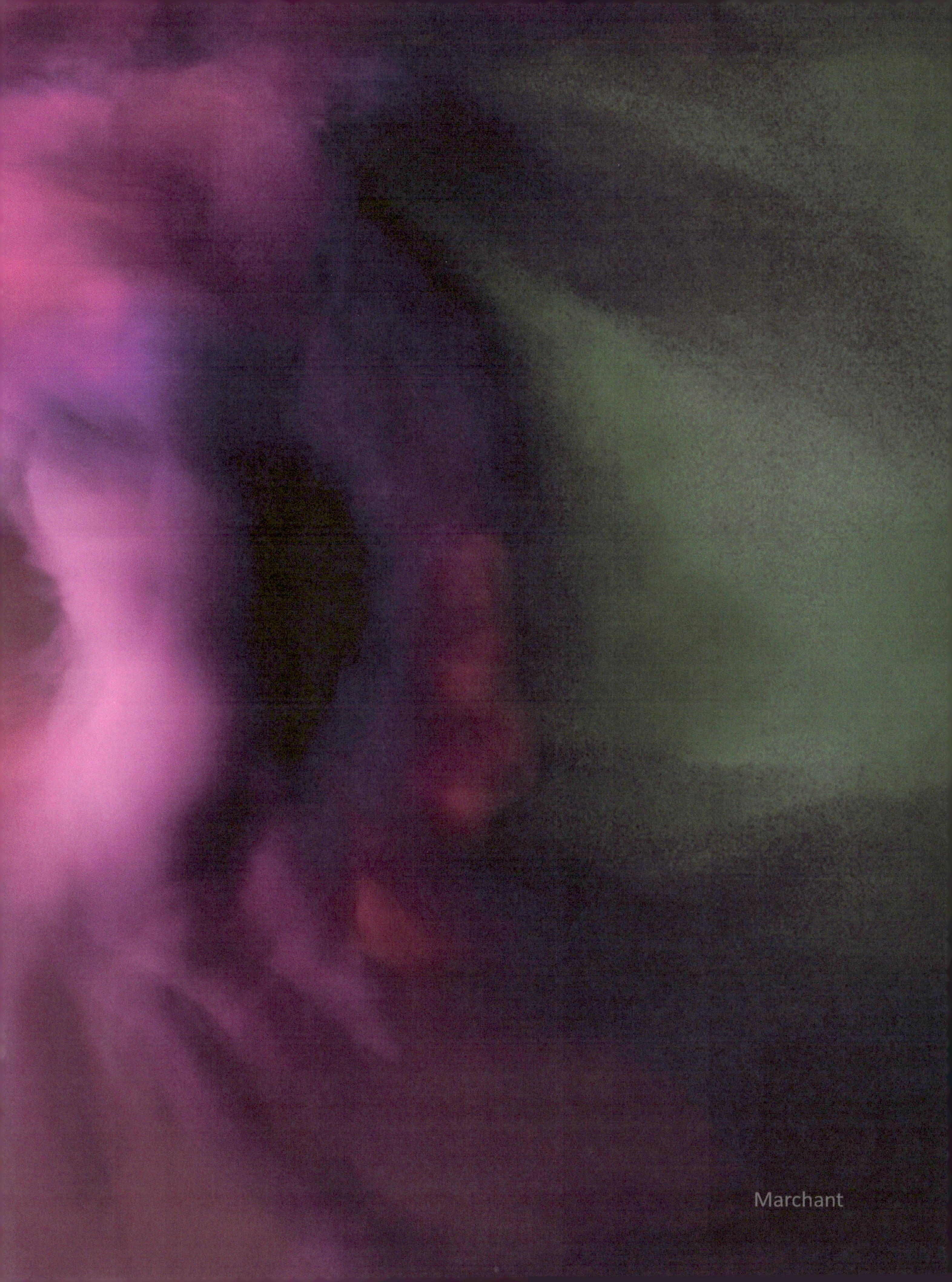

Marchant

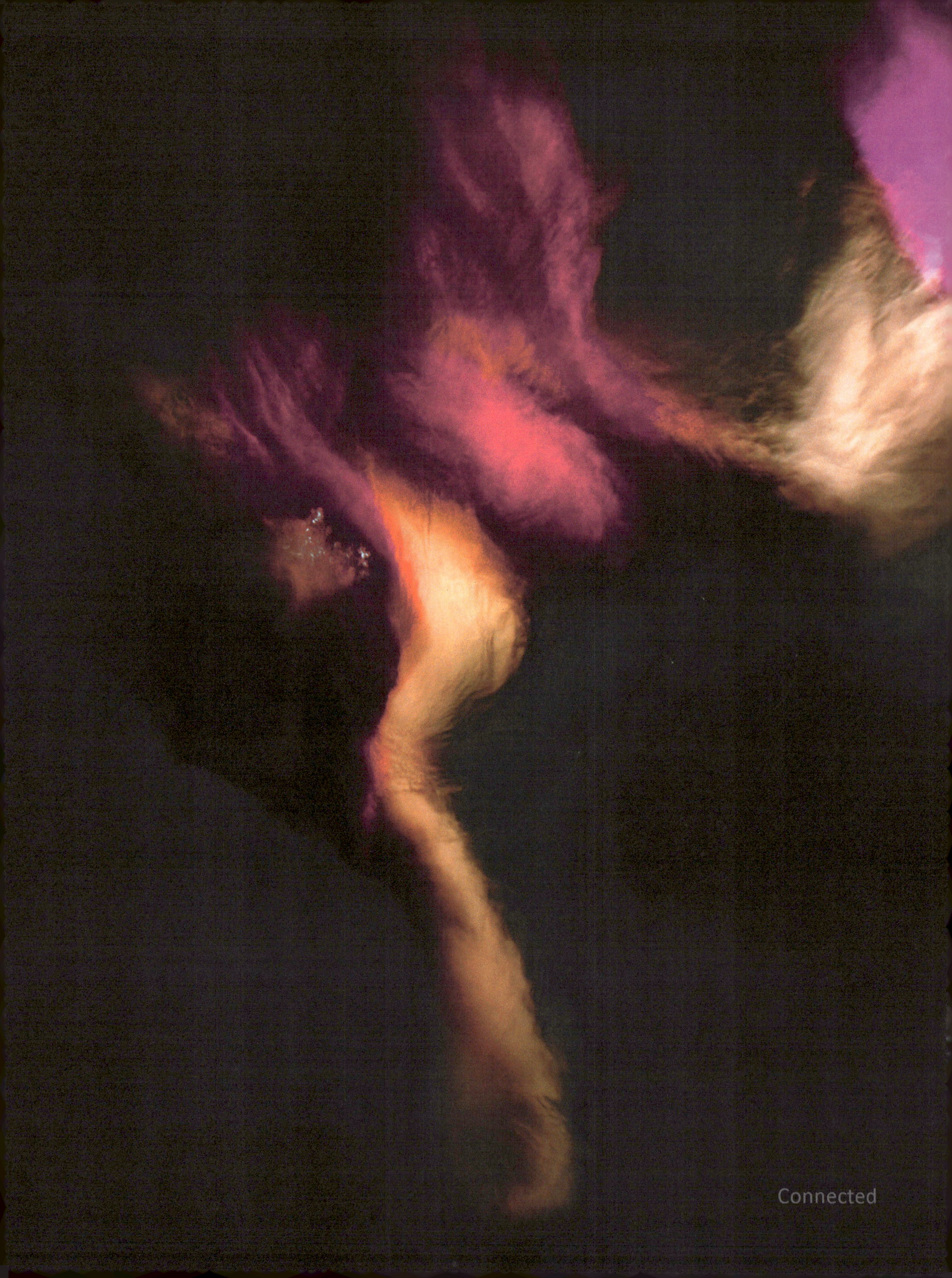

Connected

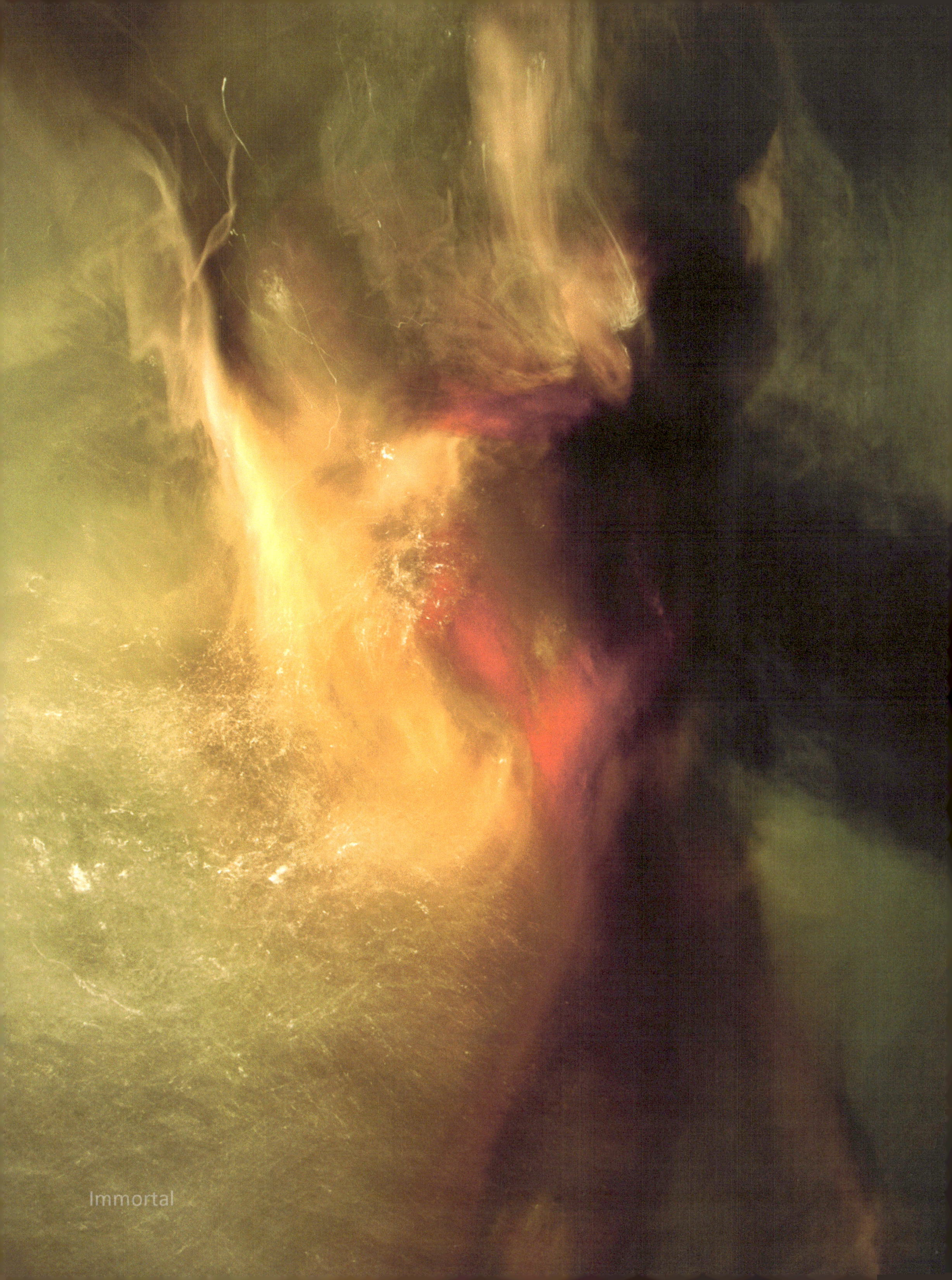
Immortal

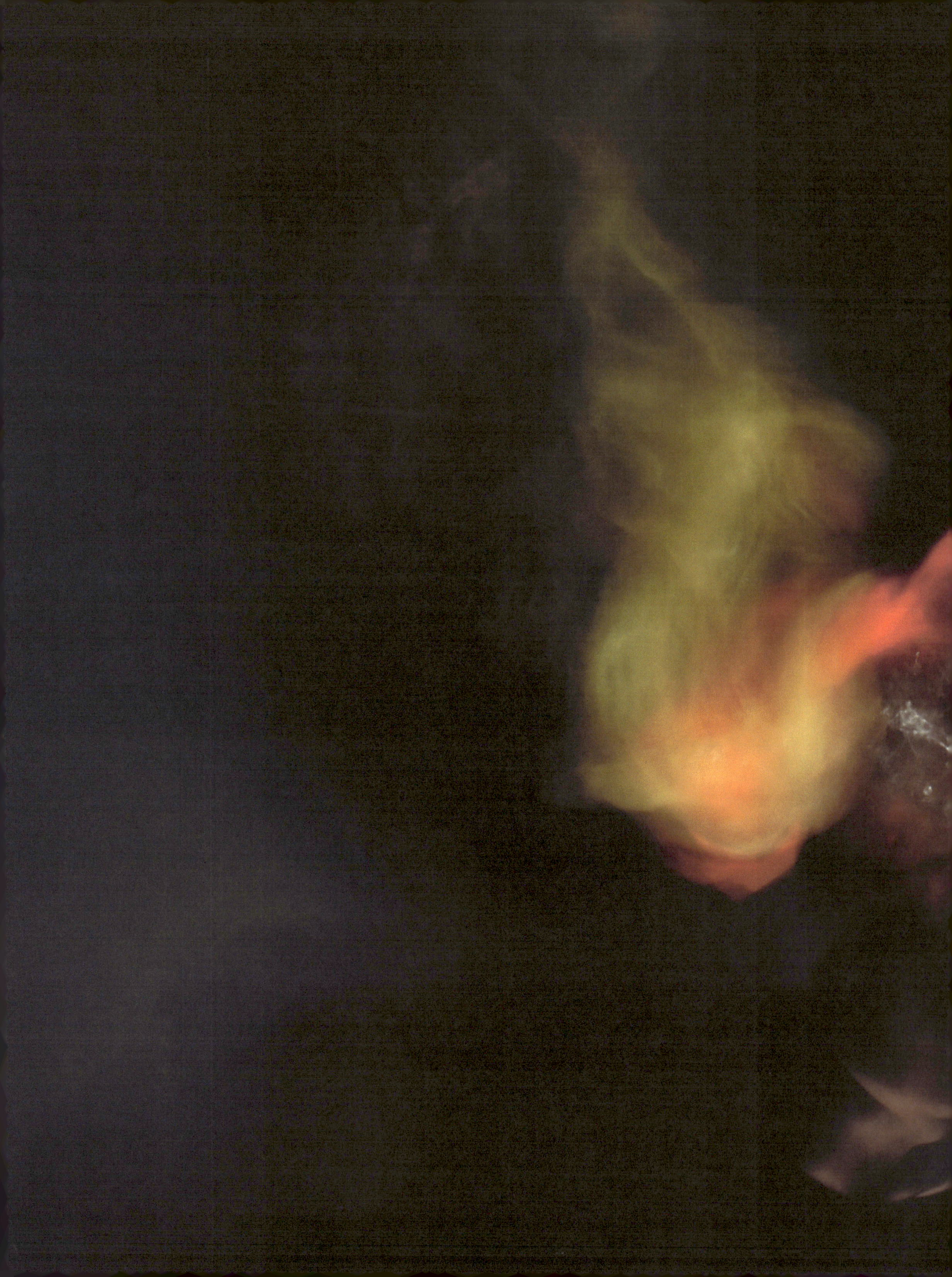

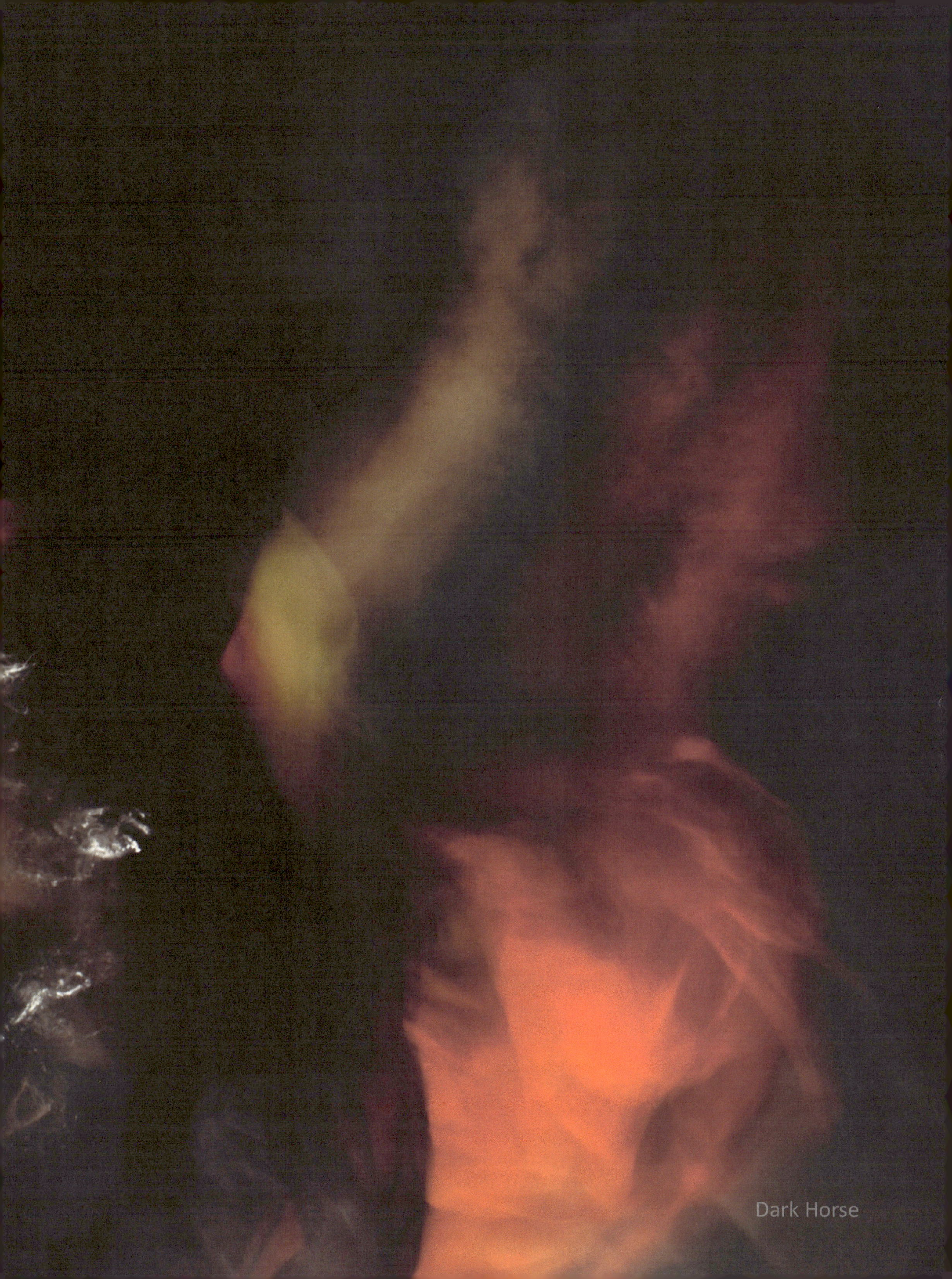

Dark Horse

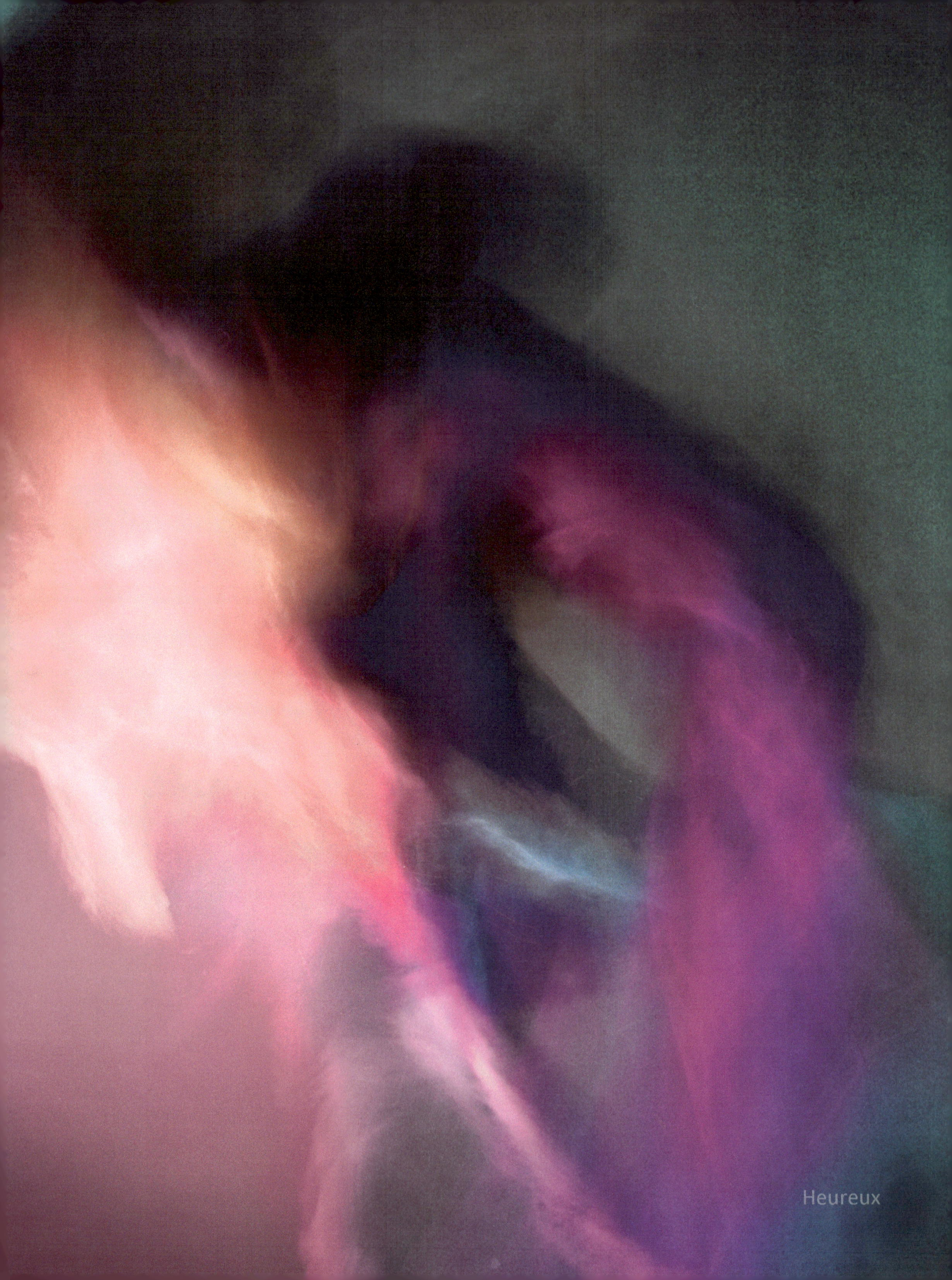
Heureux

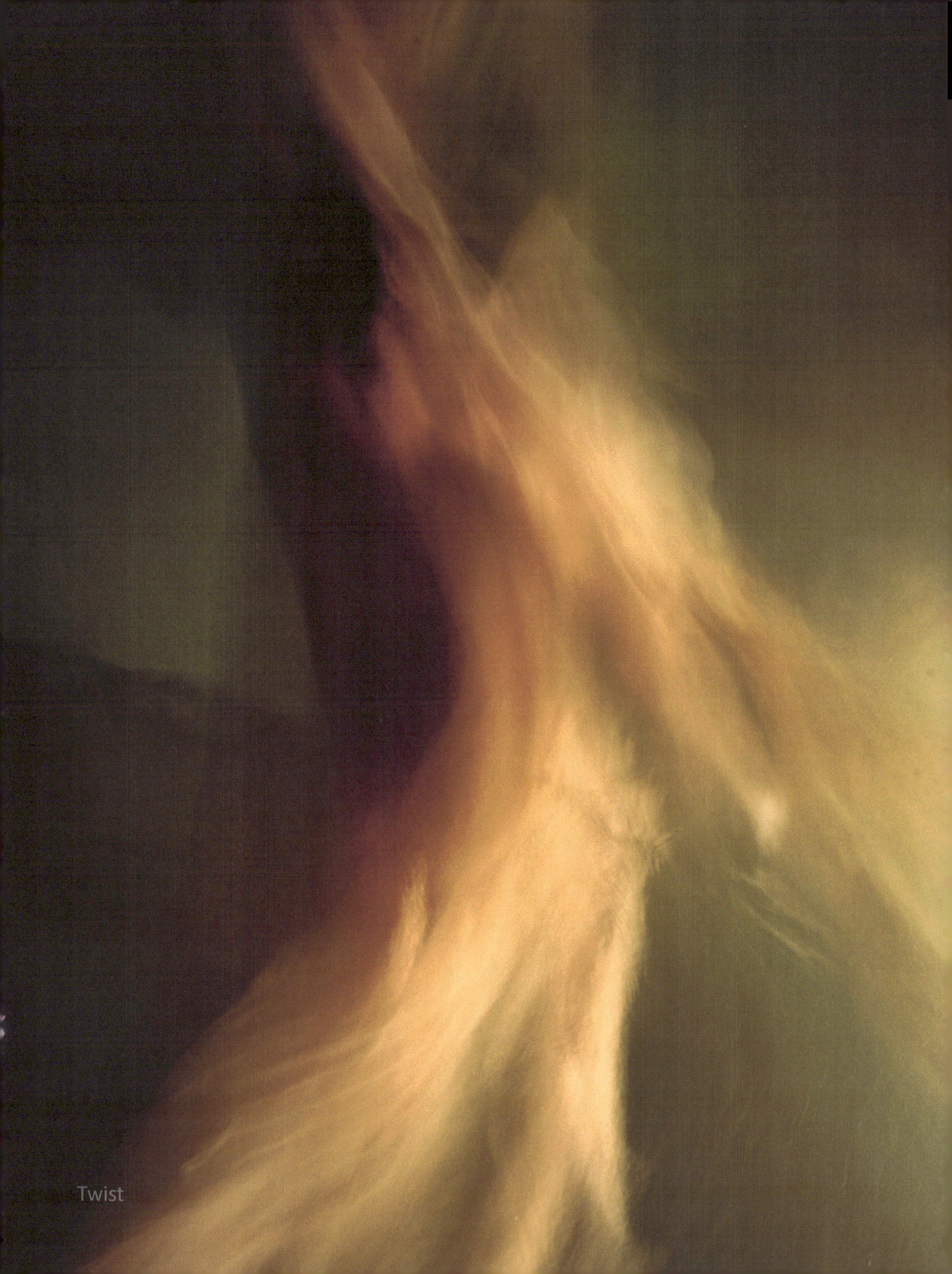

Twist

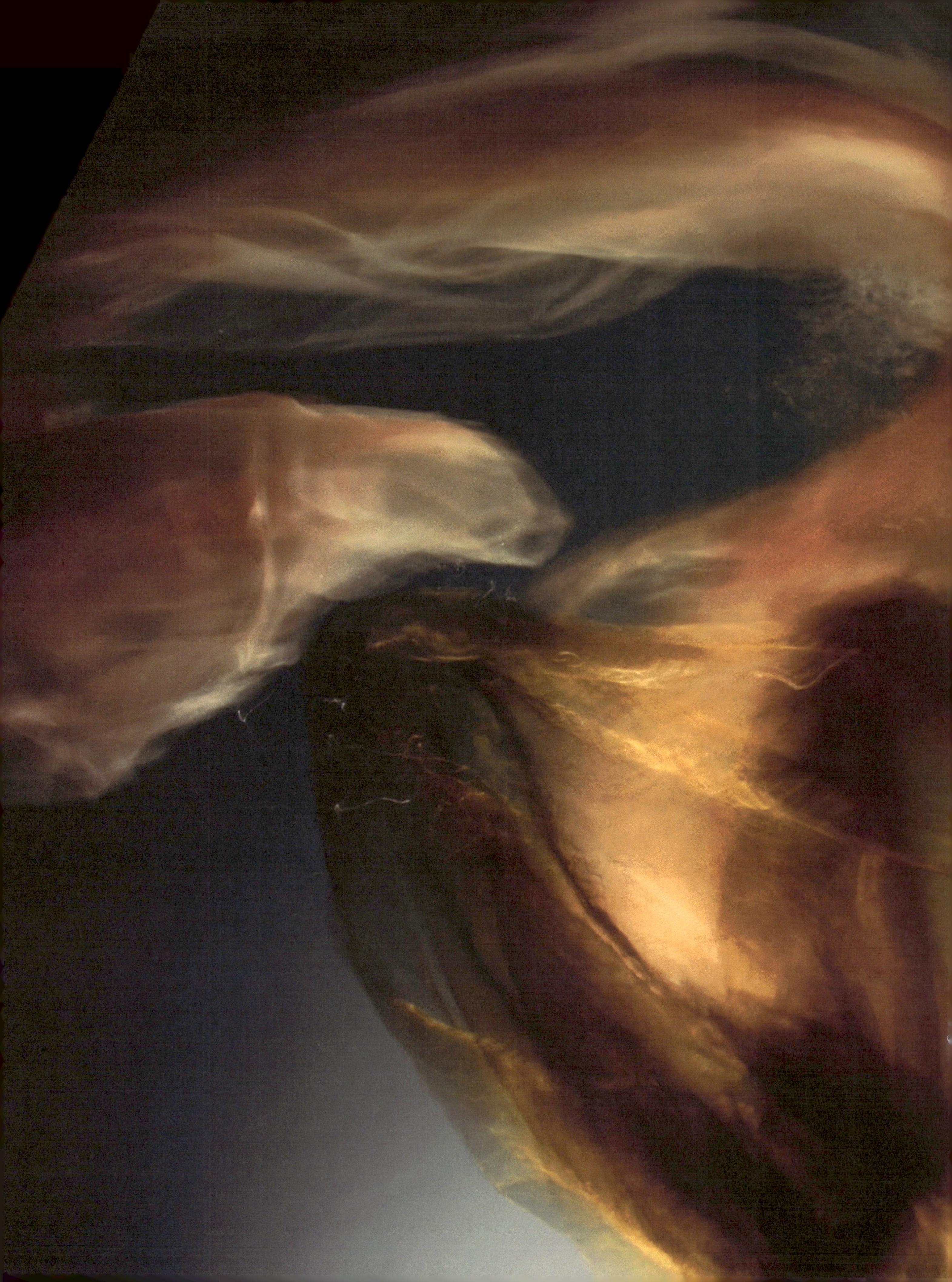

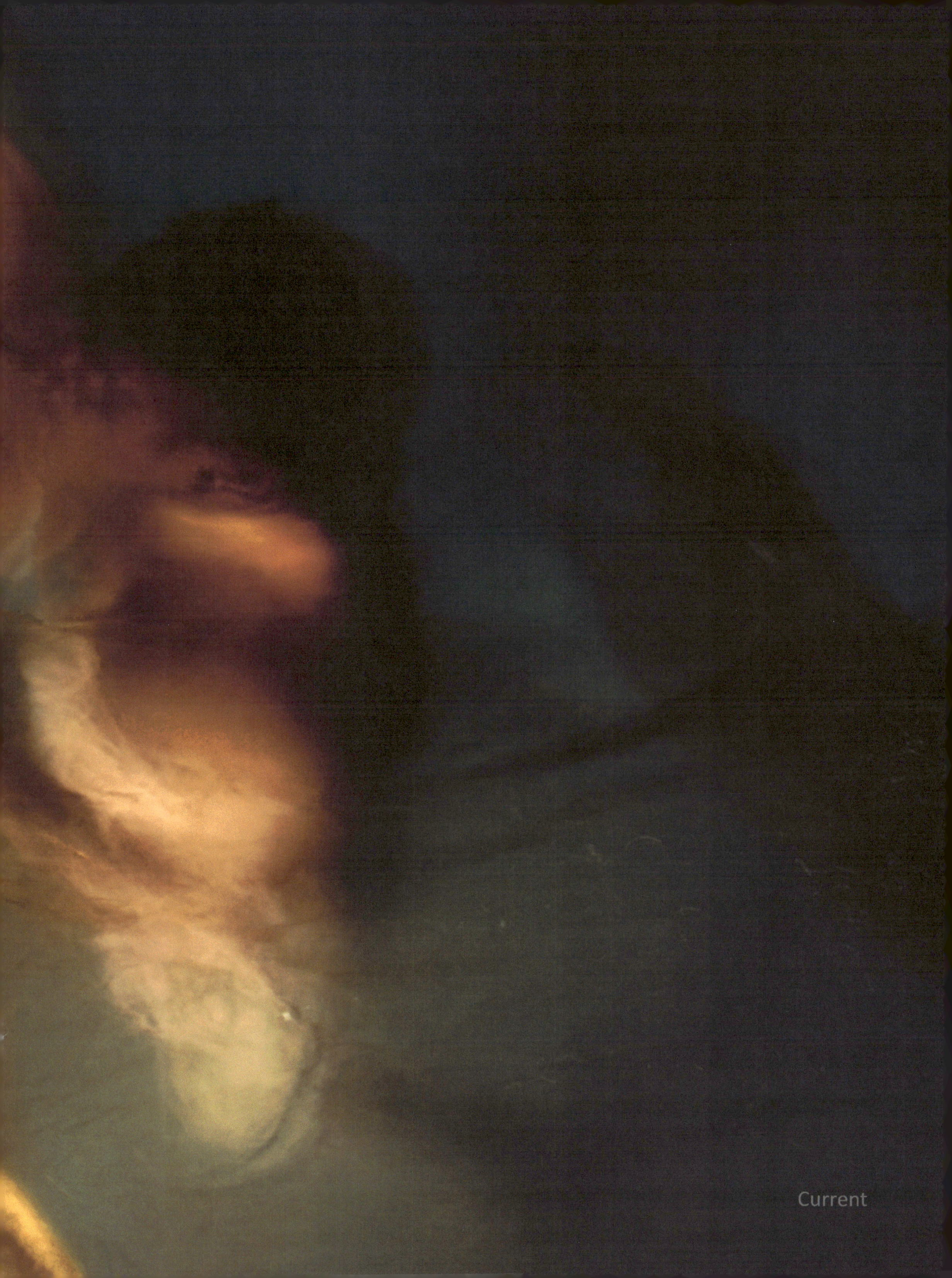
Current

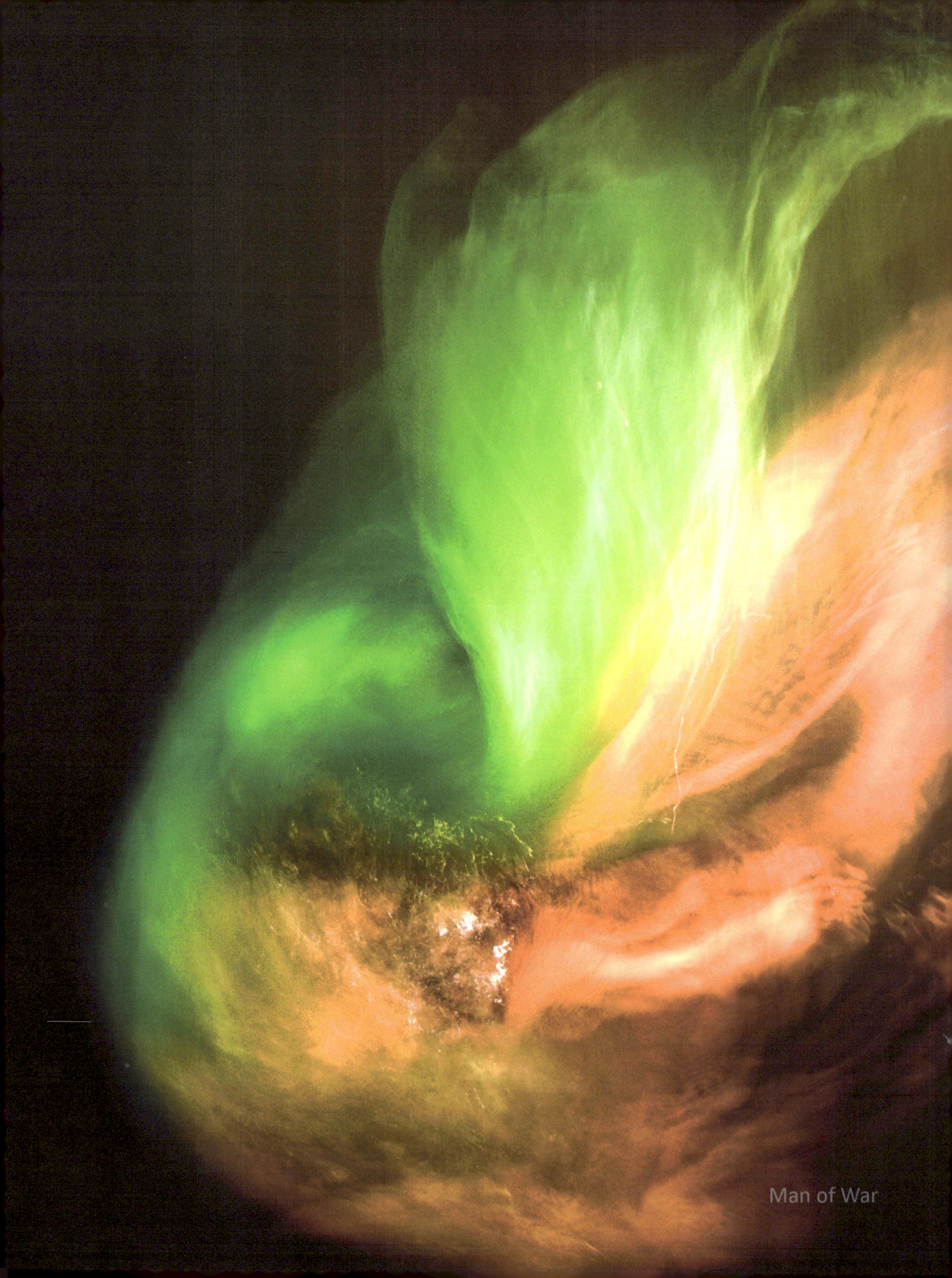

Man of War

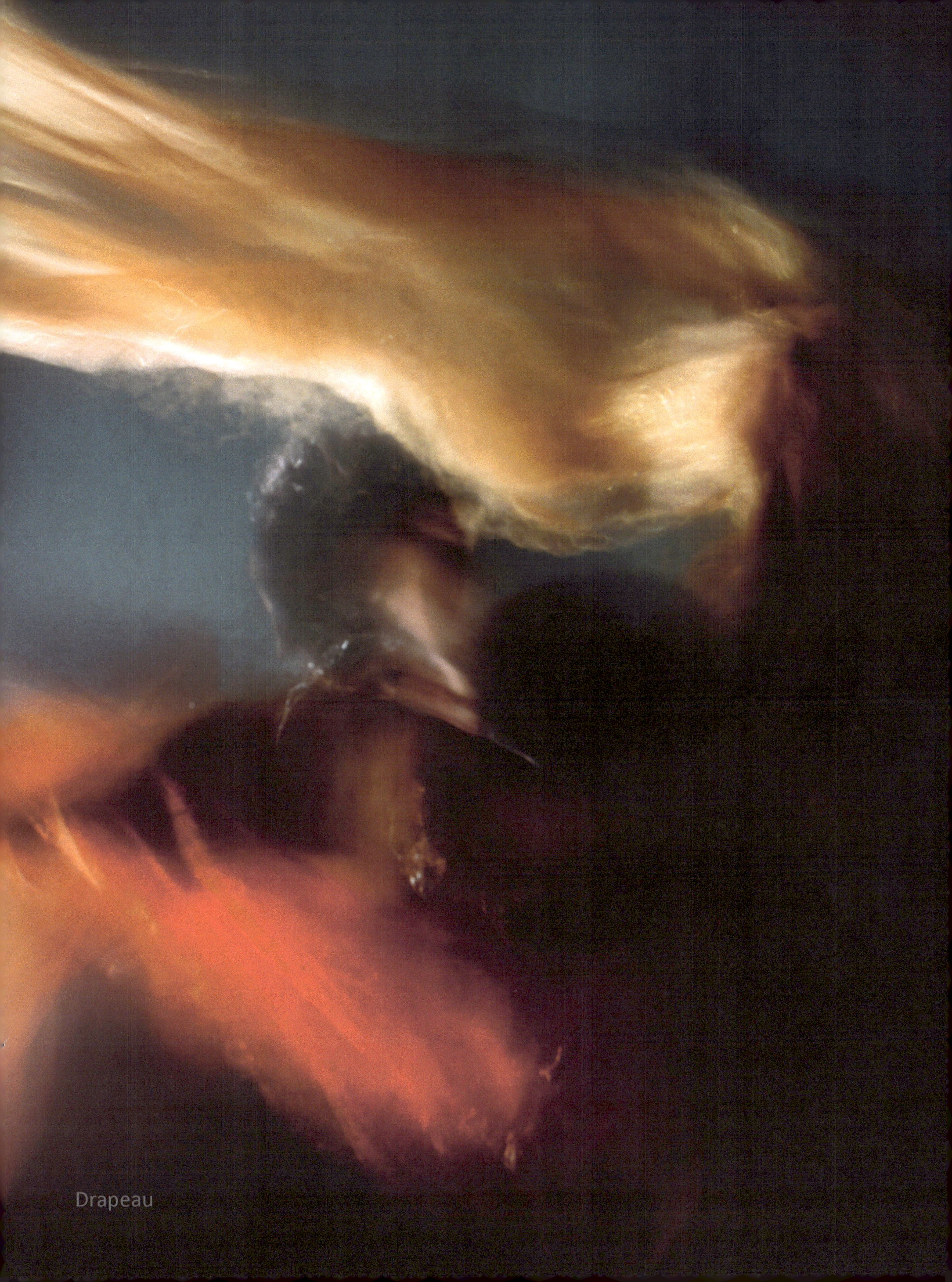

Drapeau

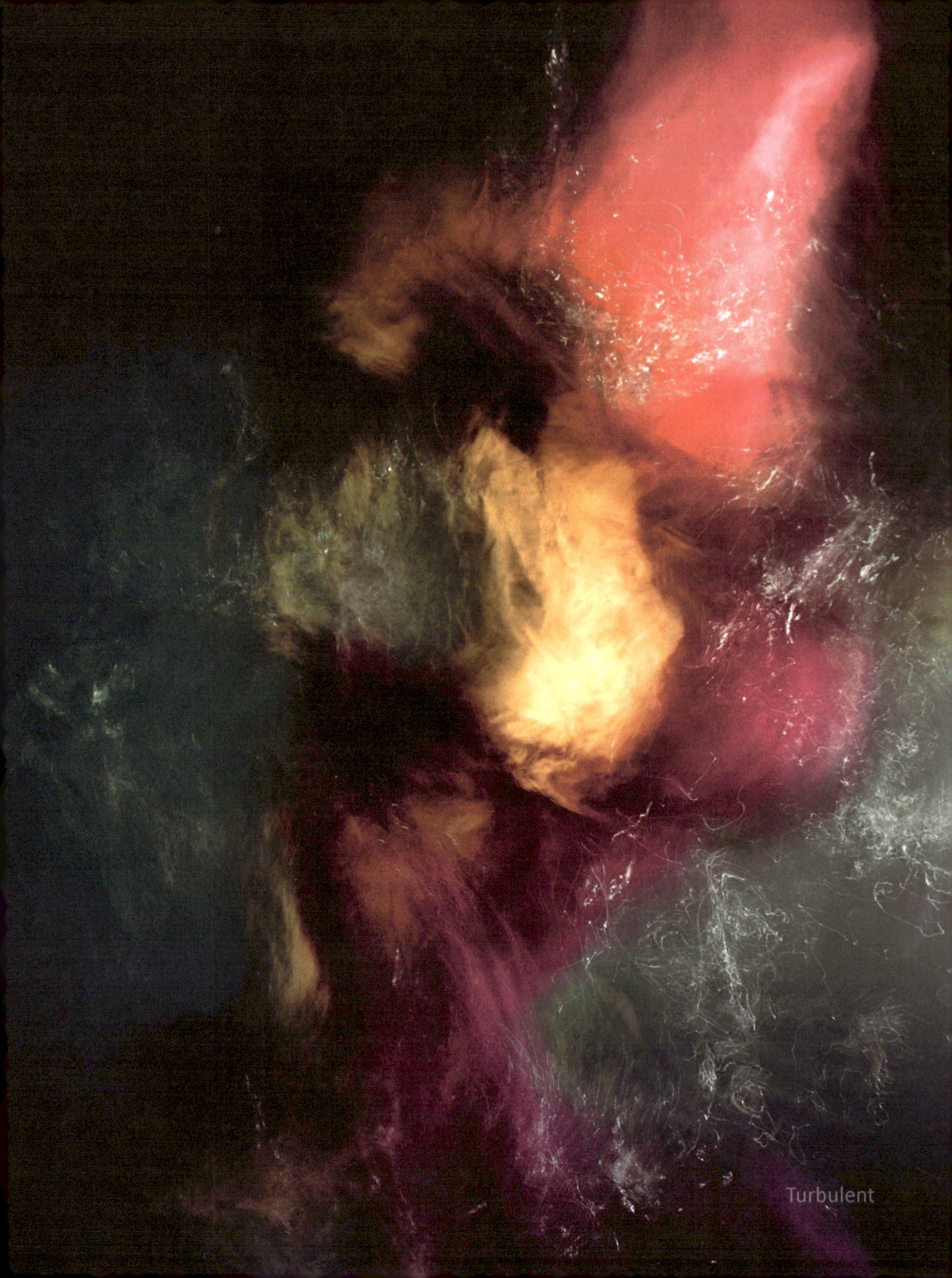
Turbulent

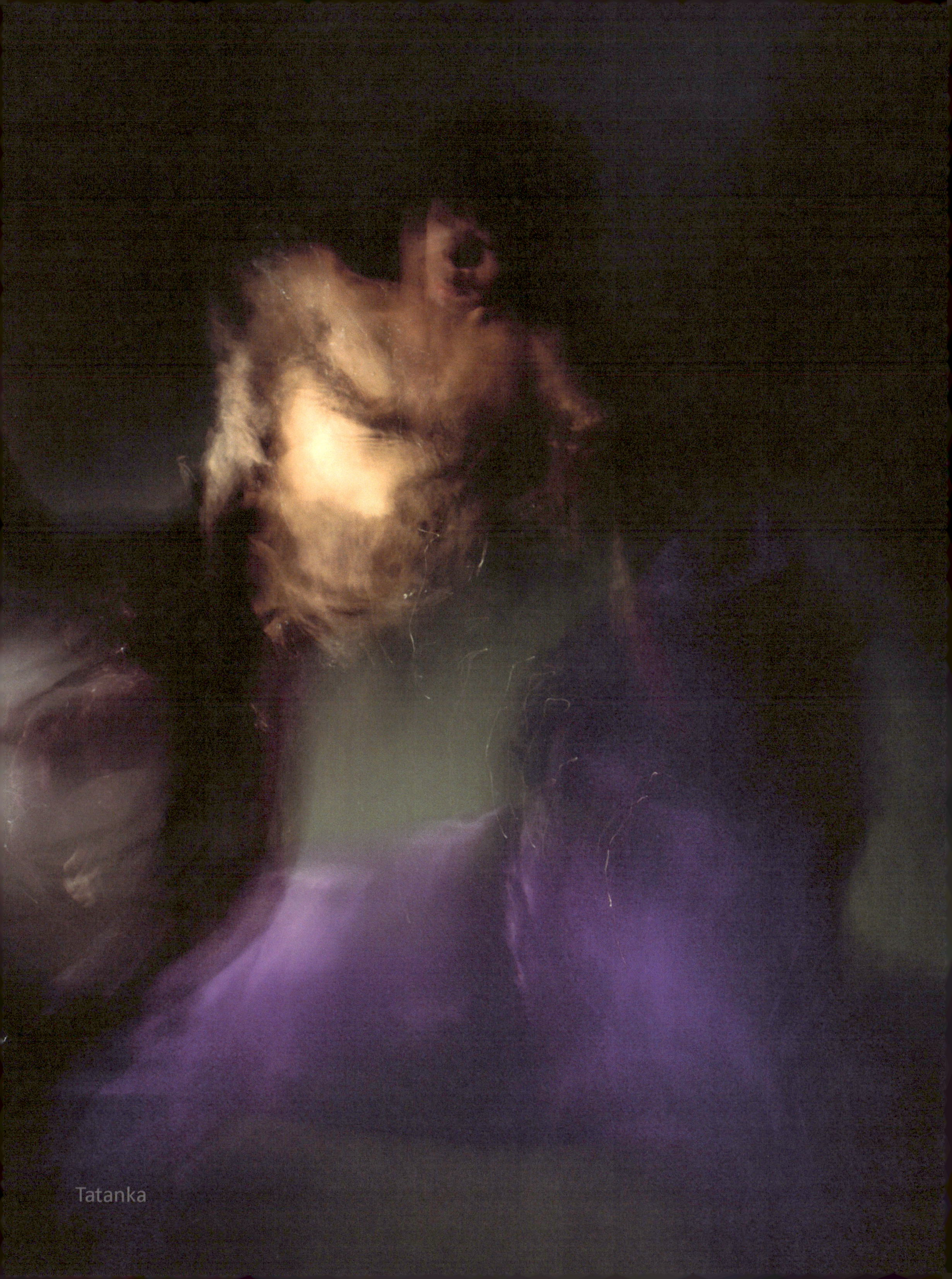

Tatanka

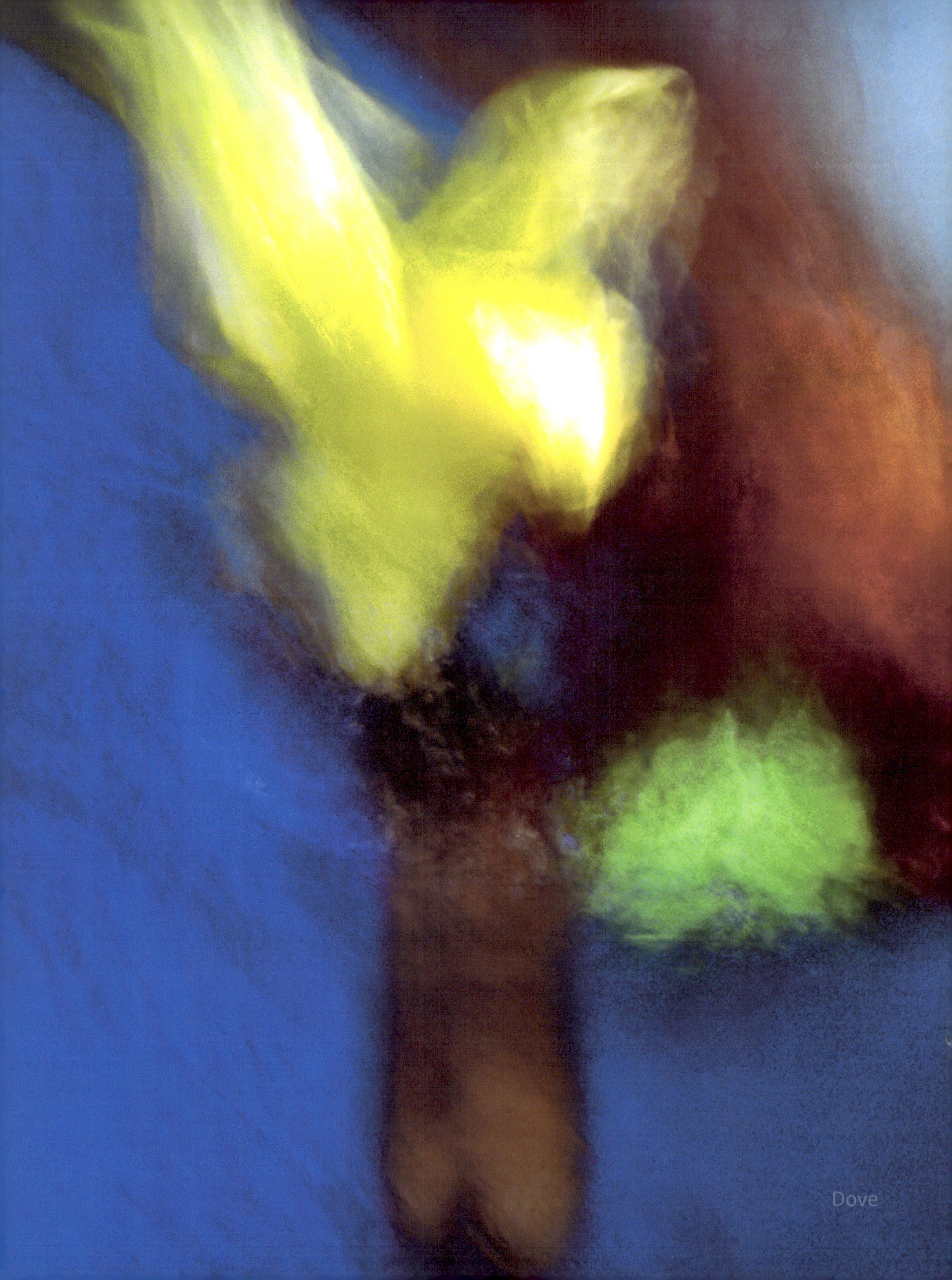

Dove

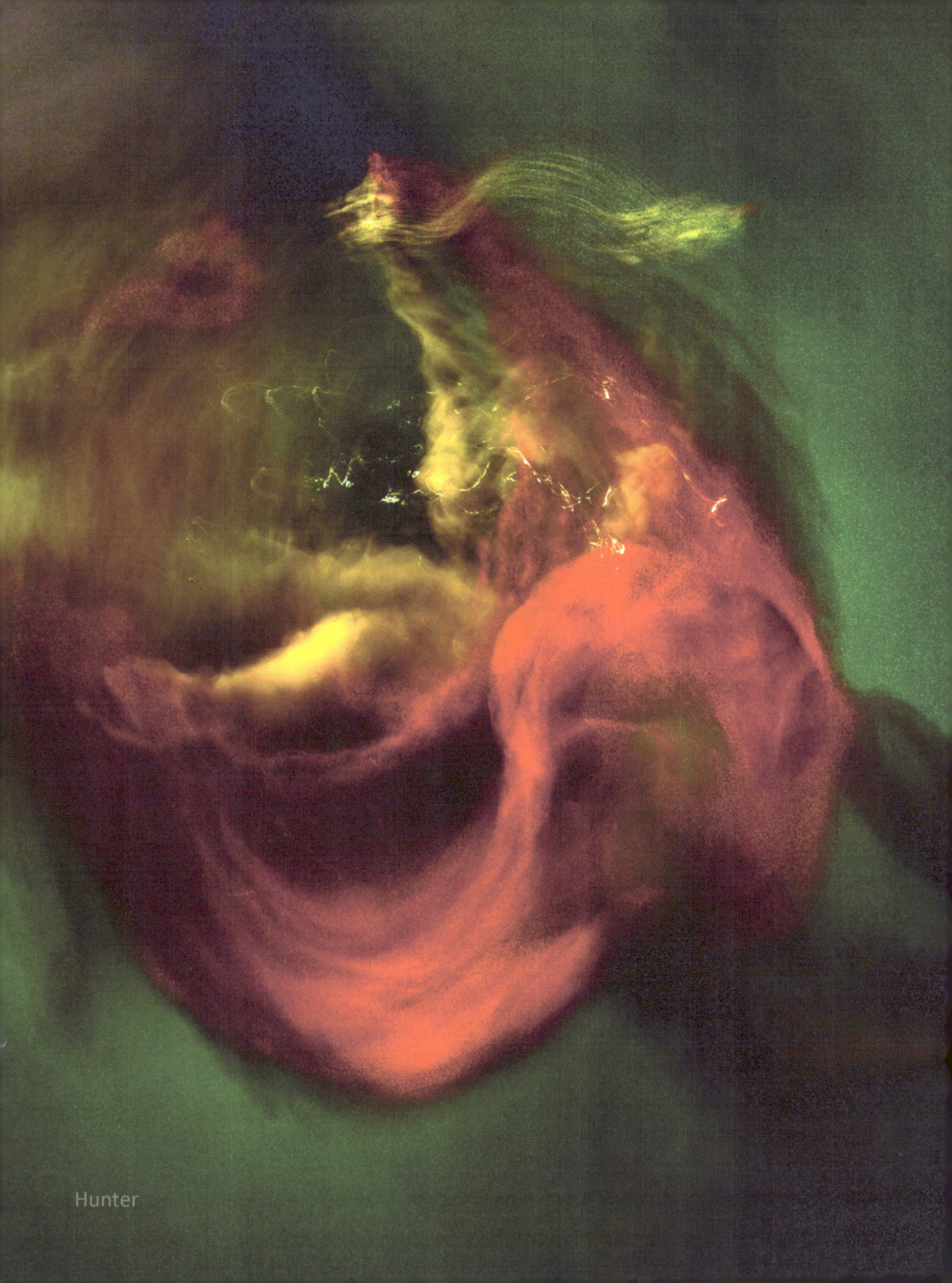

Hunter

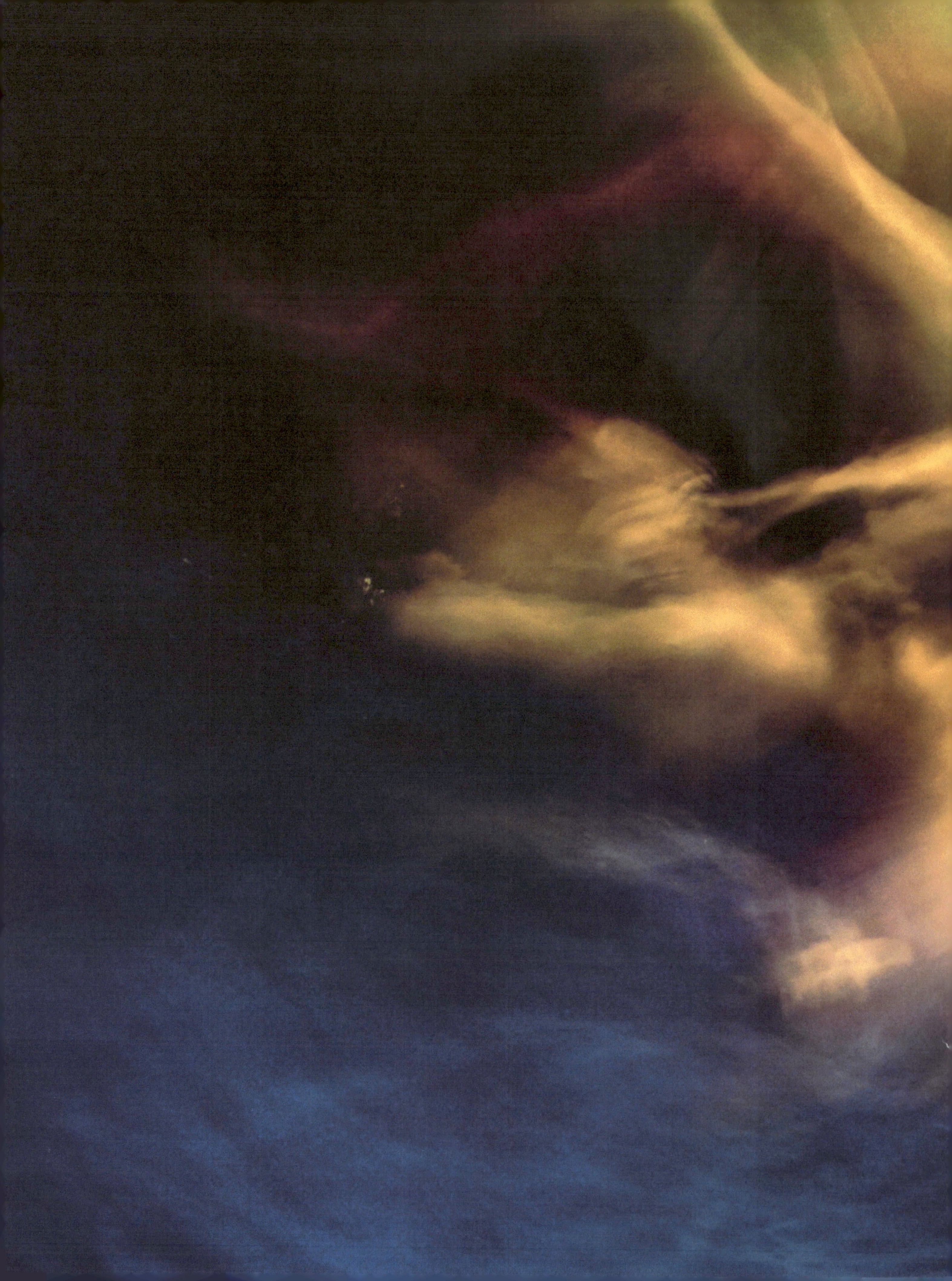

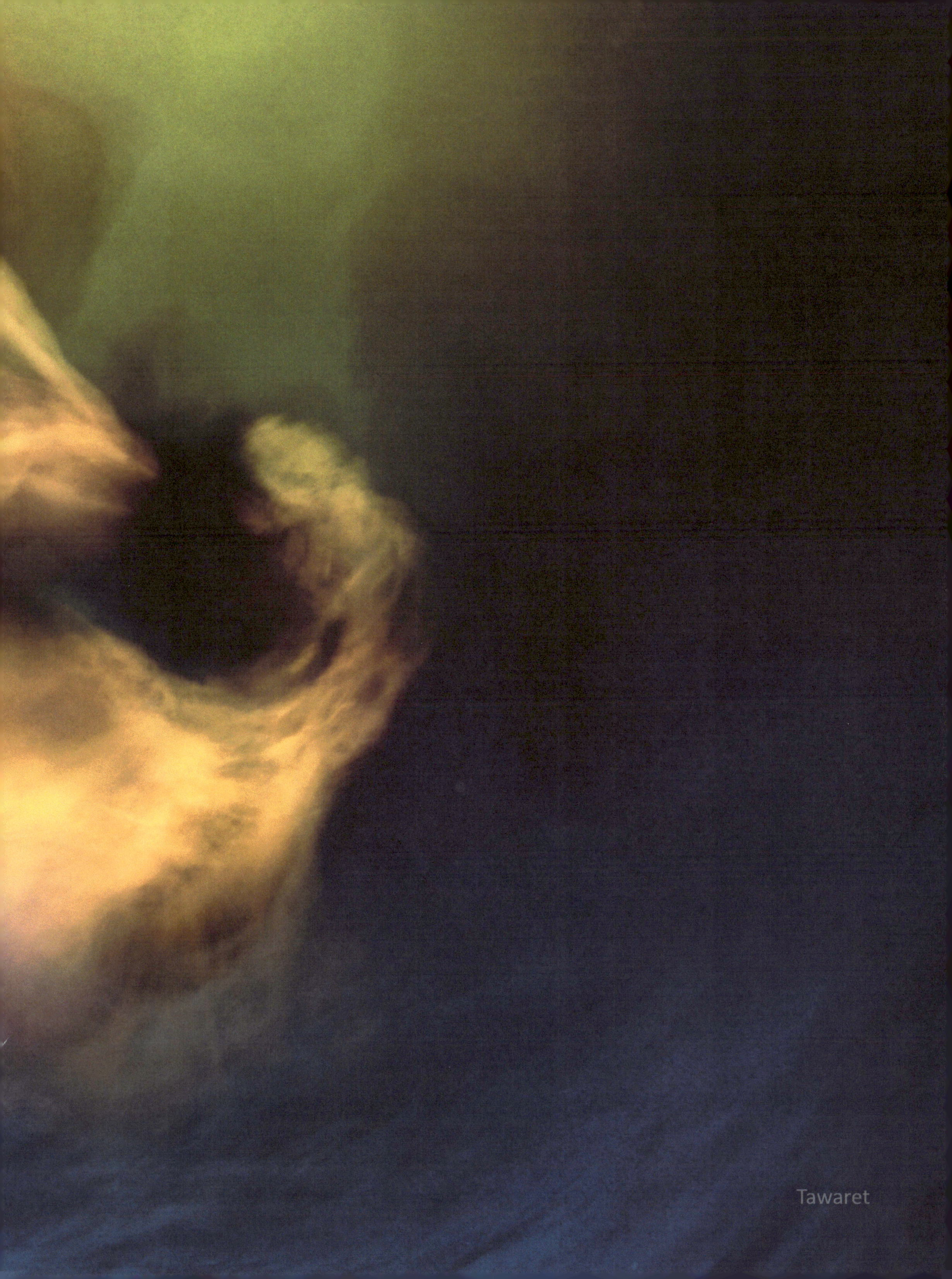

Tawaret

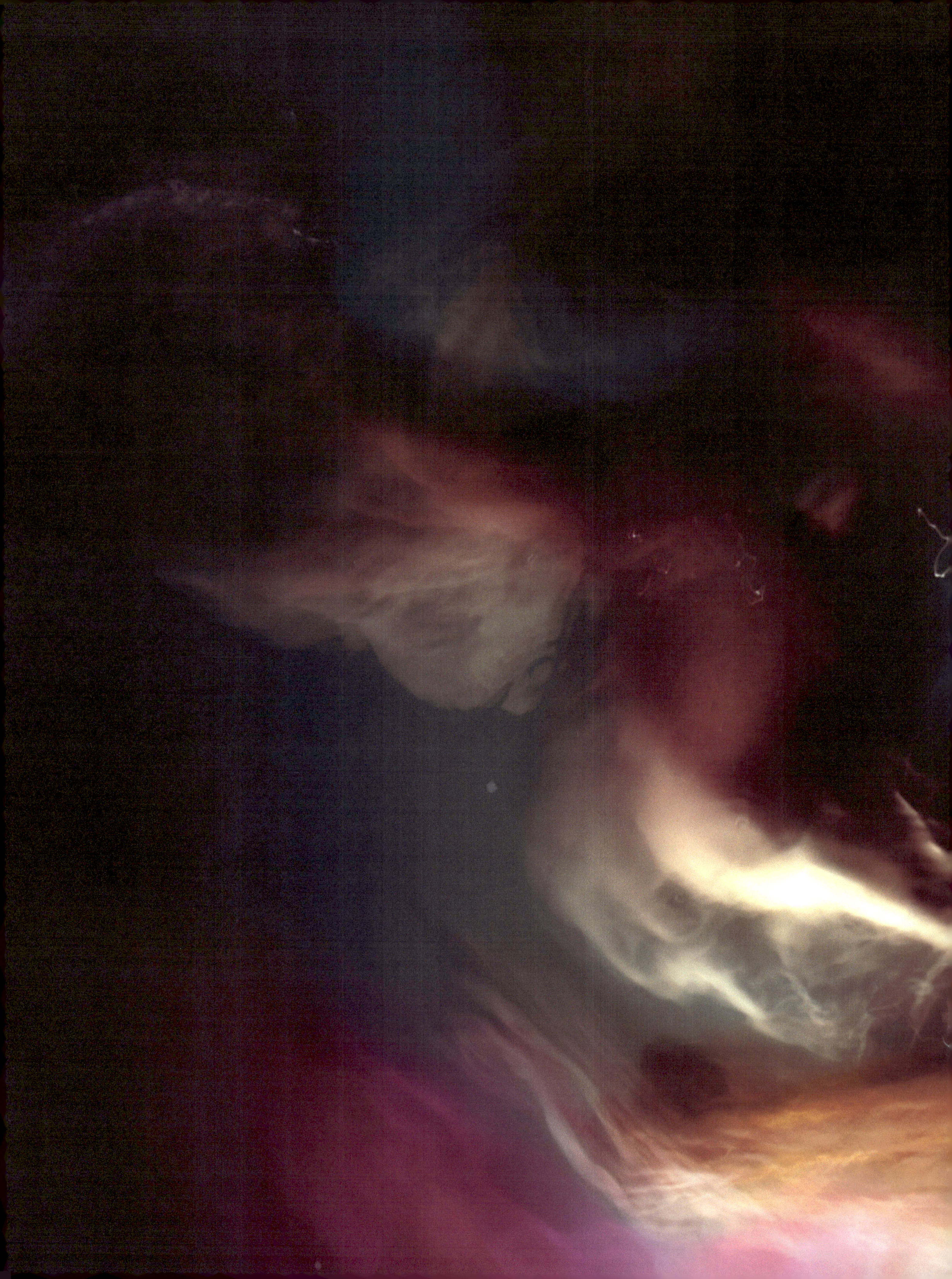

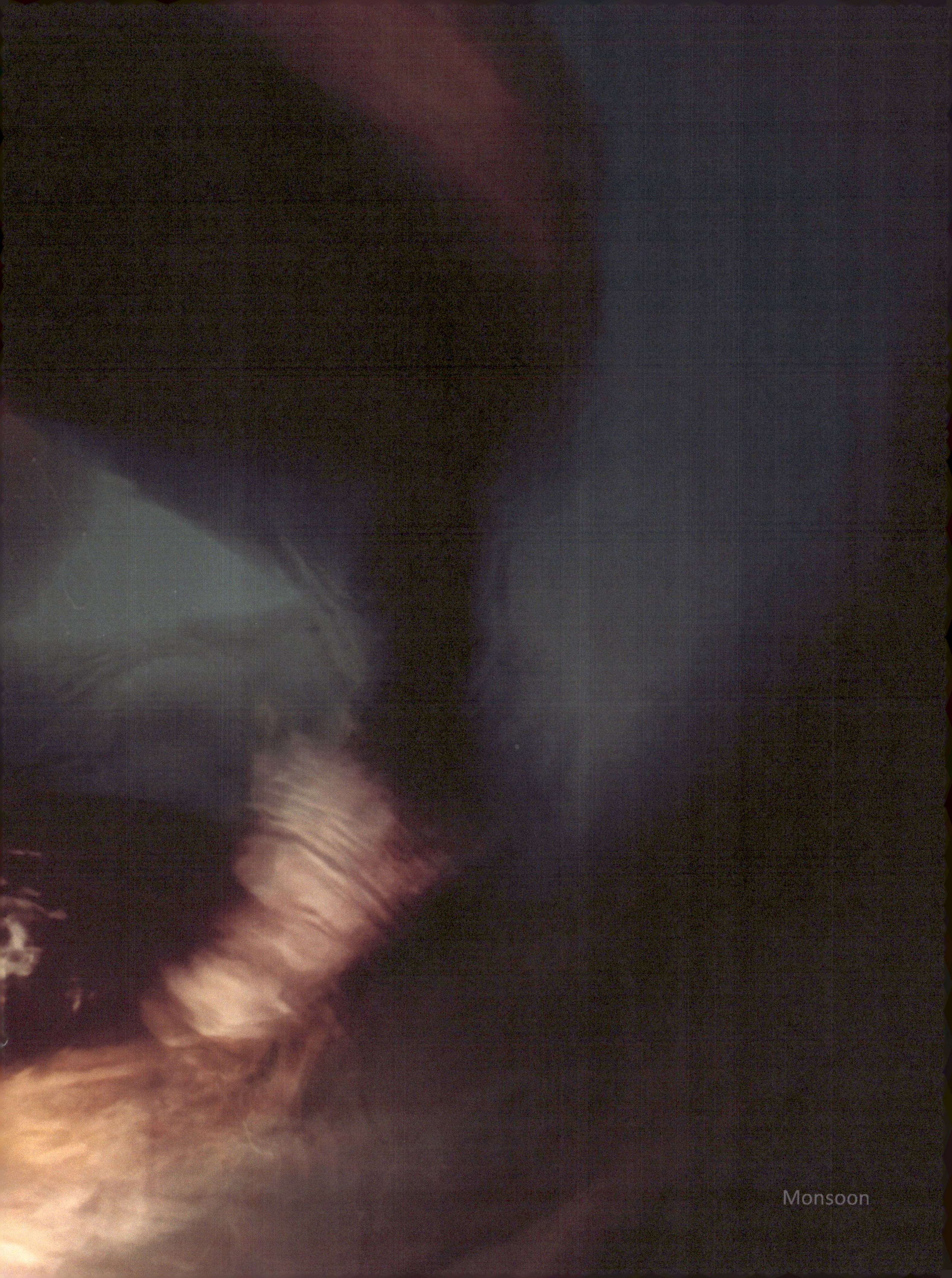
Monsoon

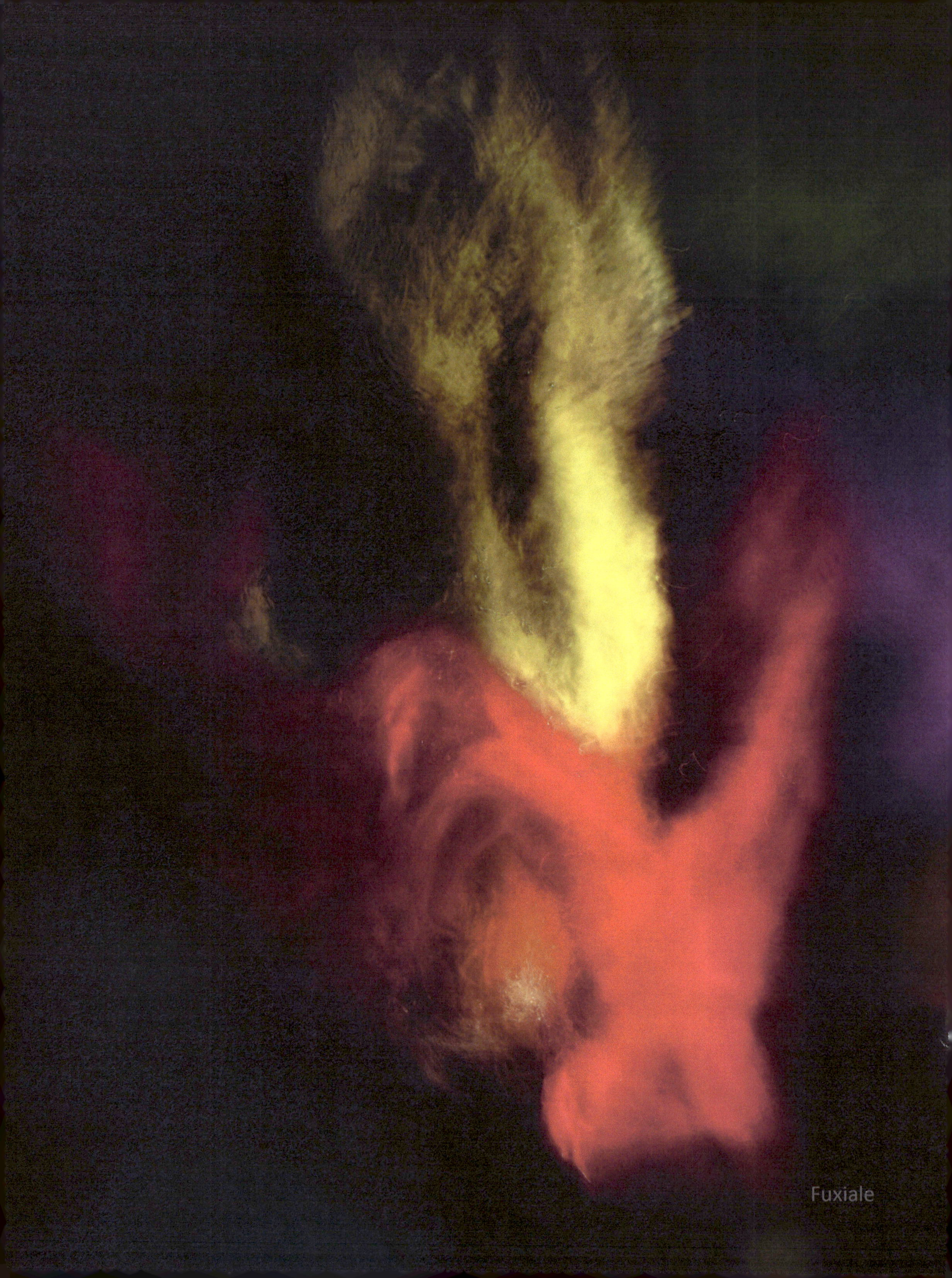

Angels & Demons

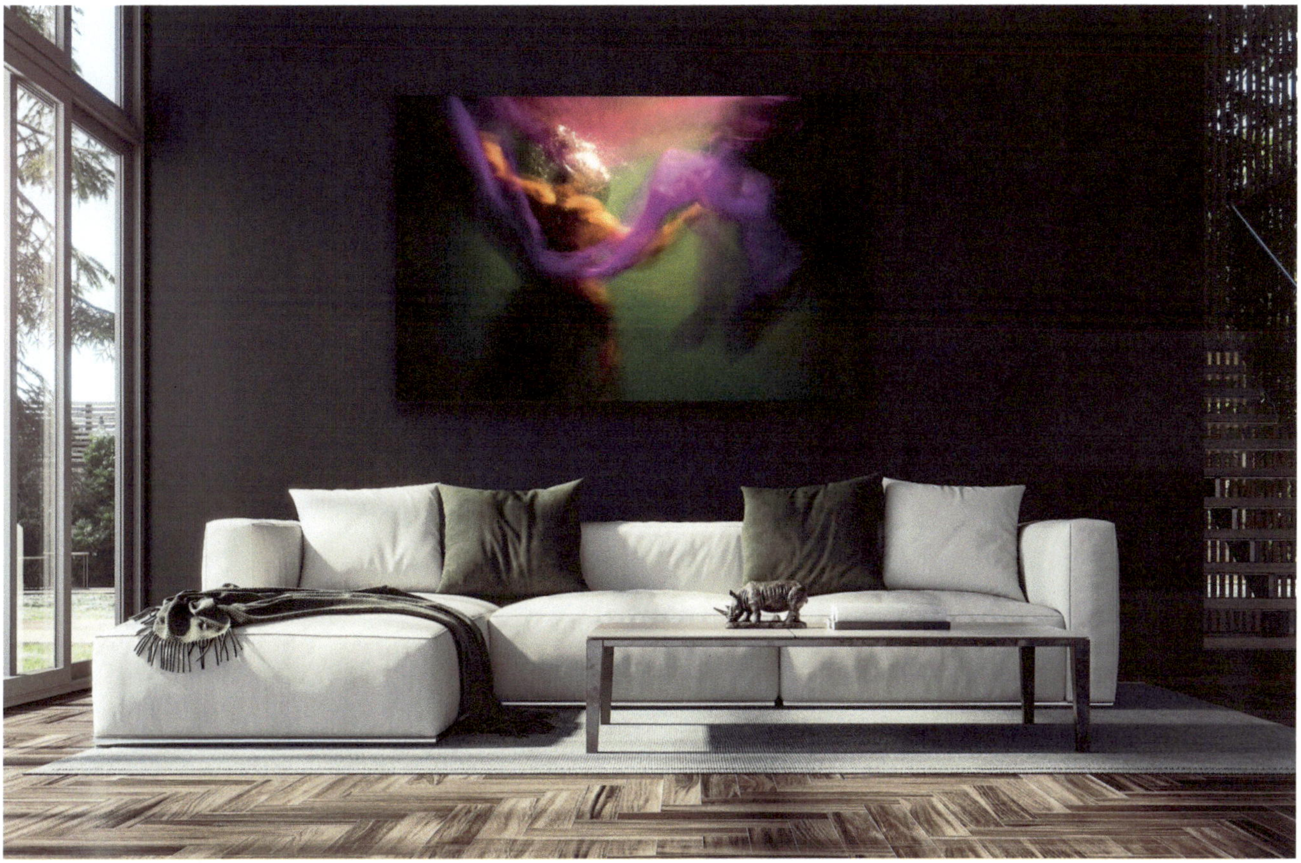

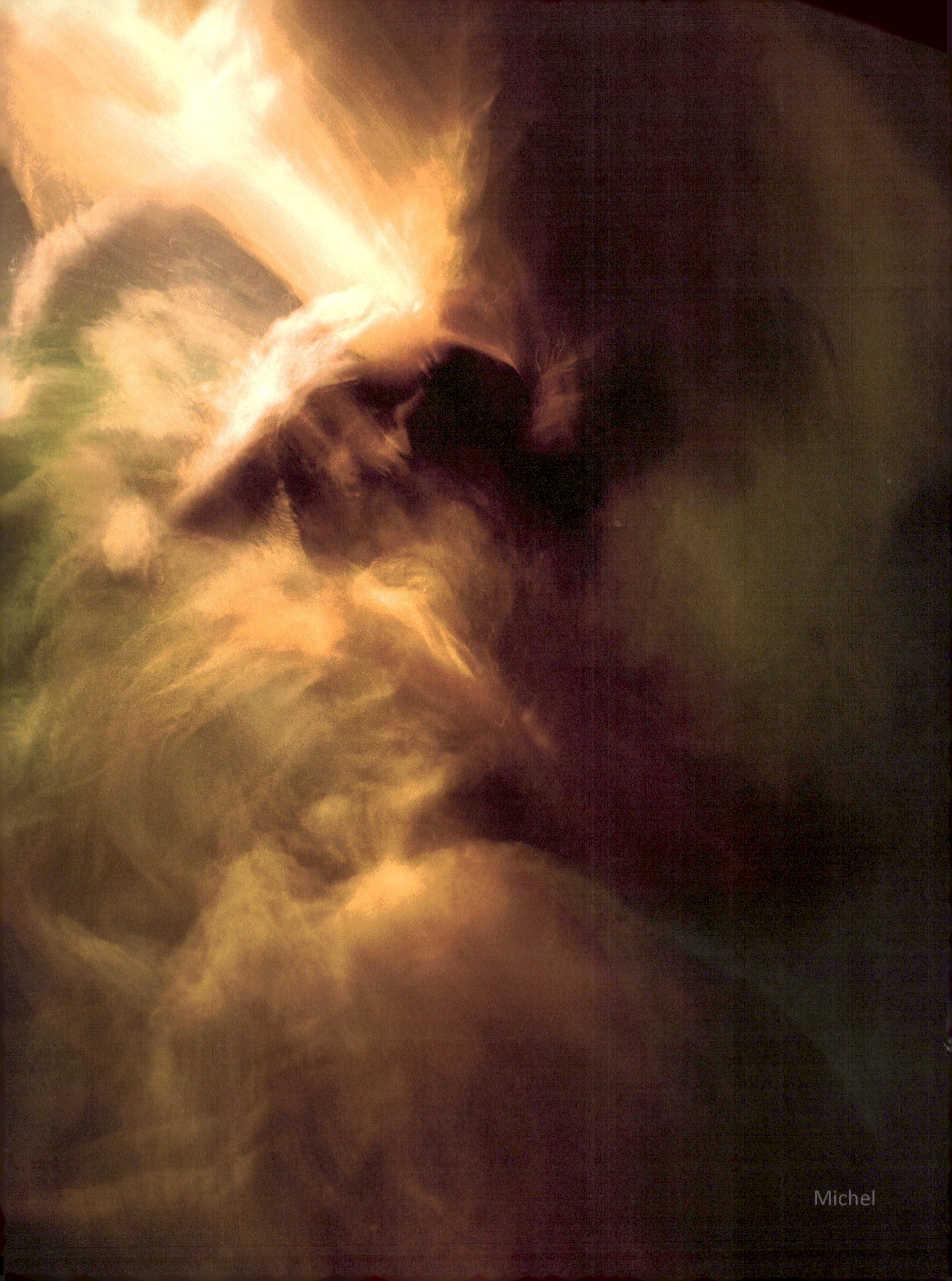
Michel

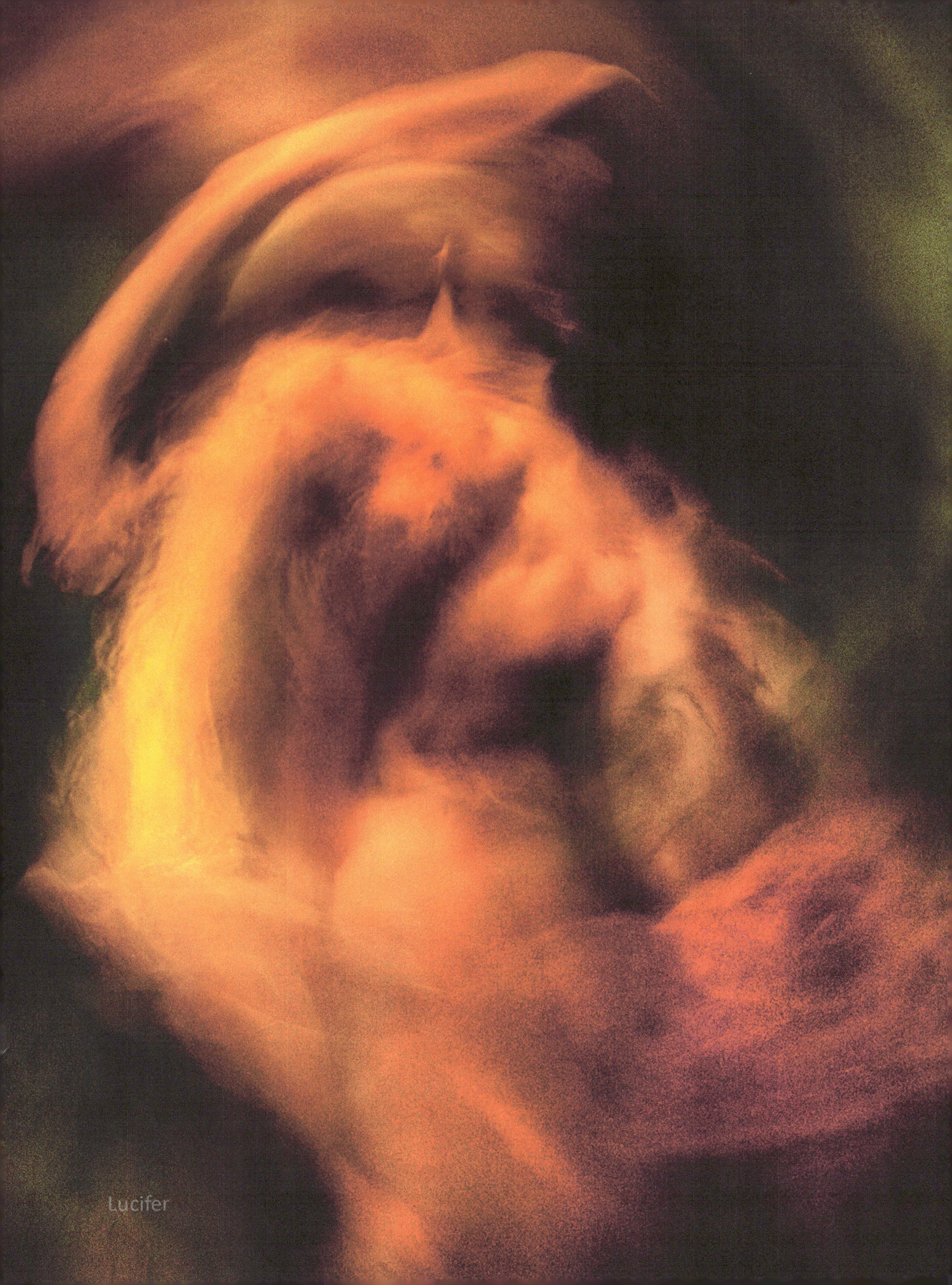

Lucifer

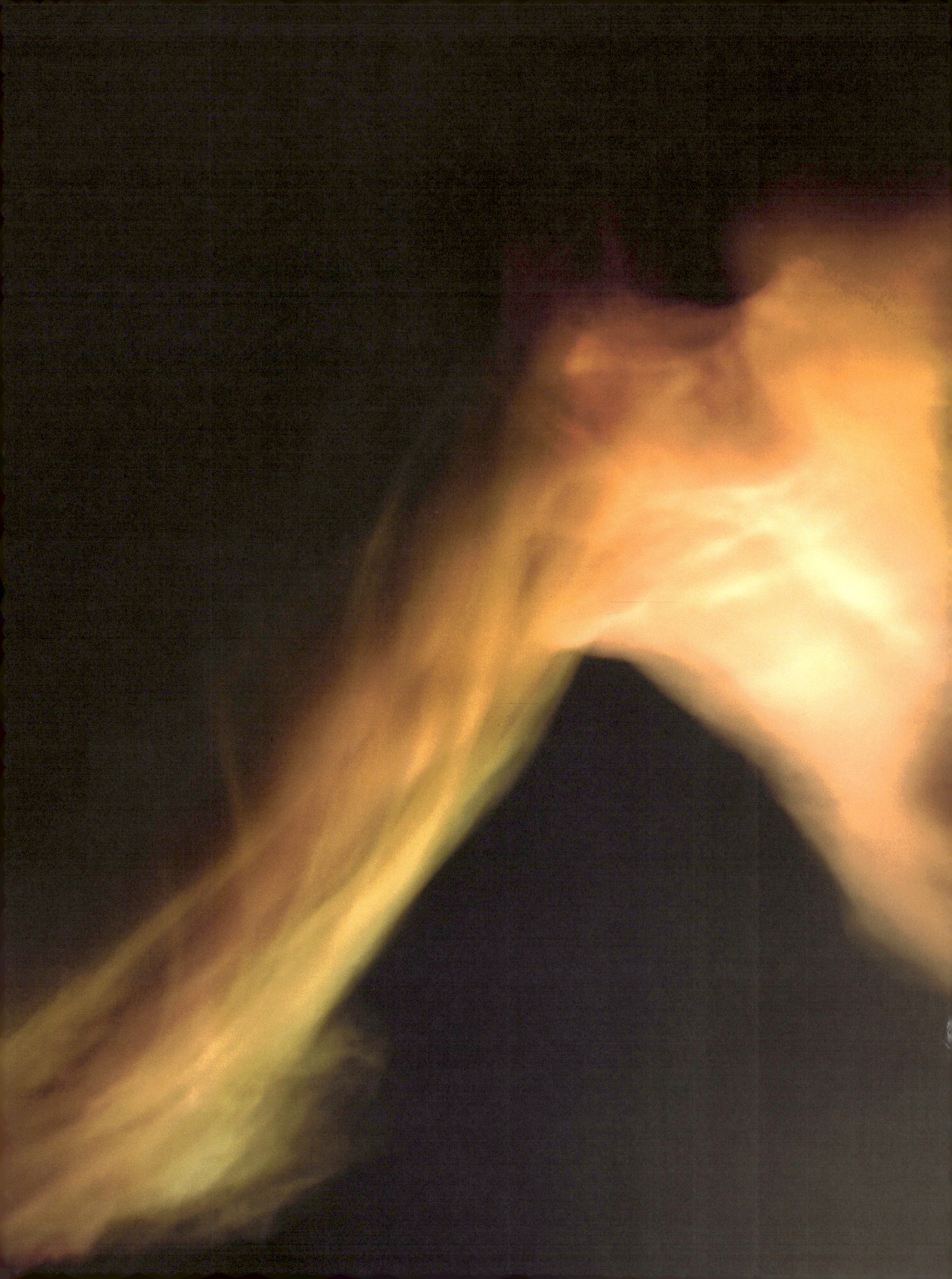

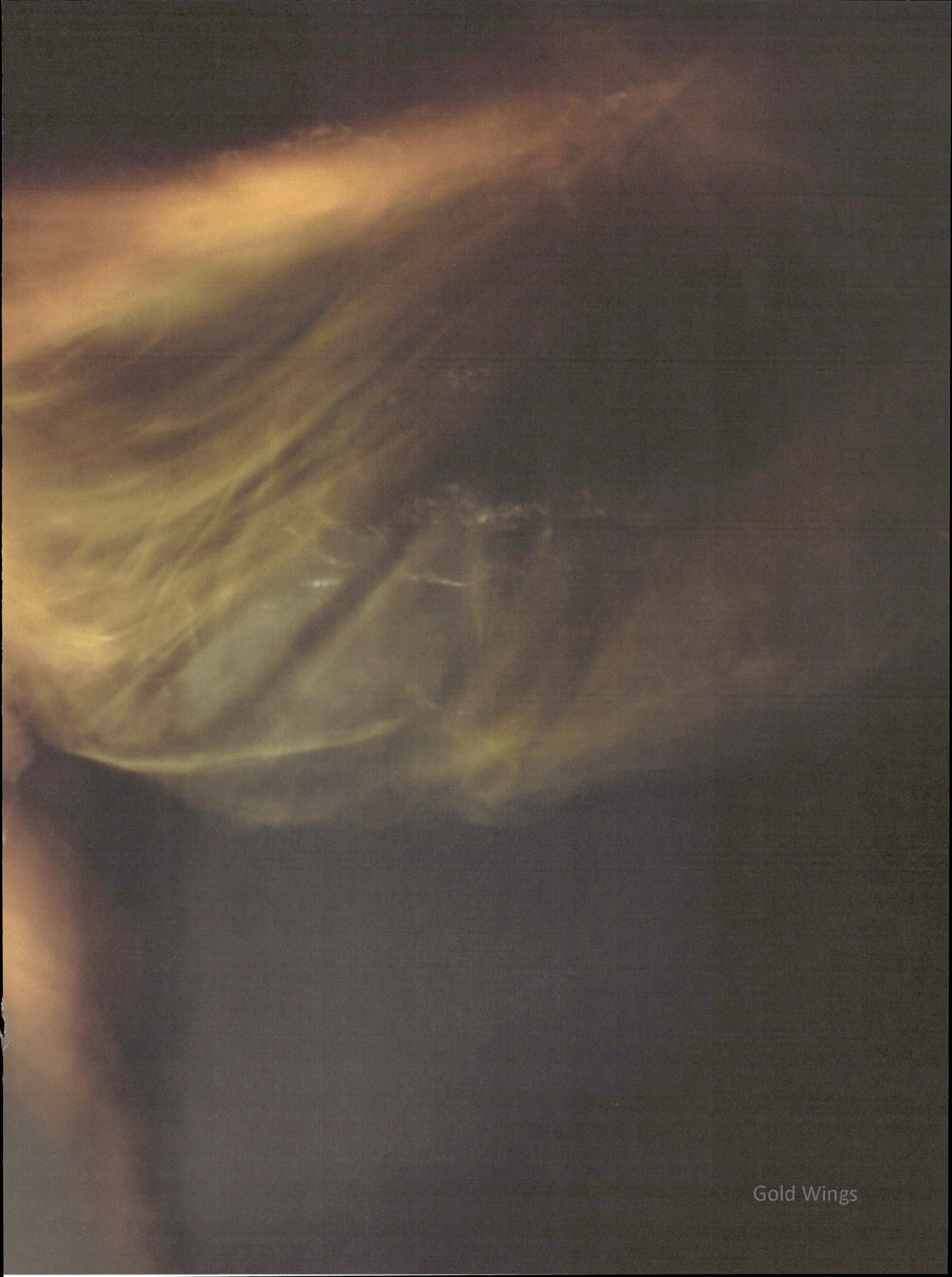

Gold Wings

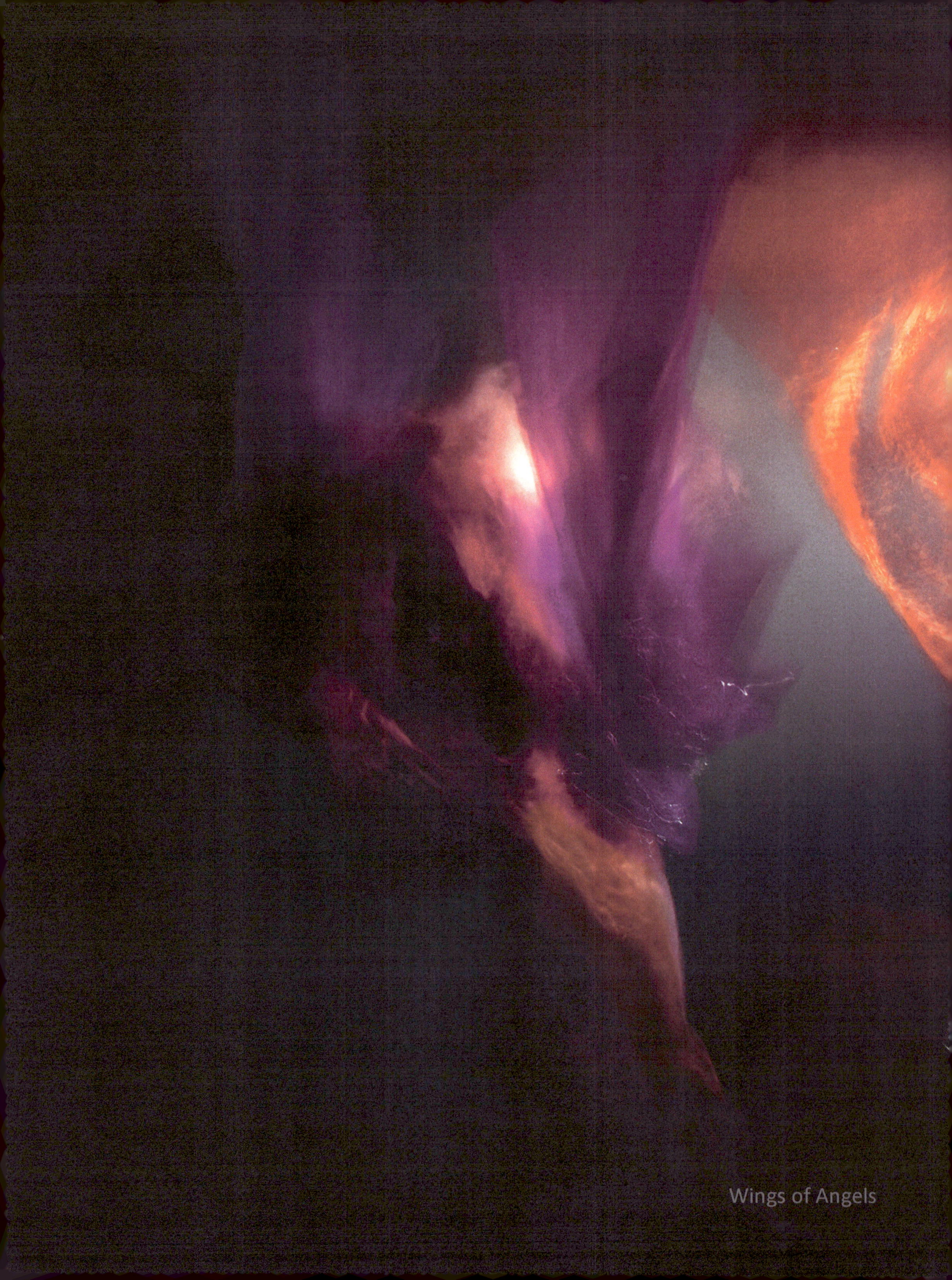

Wings of Angels

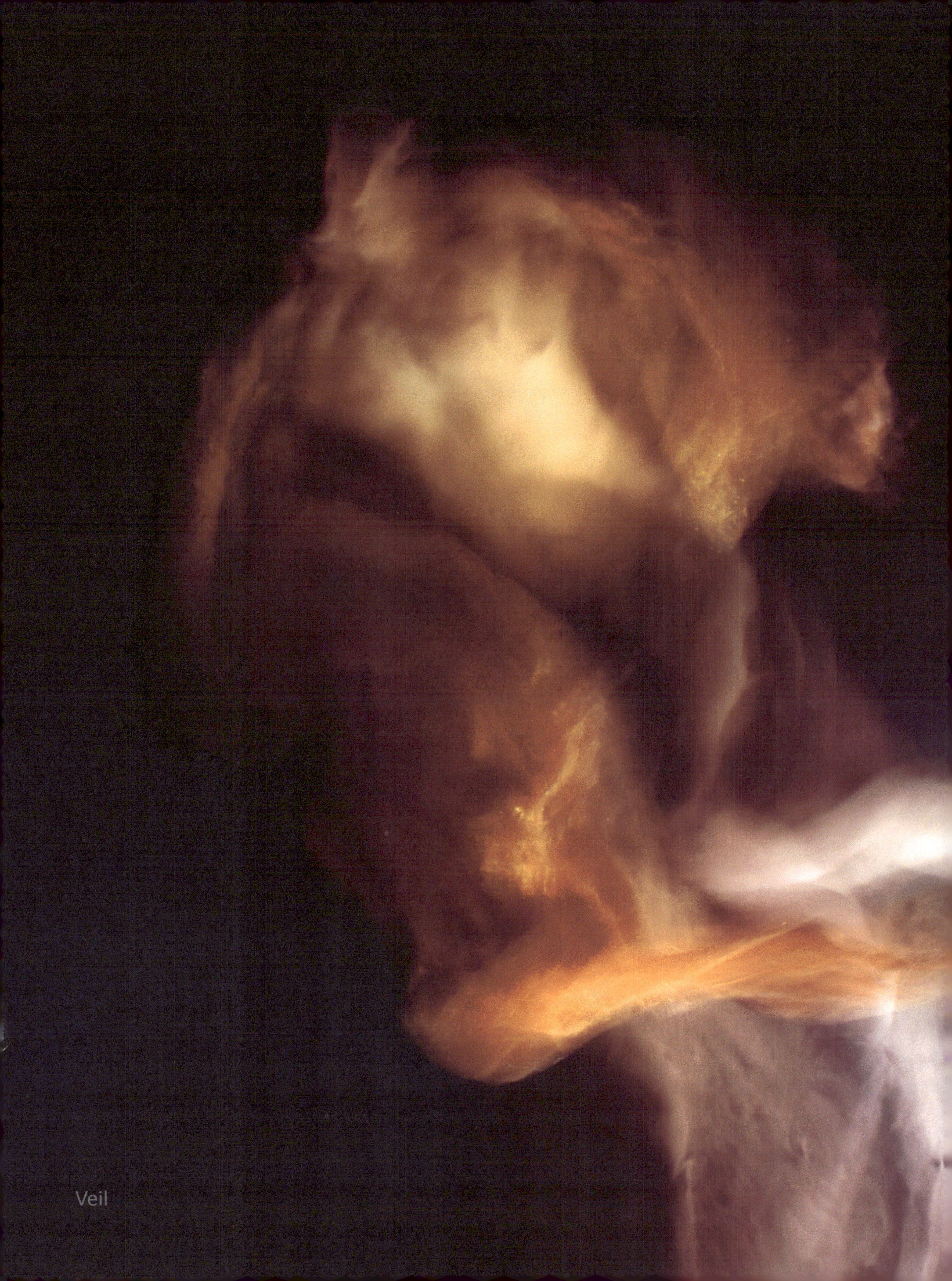

Veil

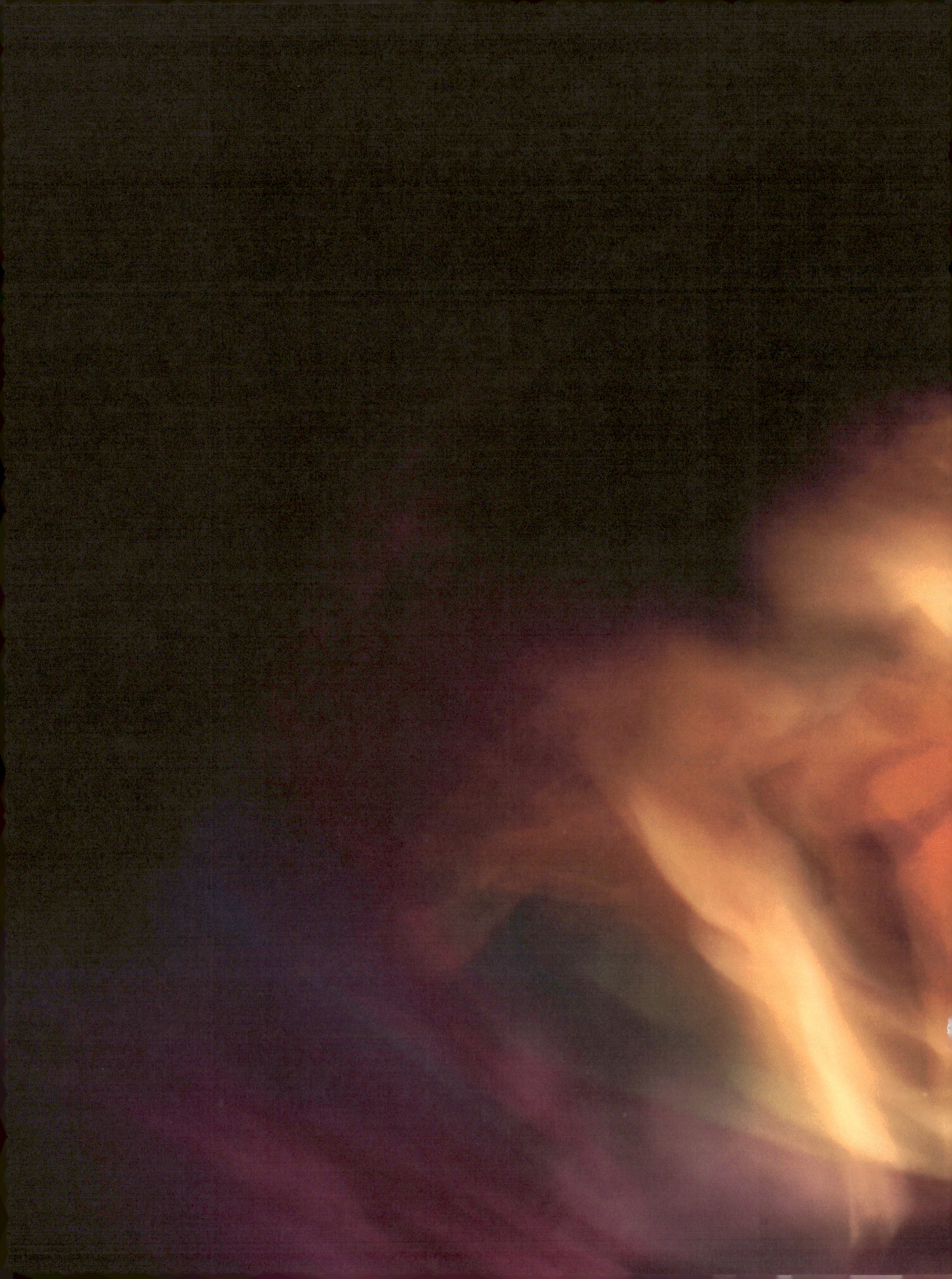

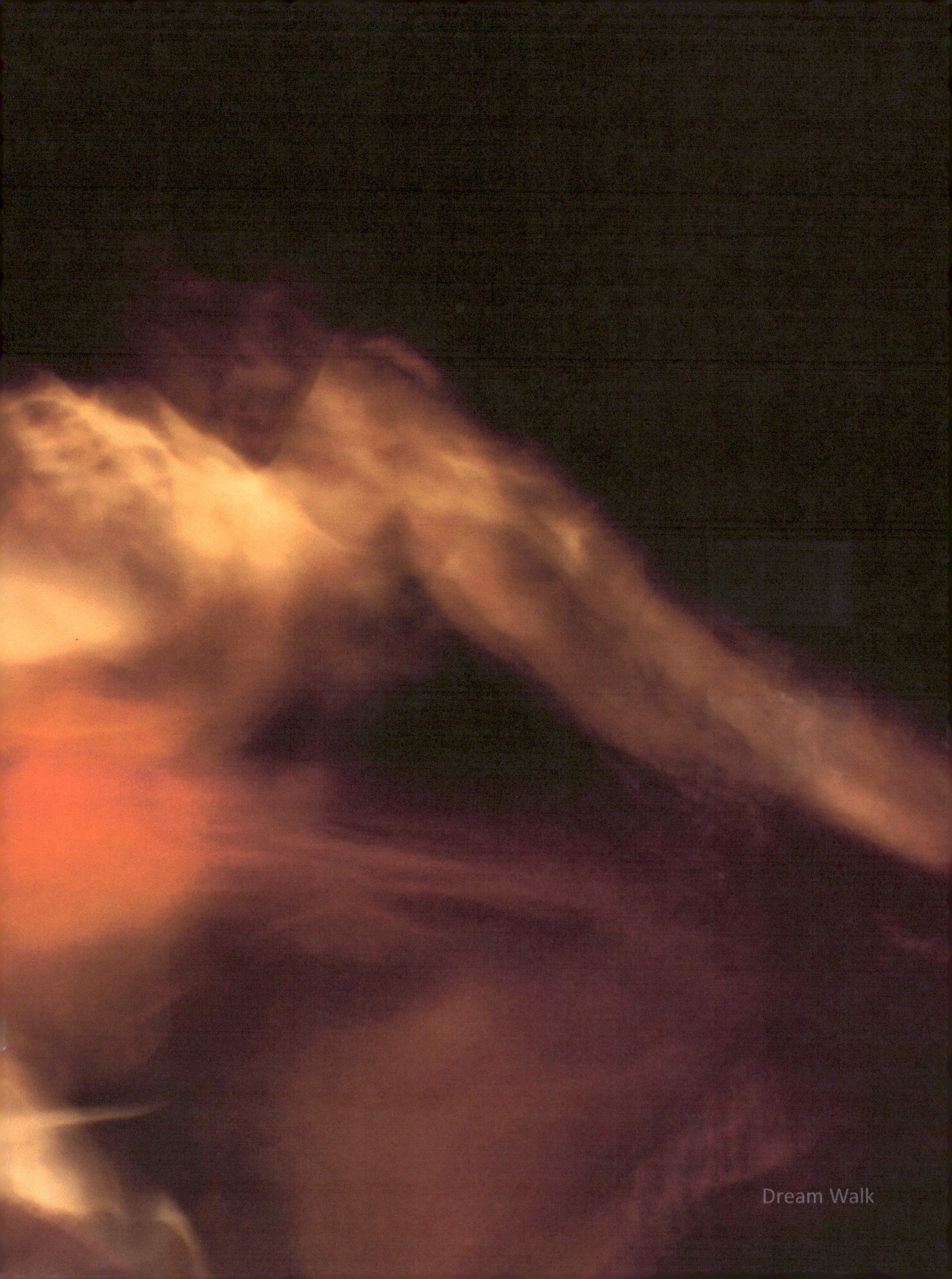

Dream Walk

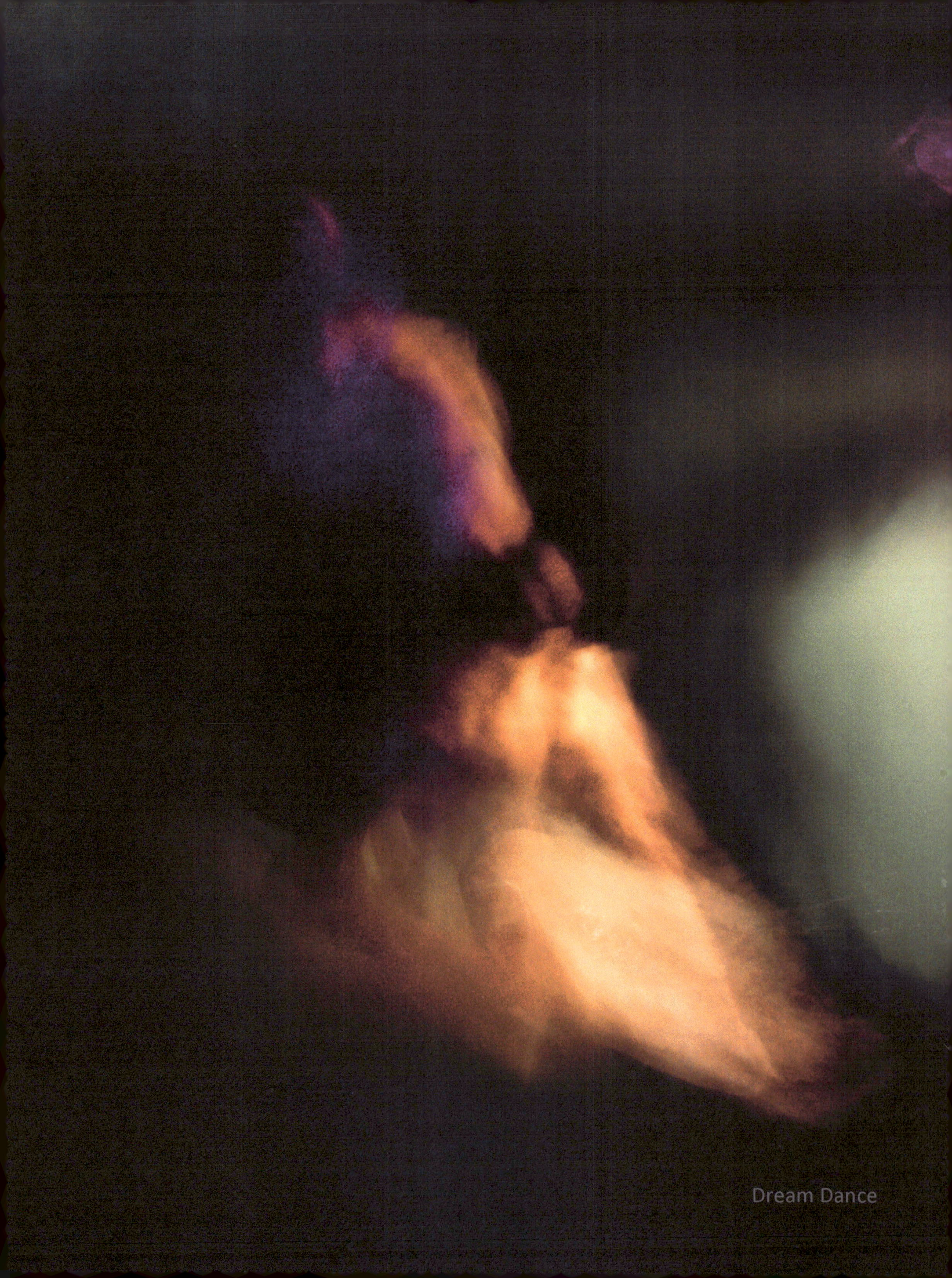

Dream Dance

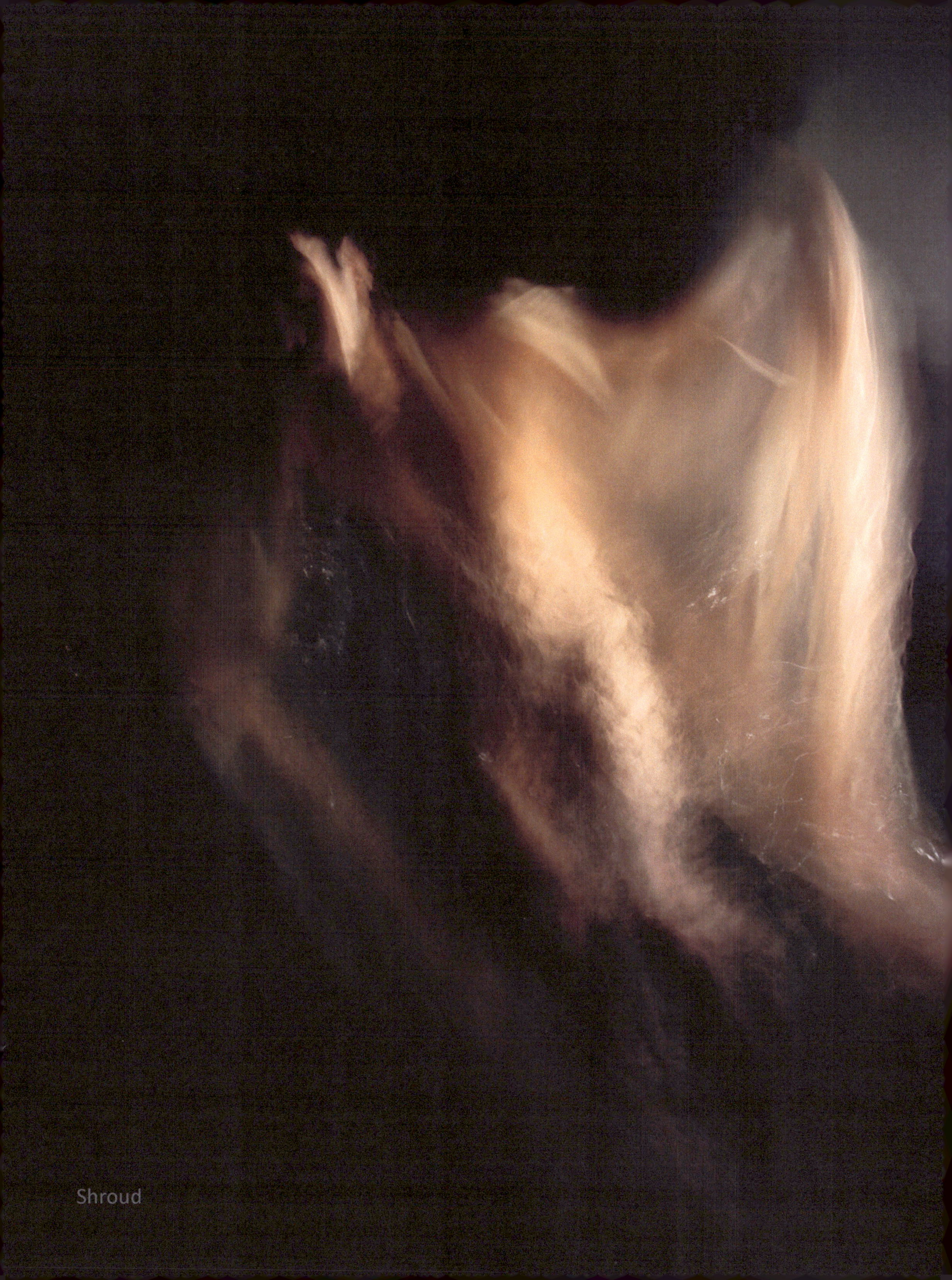

Shroud

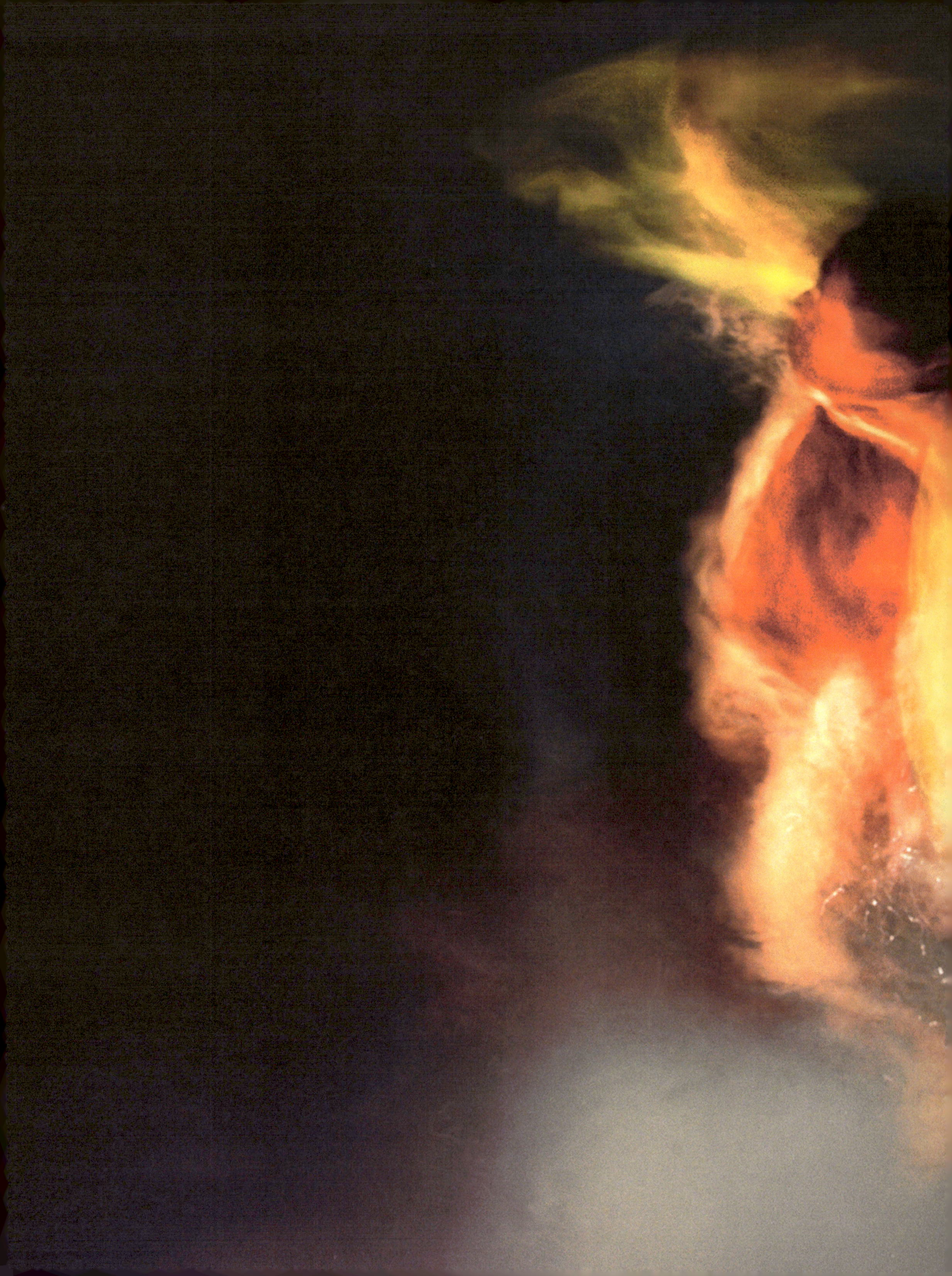

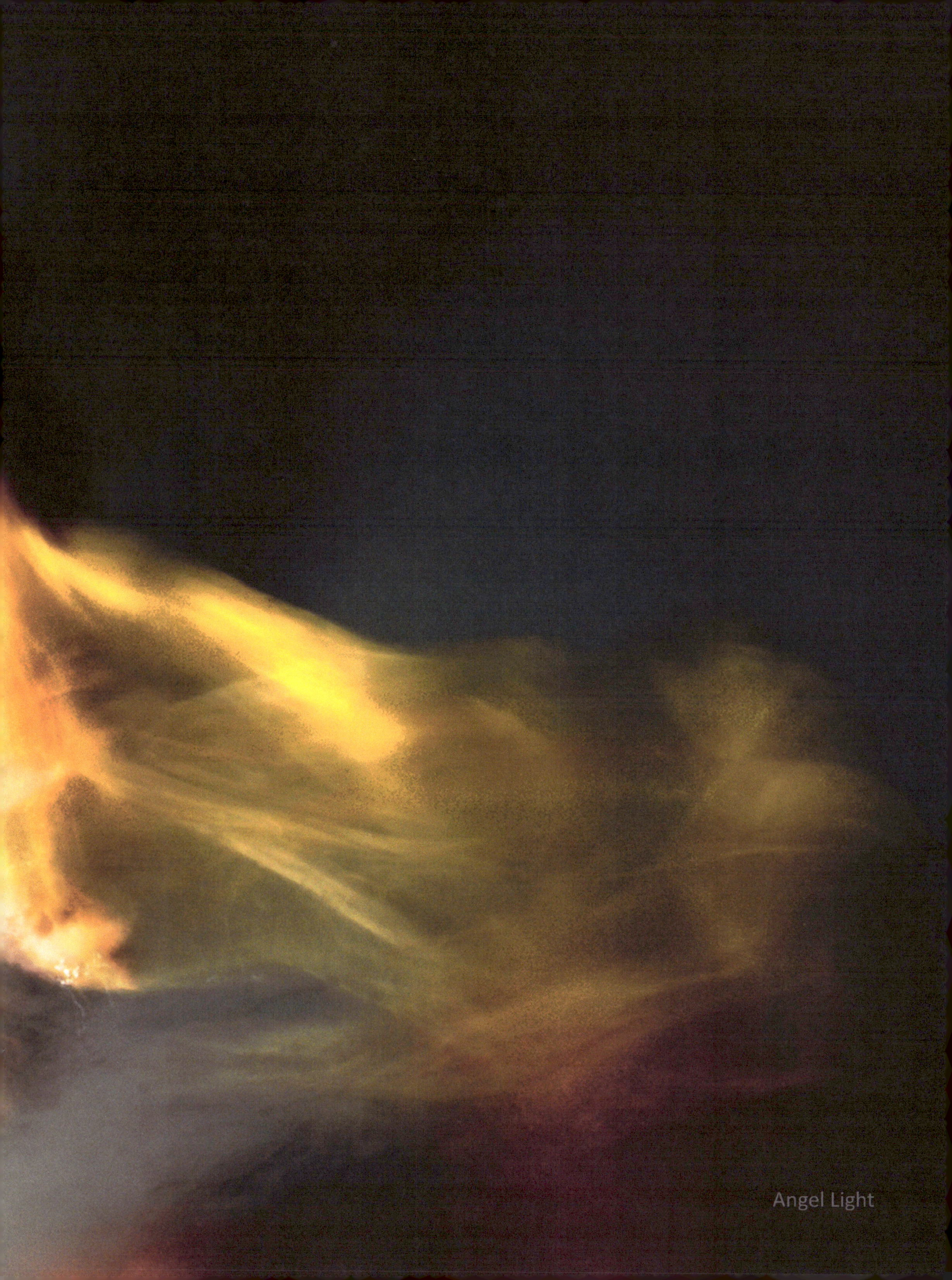
Angel Light

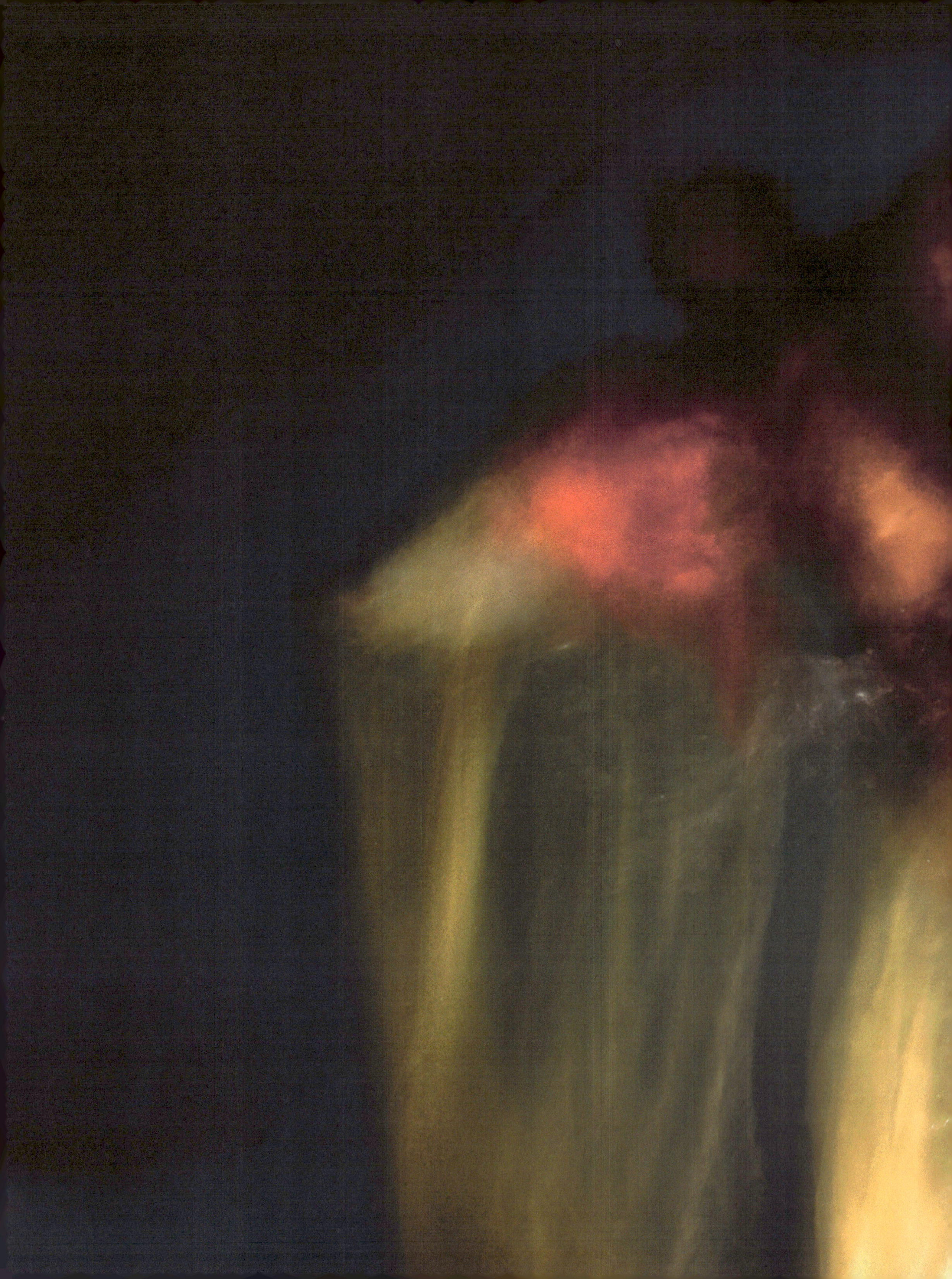

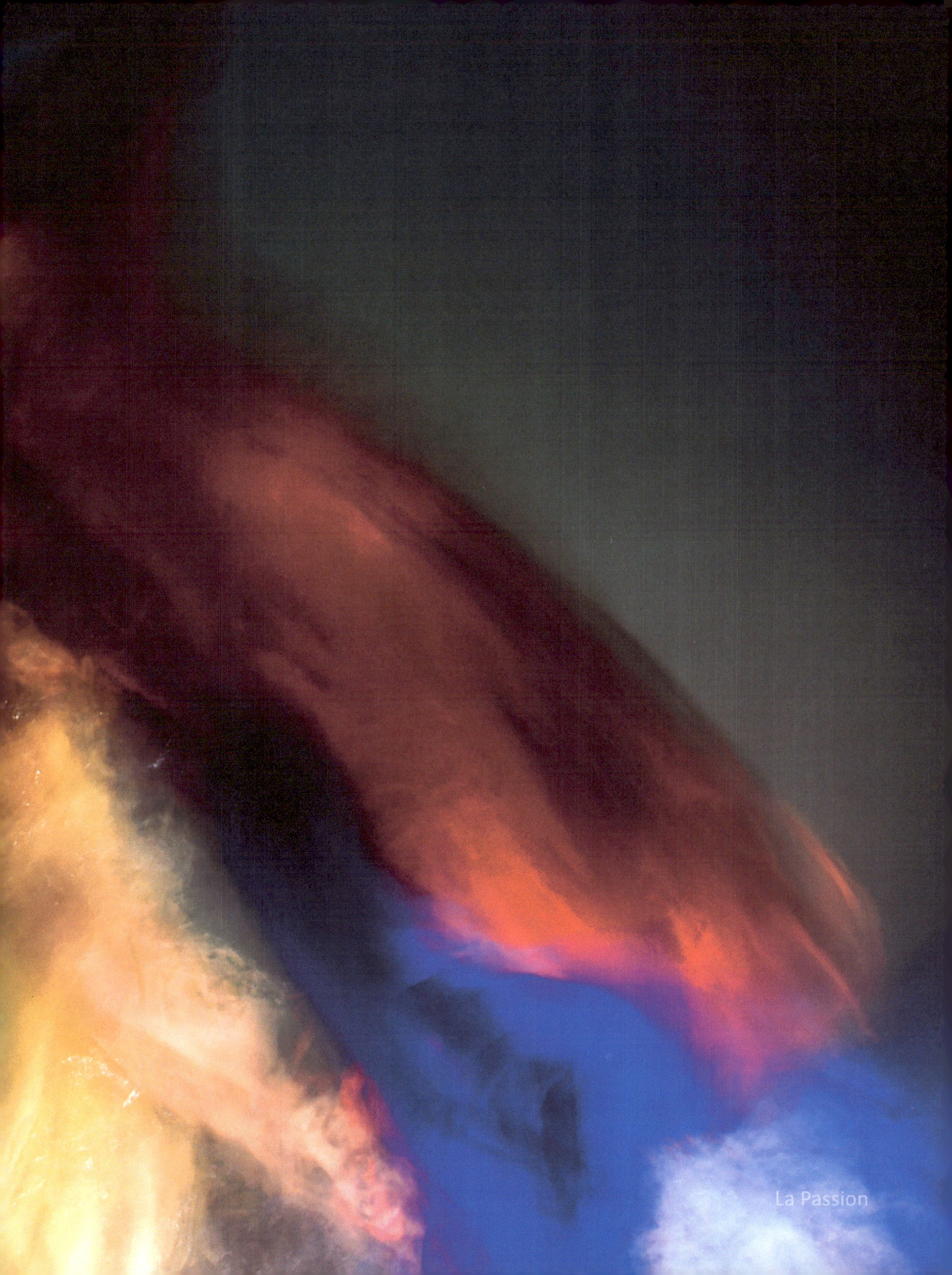
La Passion

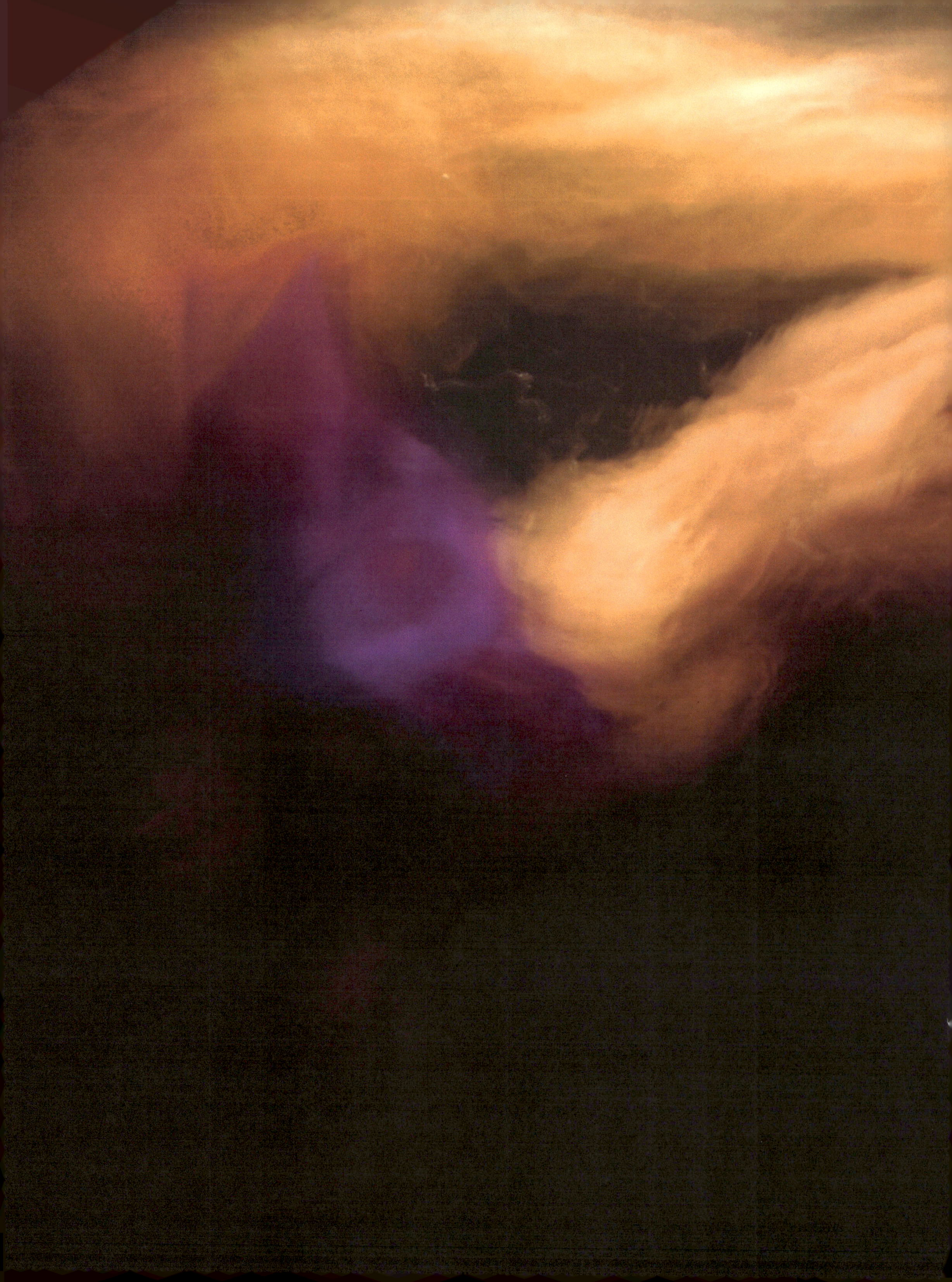

Through the Veil

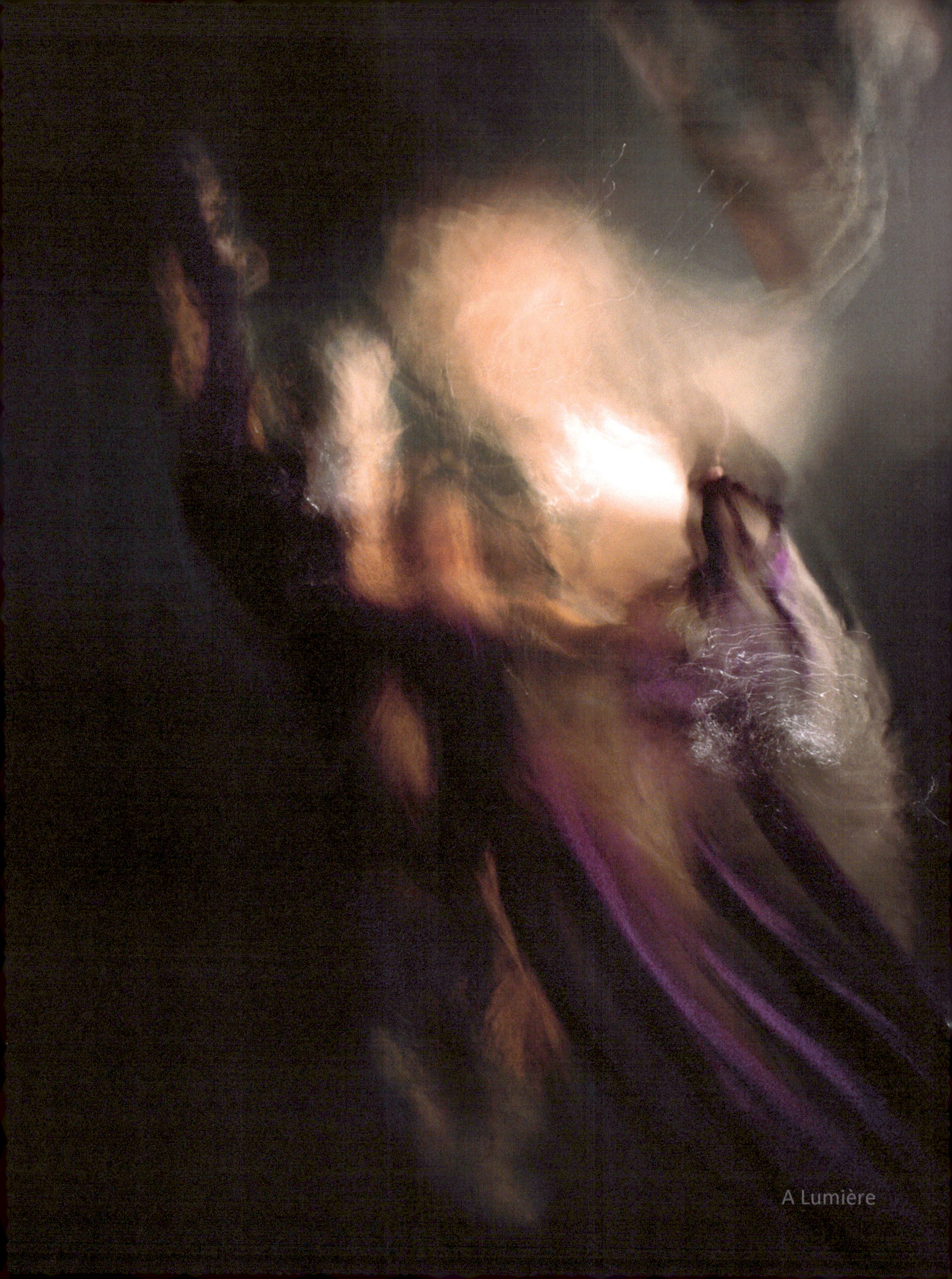

A Lumière

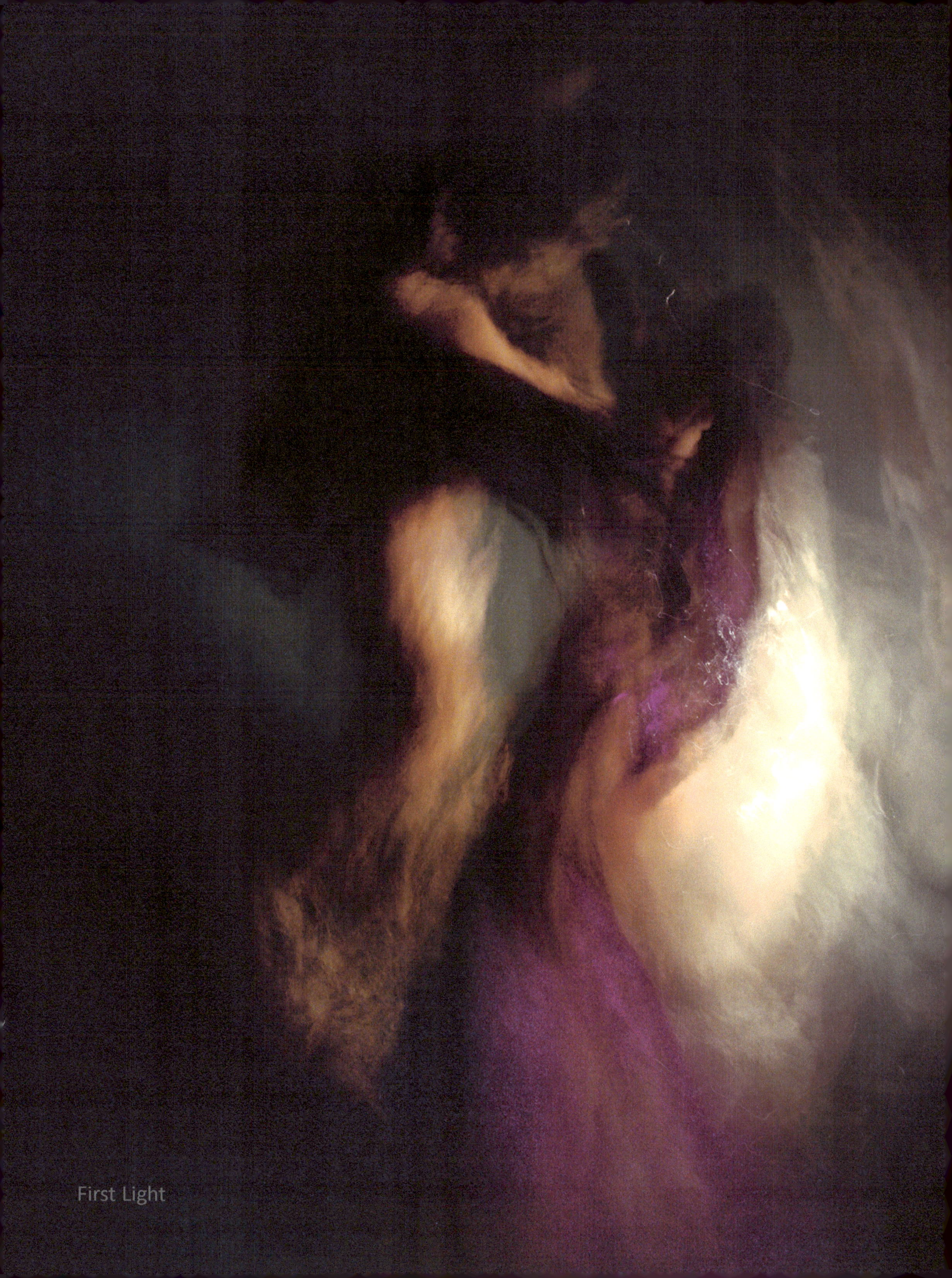

First Light

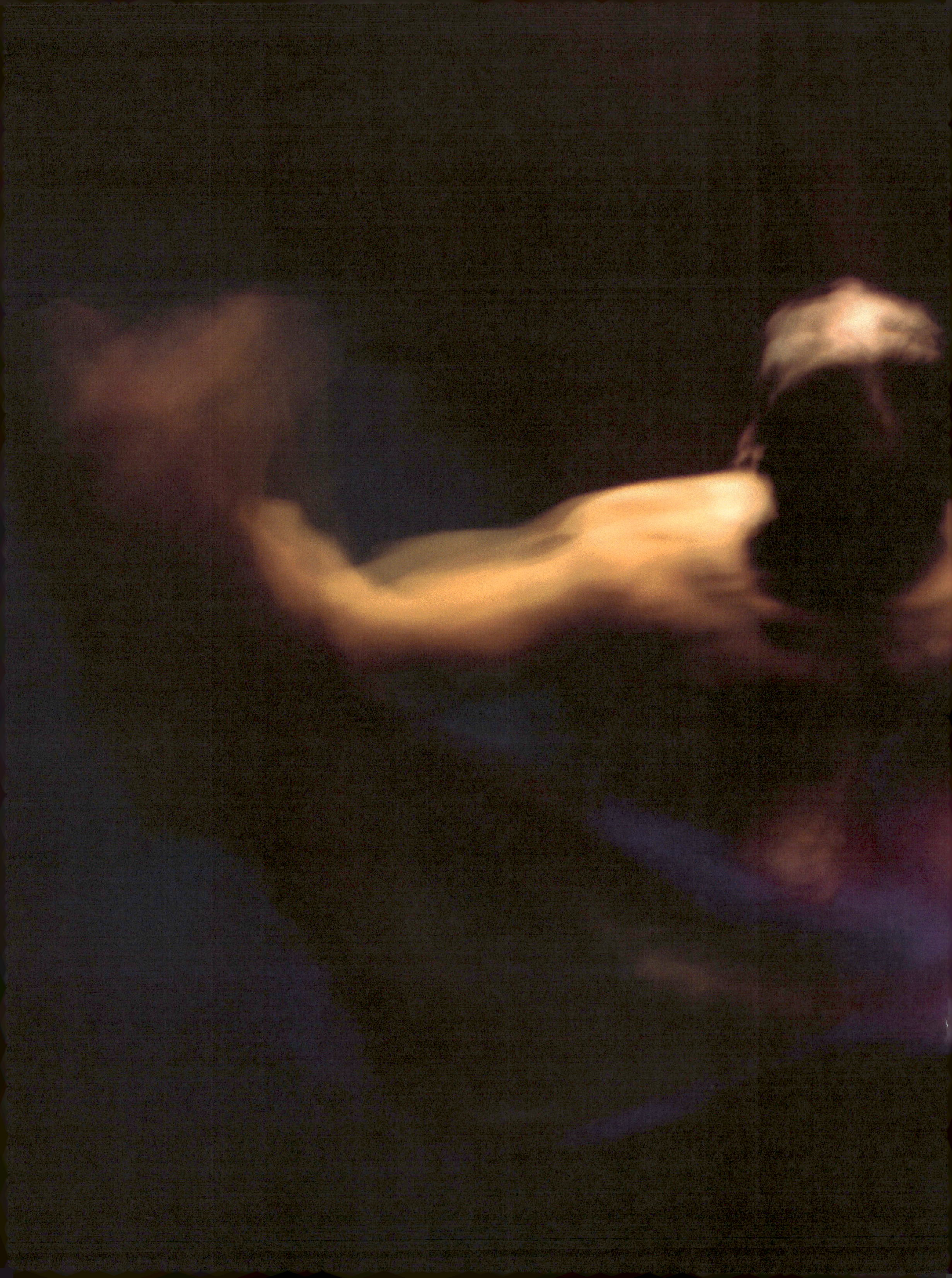

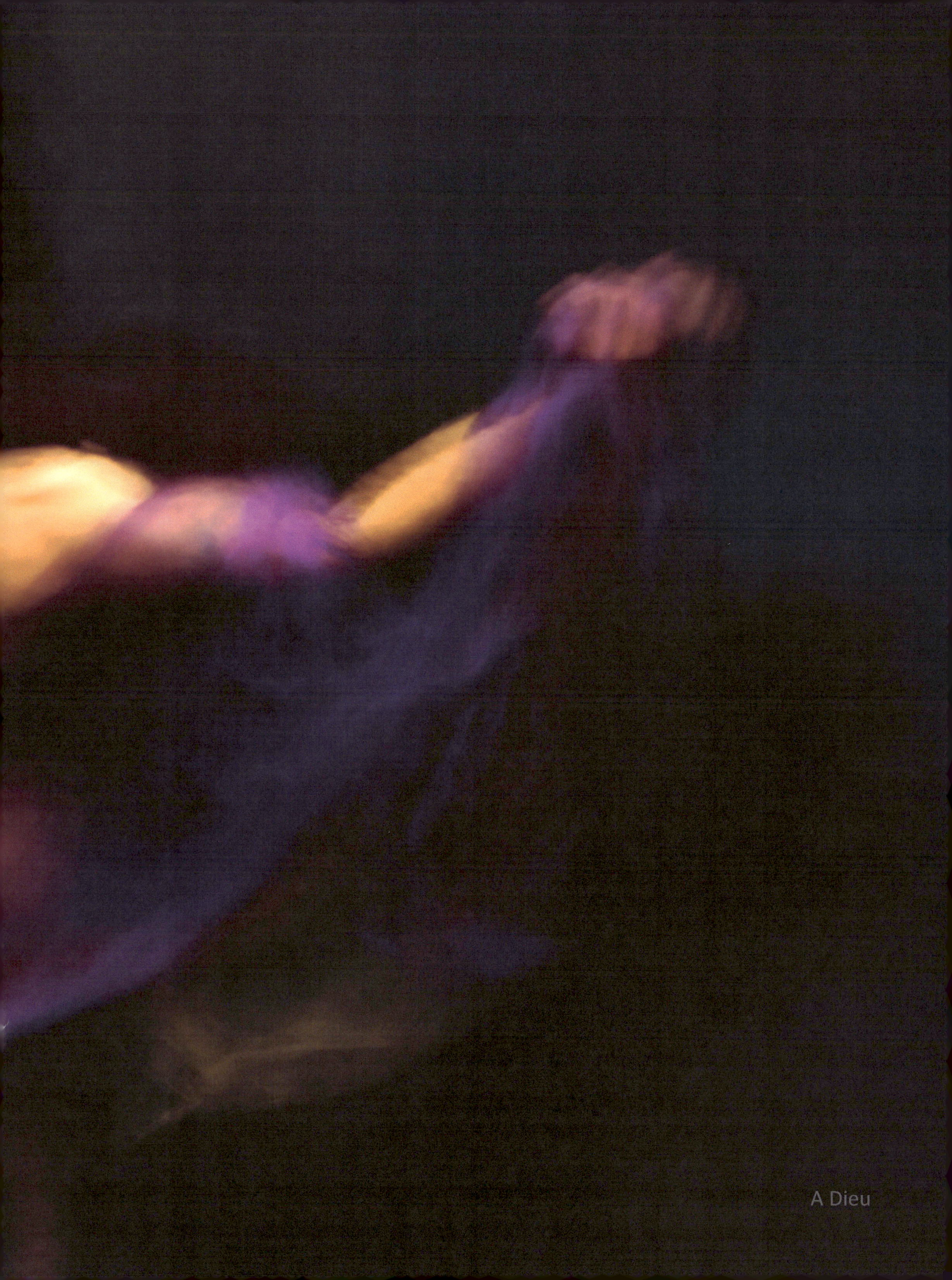

A Dieu

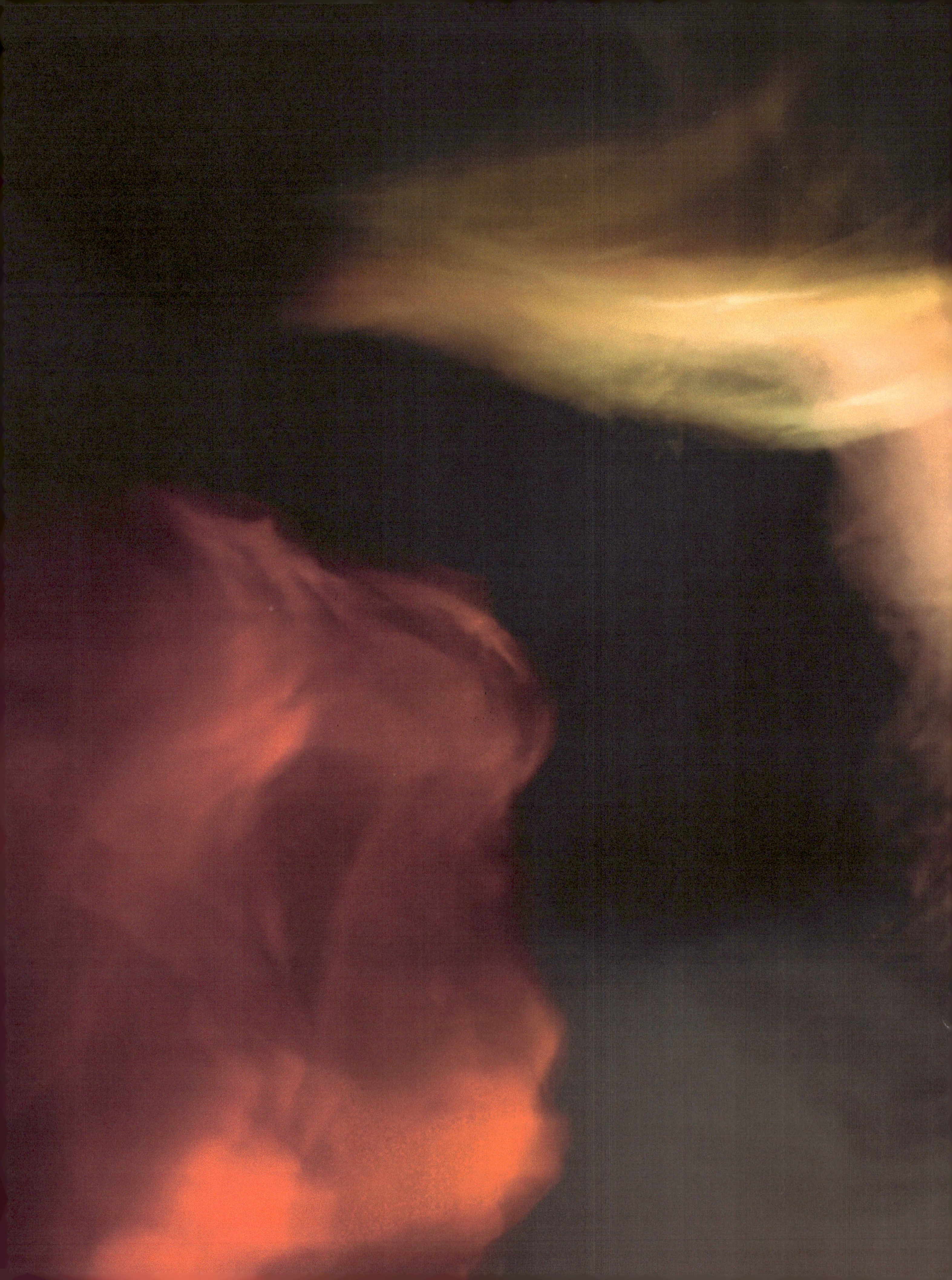

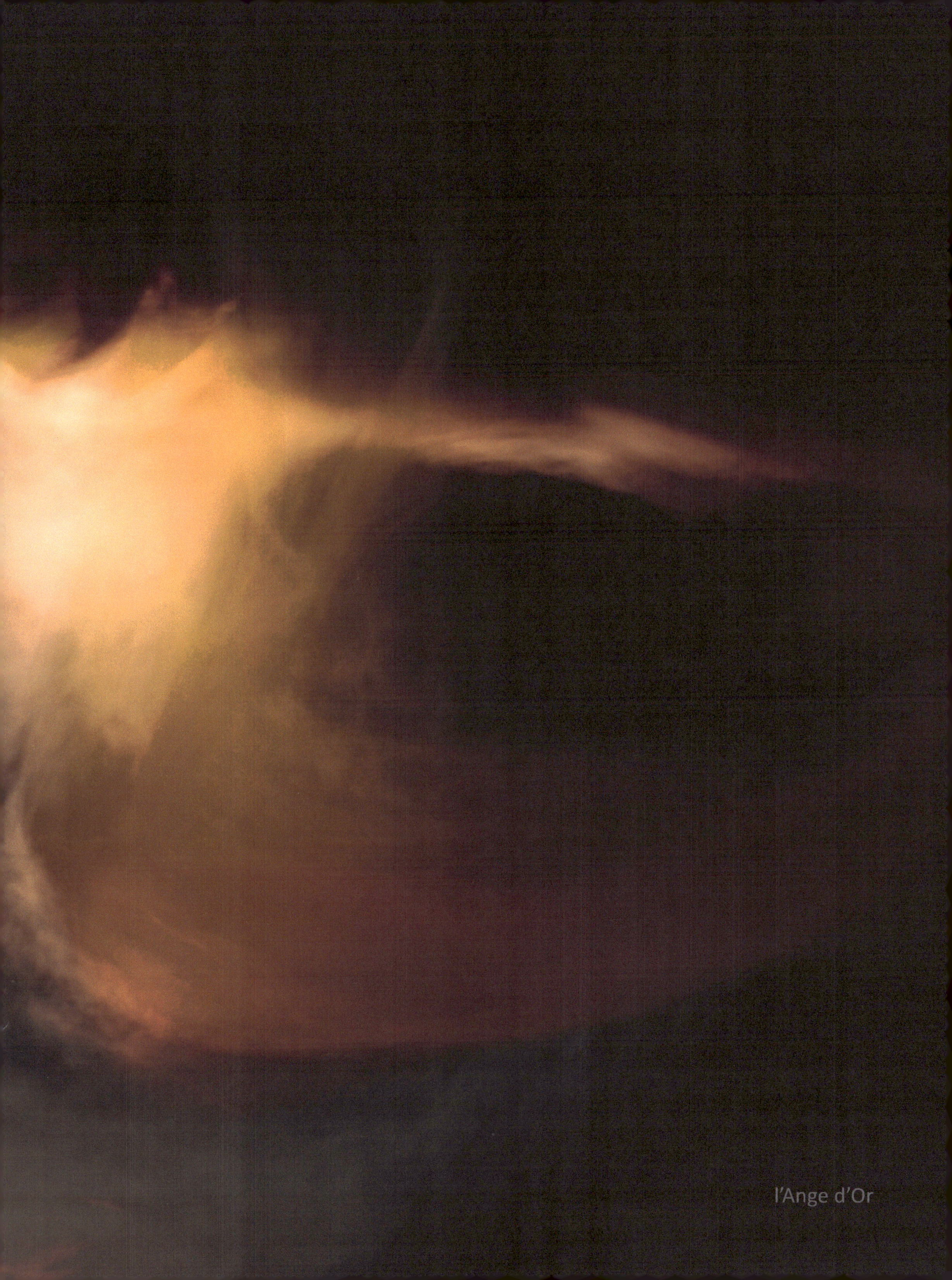

l'Ange d'Or

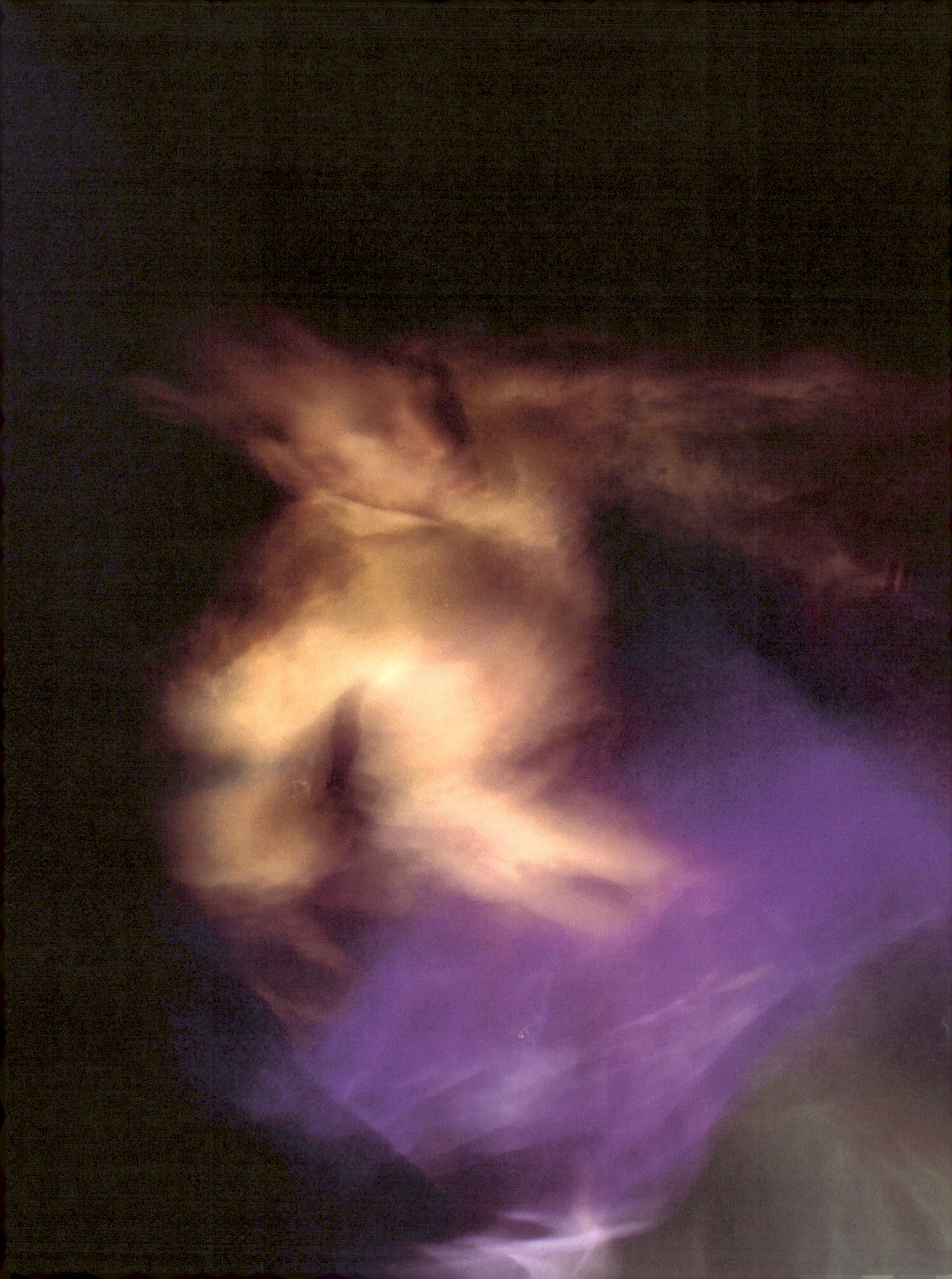

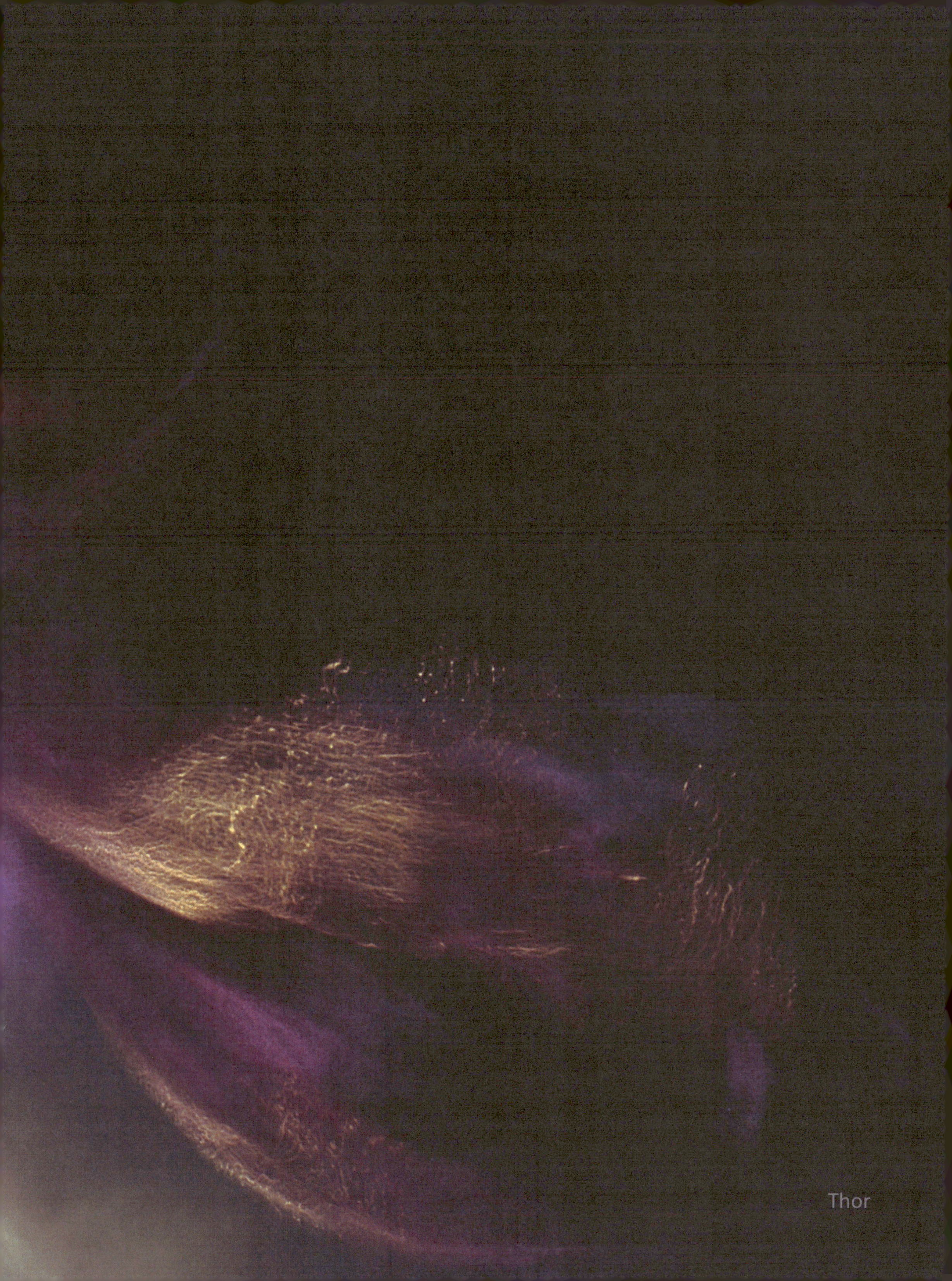

Thor

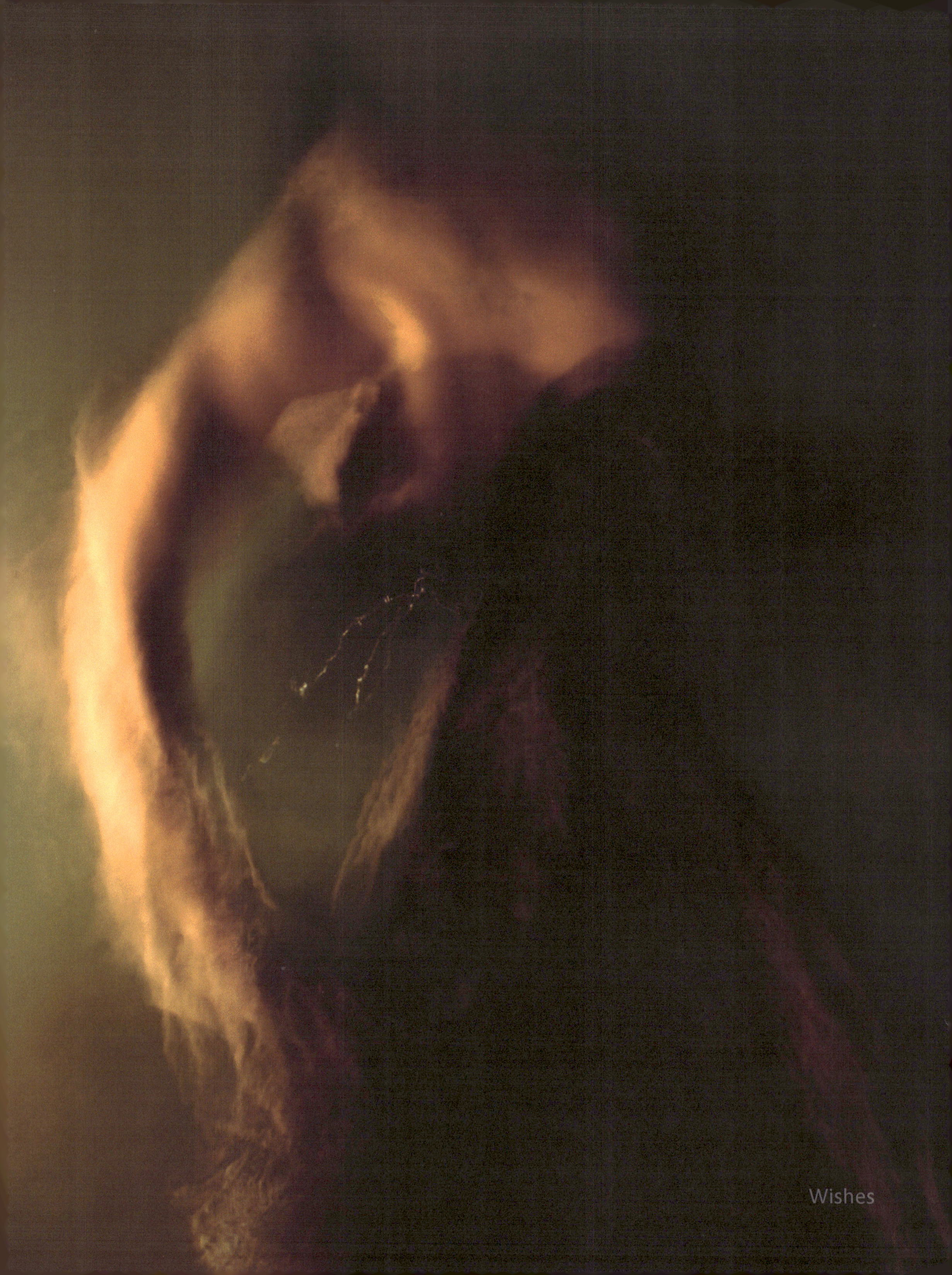

Wishes

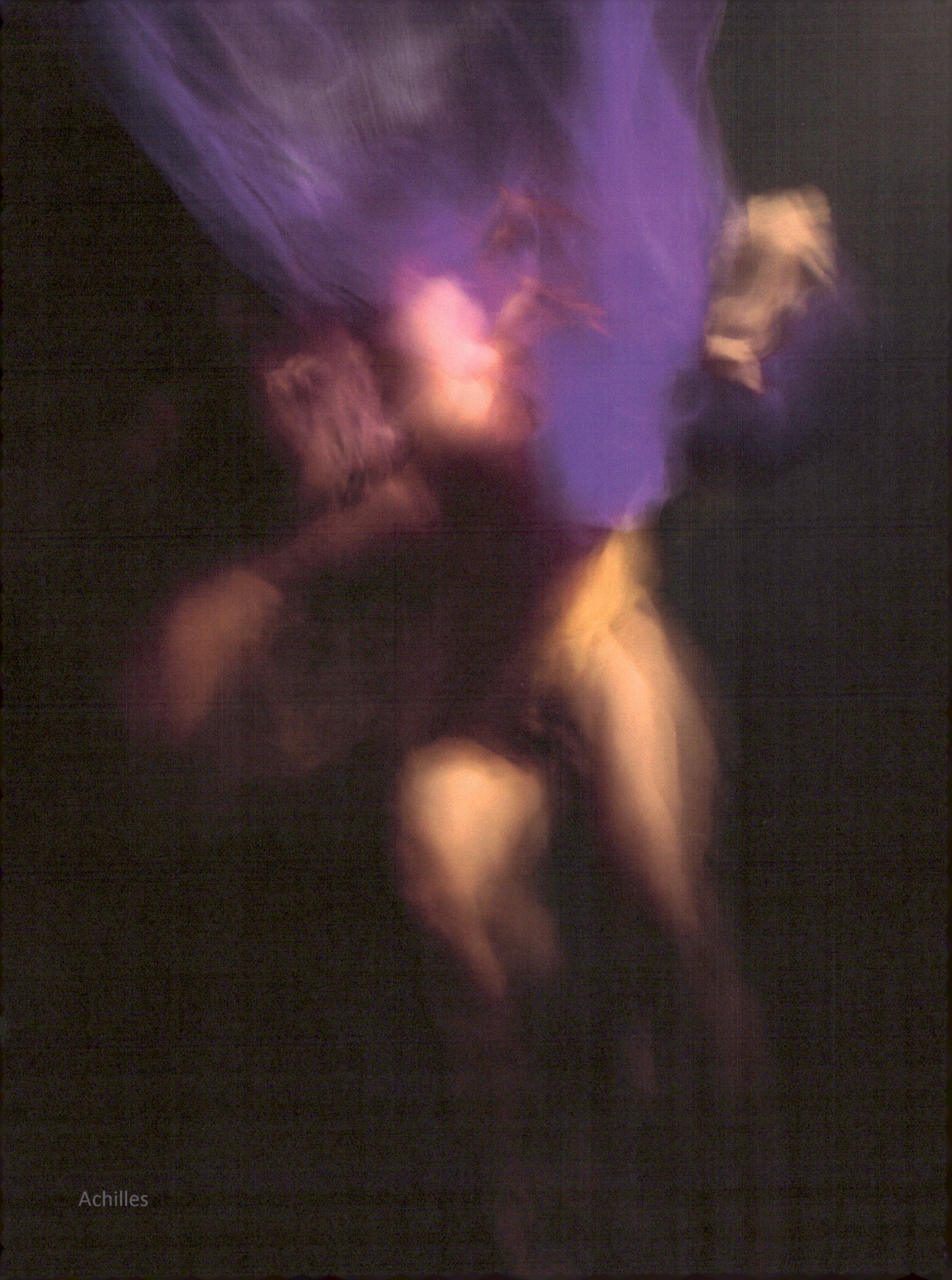

Achilles

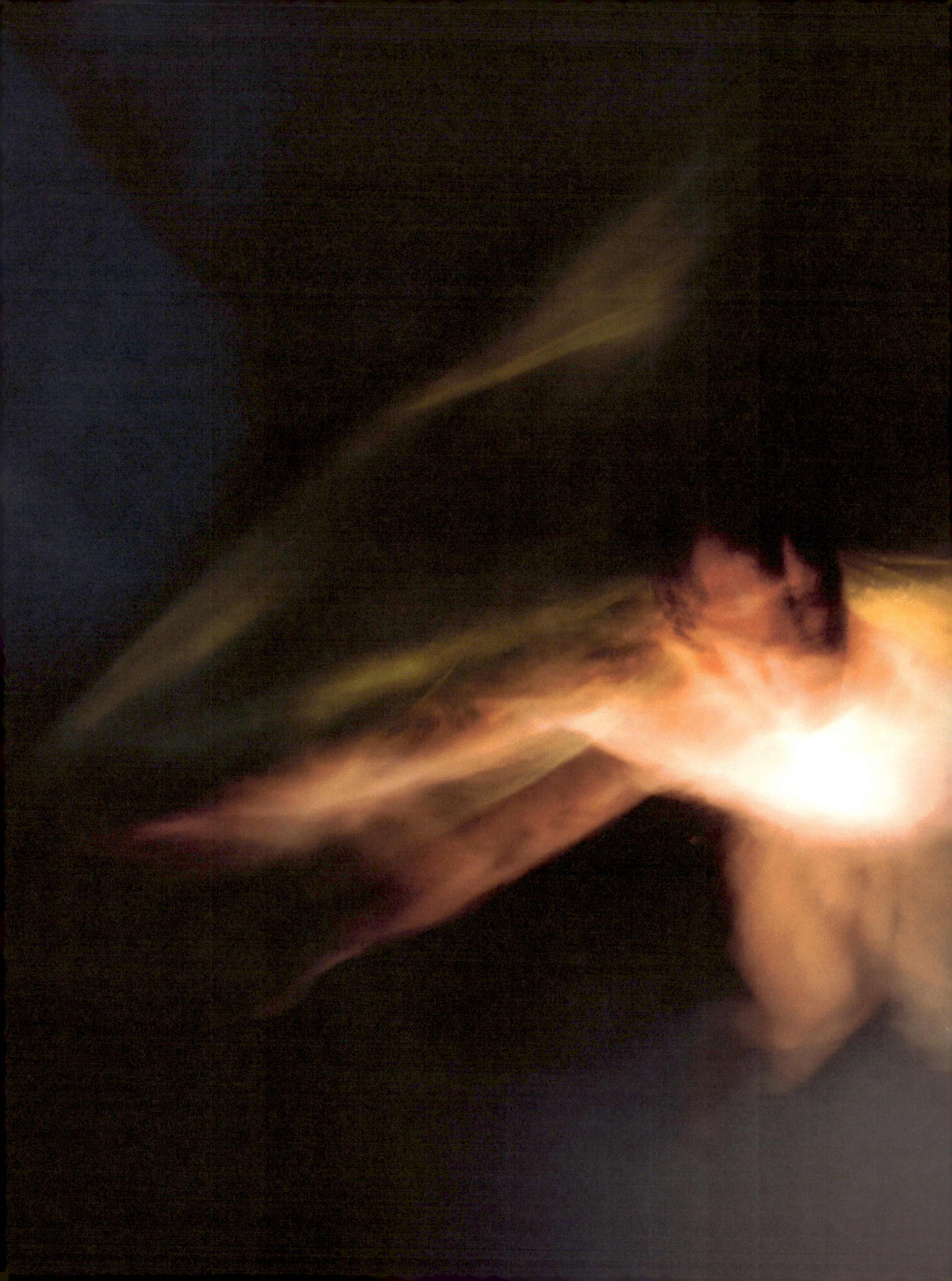

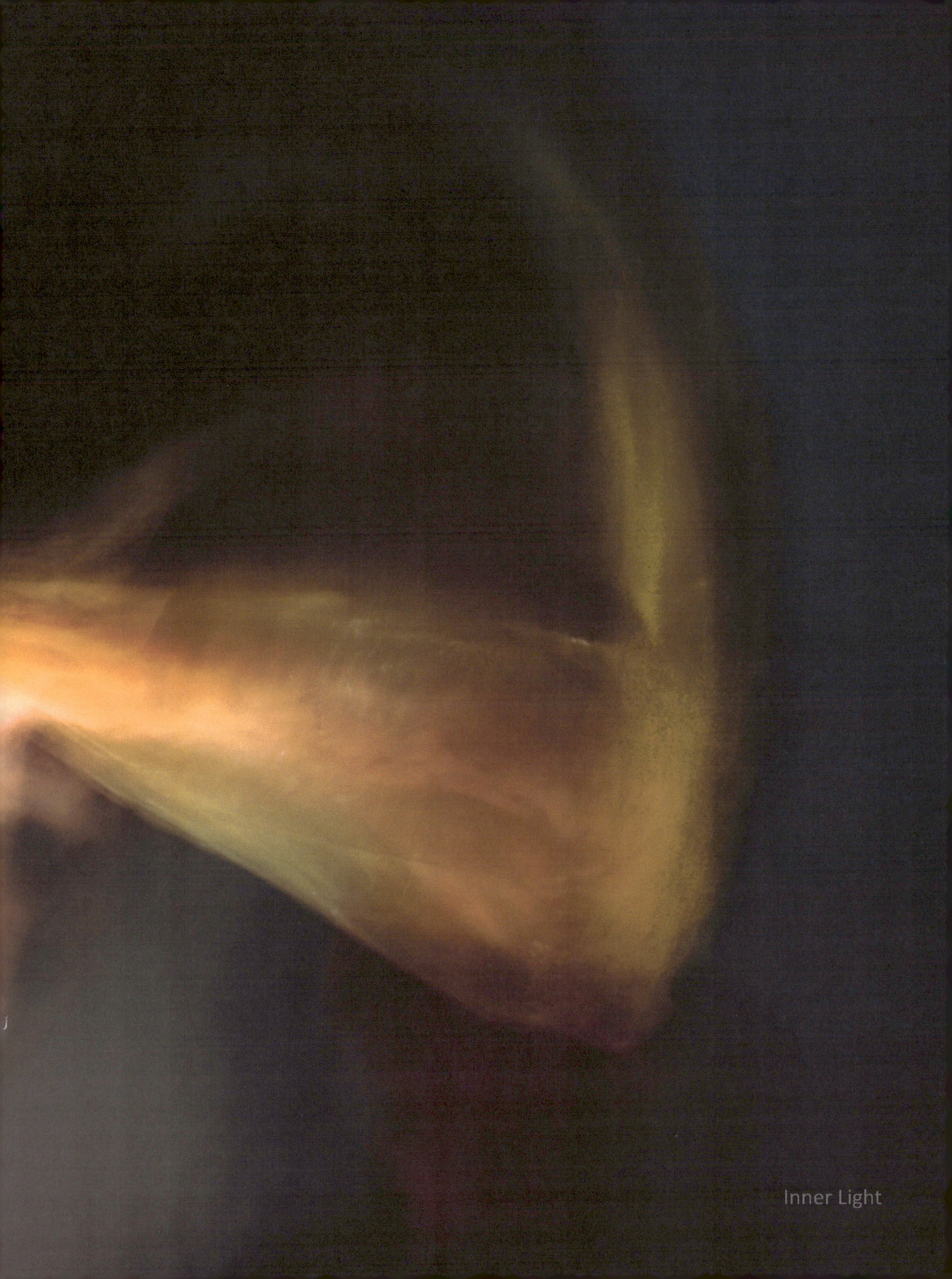

Inner Light

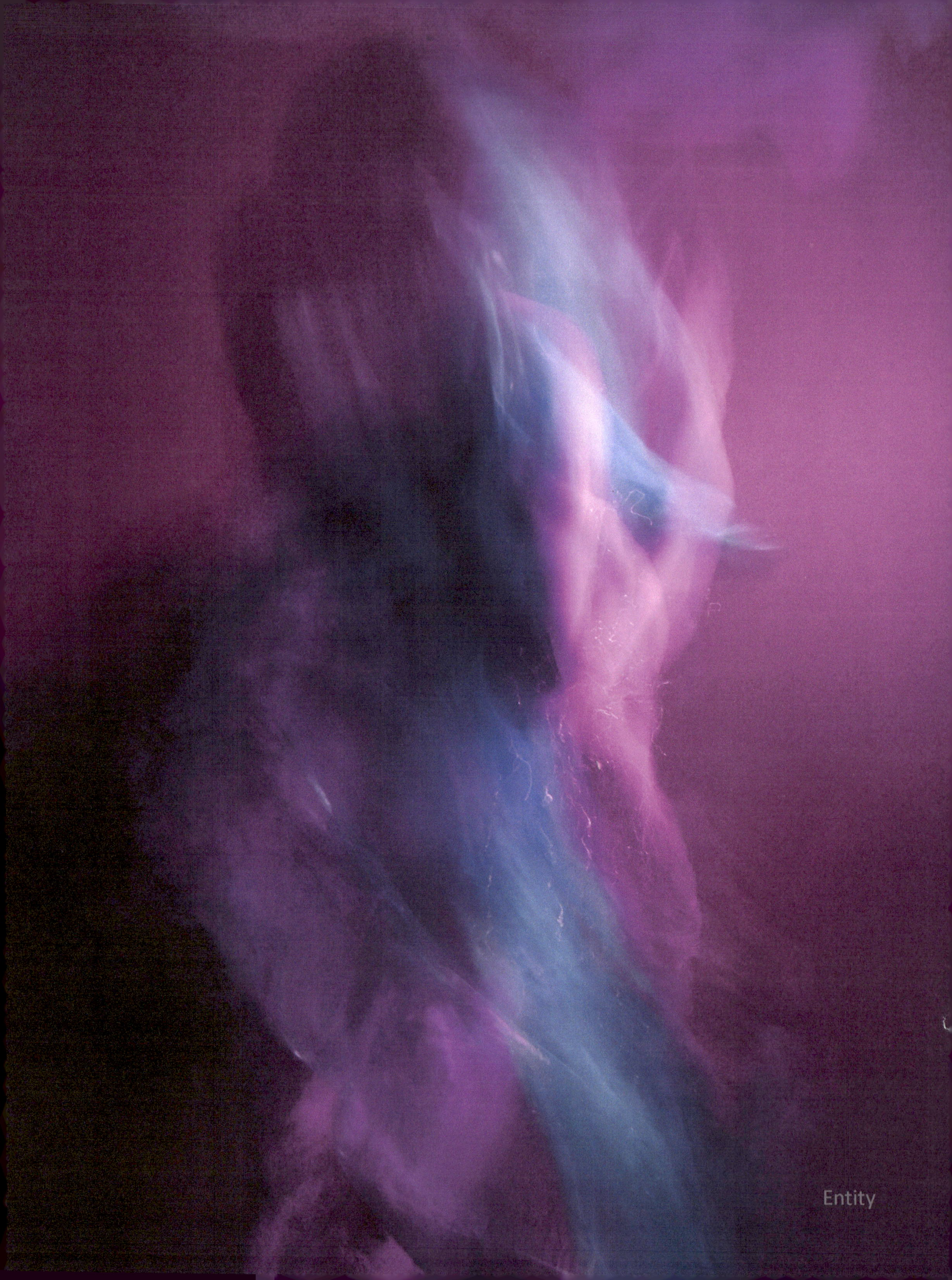

Entity

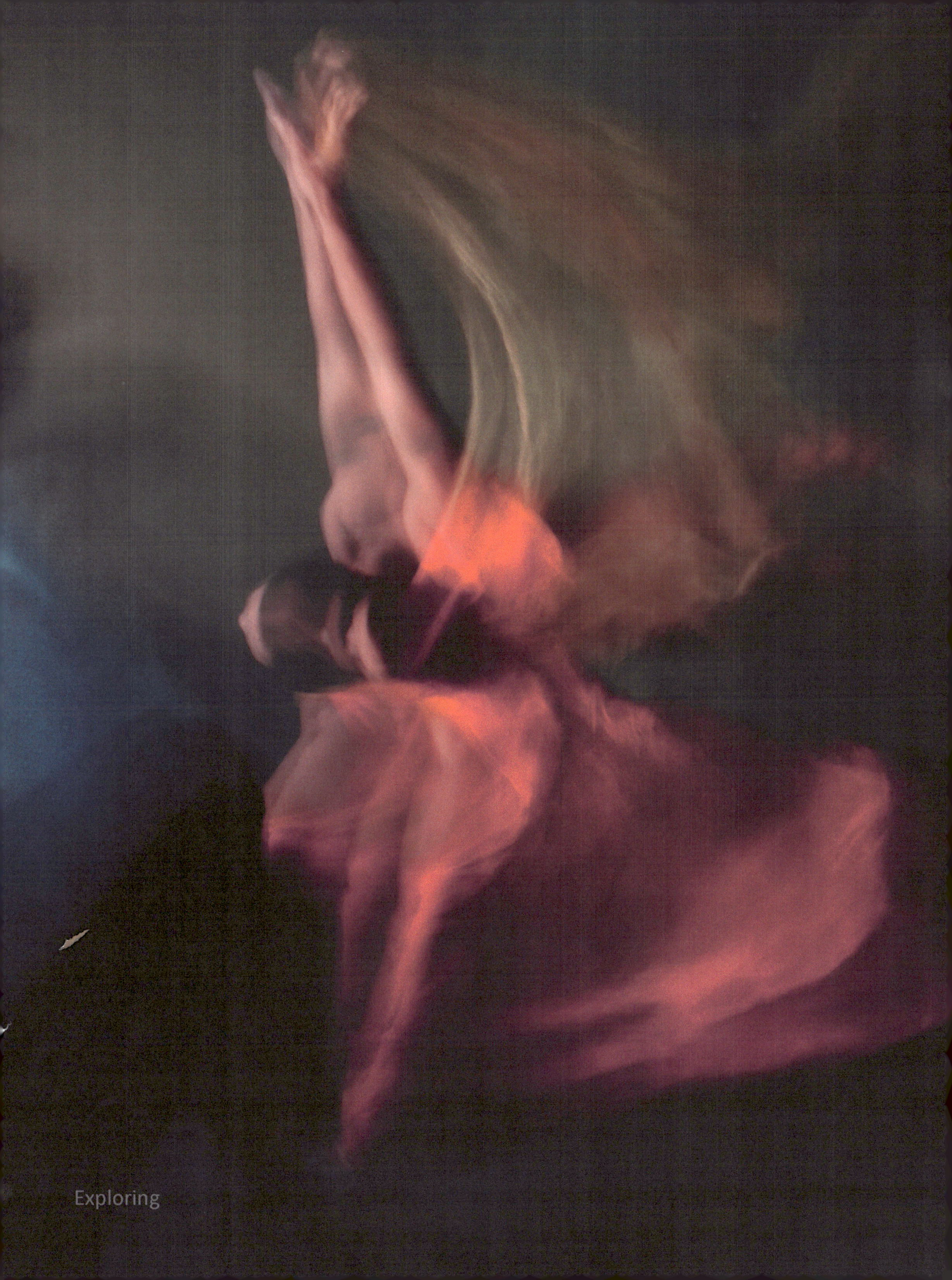
Exploring

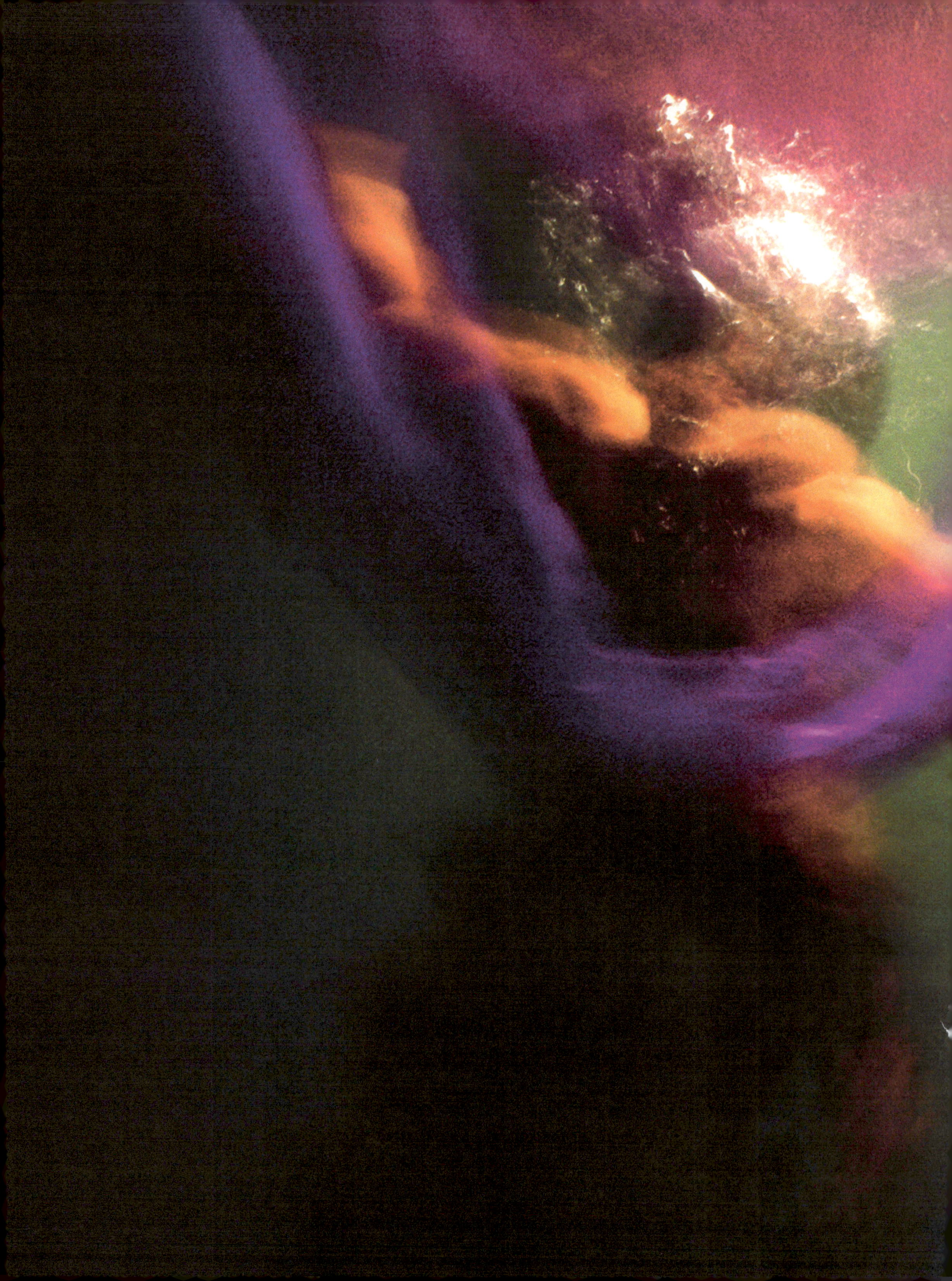

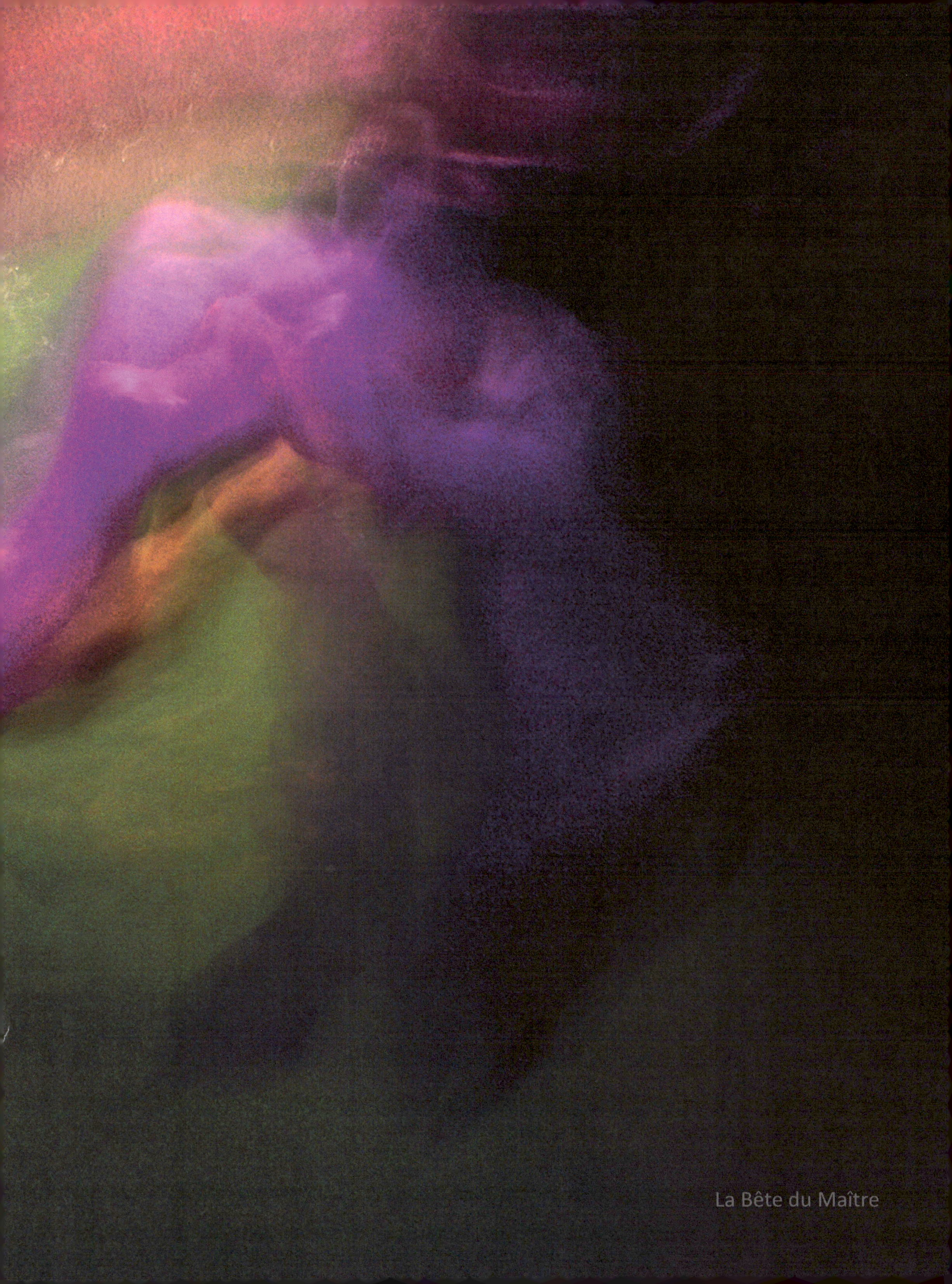

La Bête du Maître

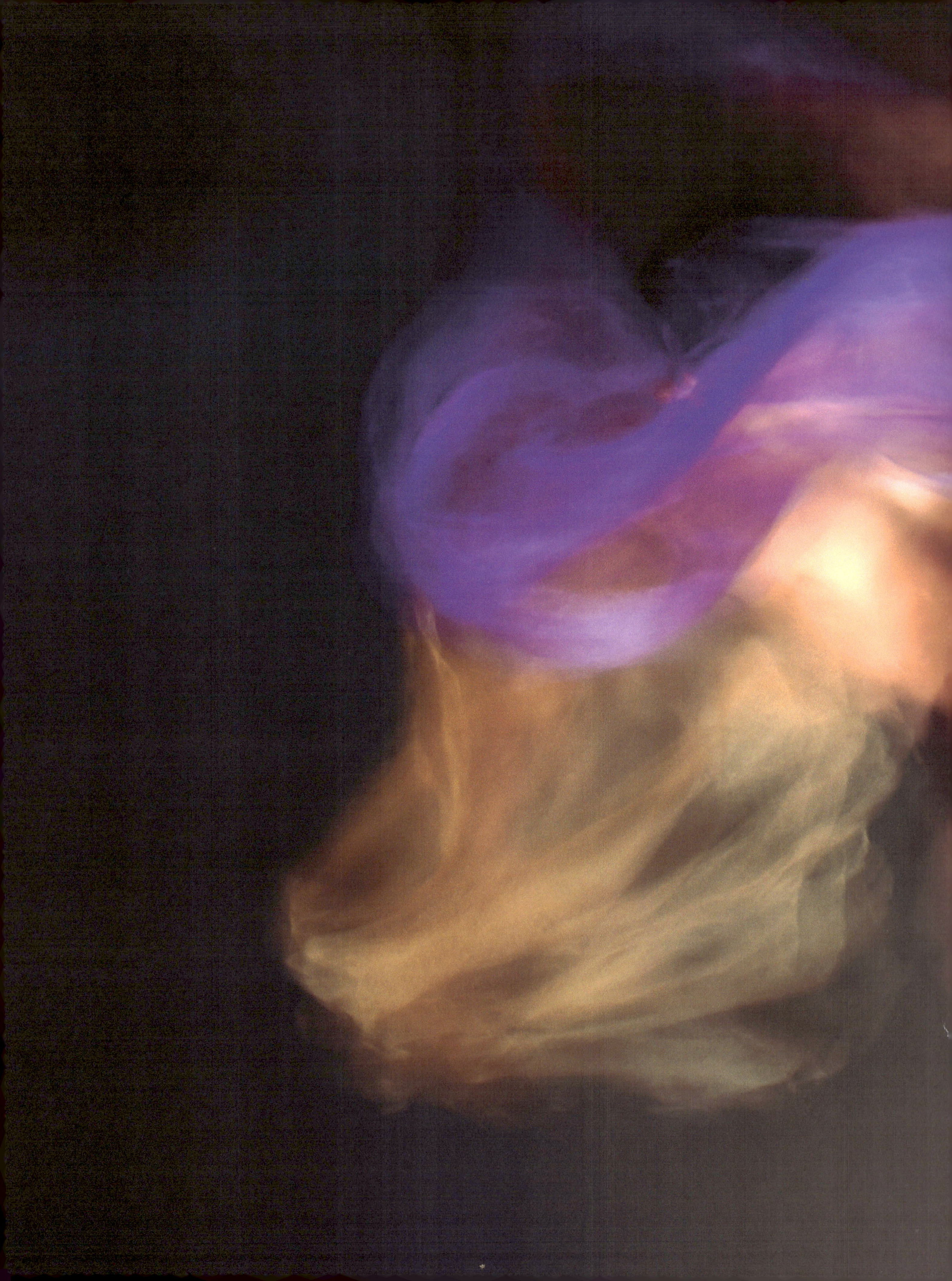

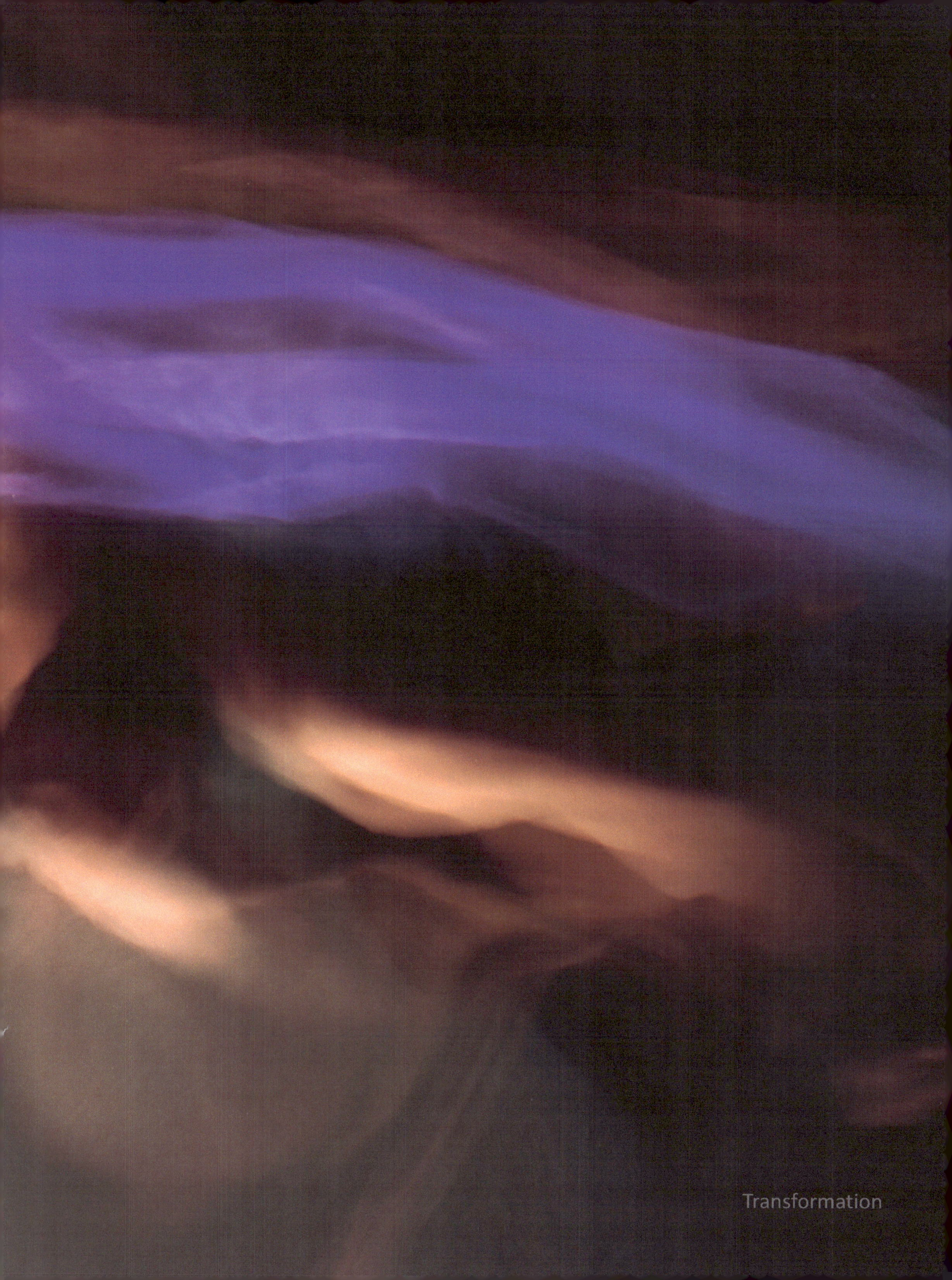

Transformation

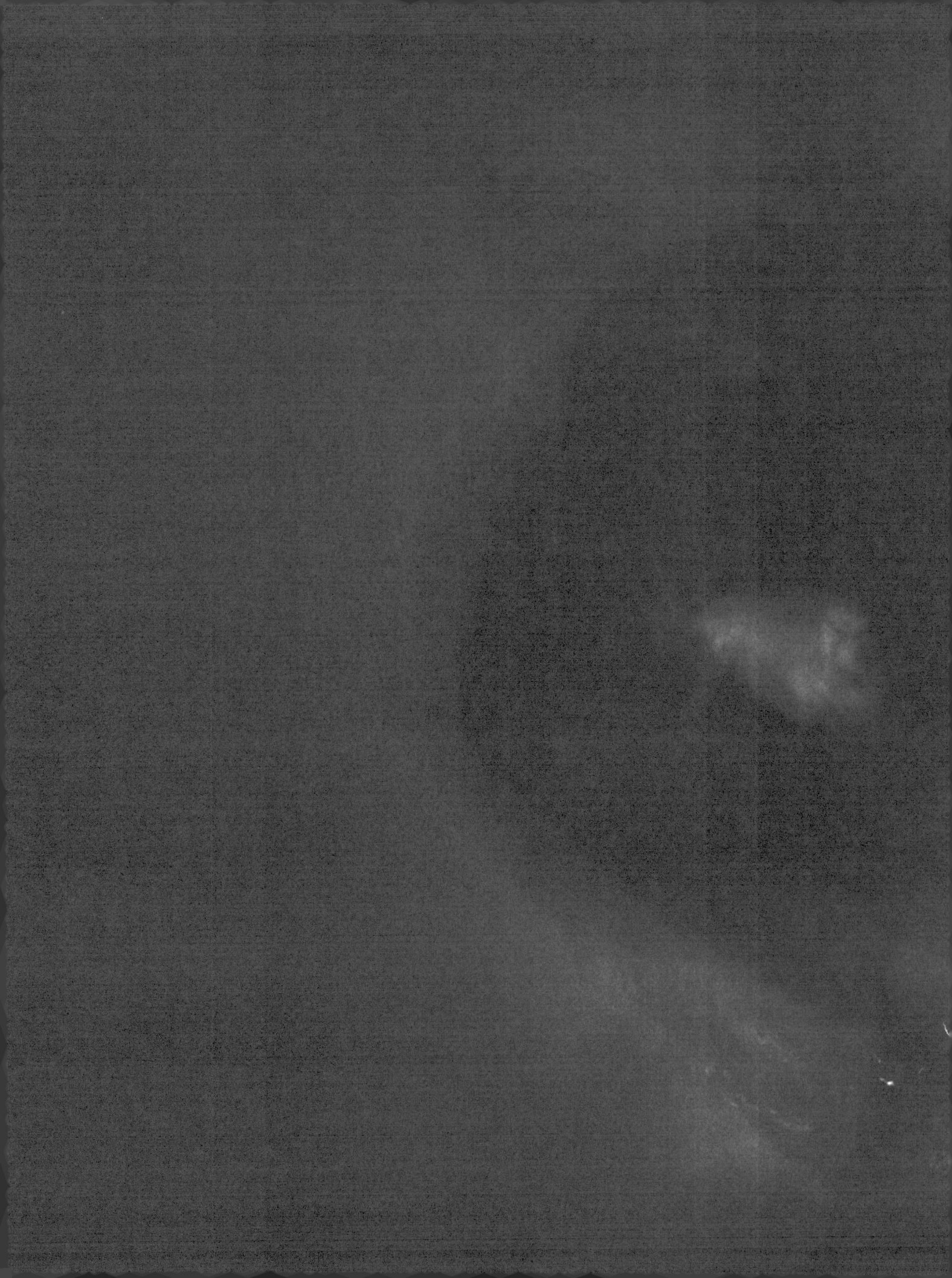

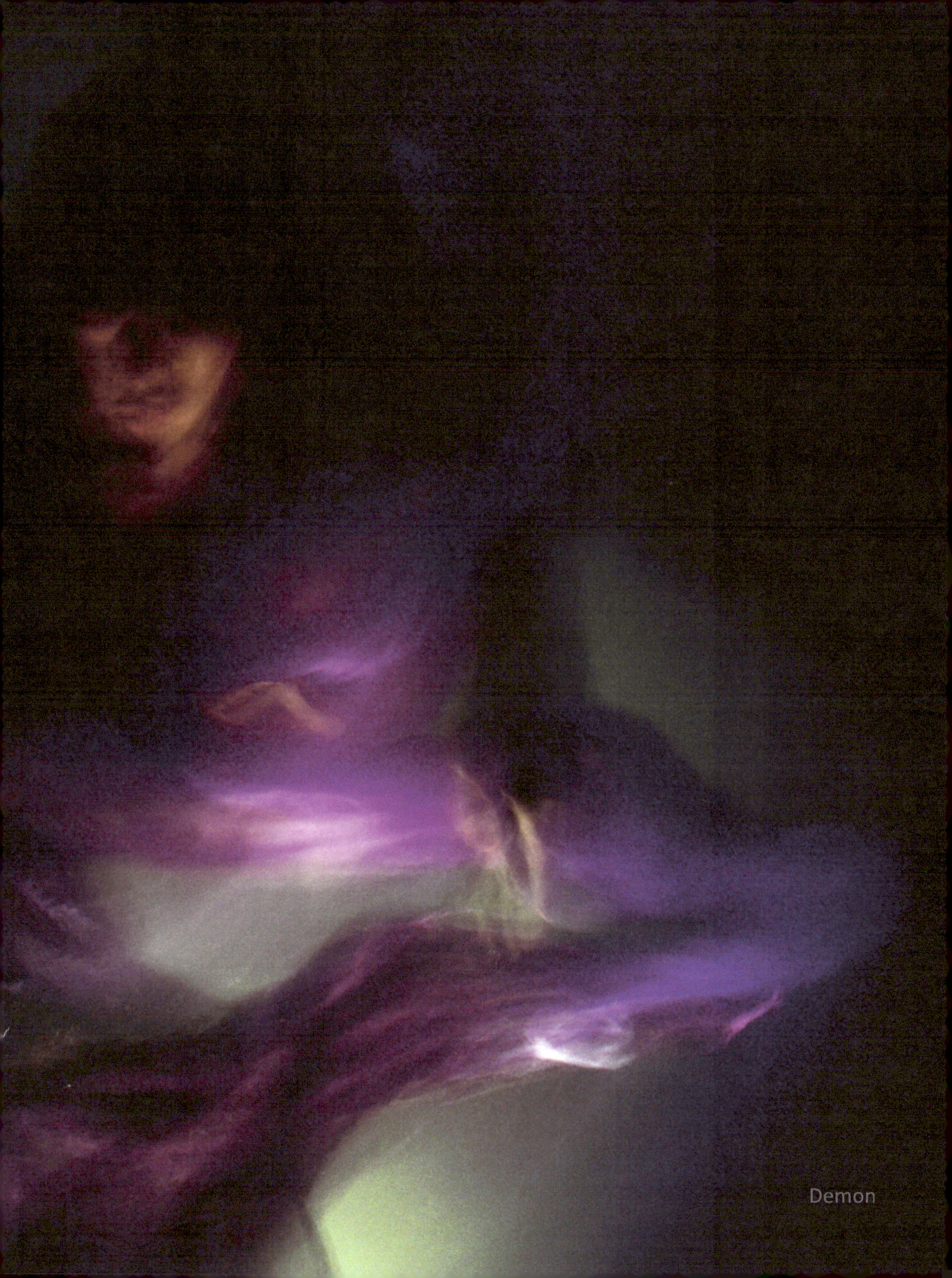

Demon

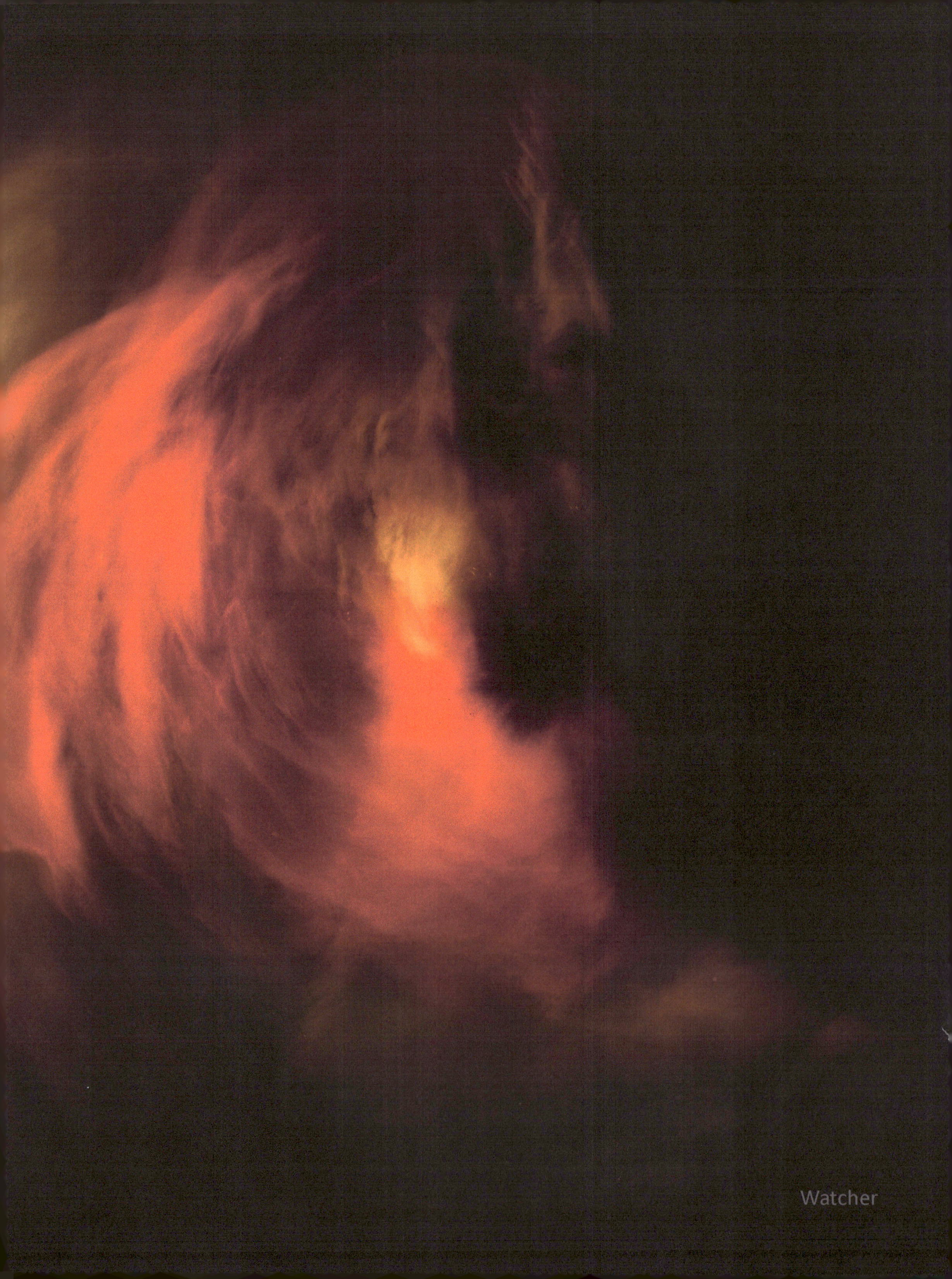

Watcher

L'Homme

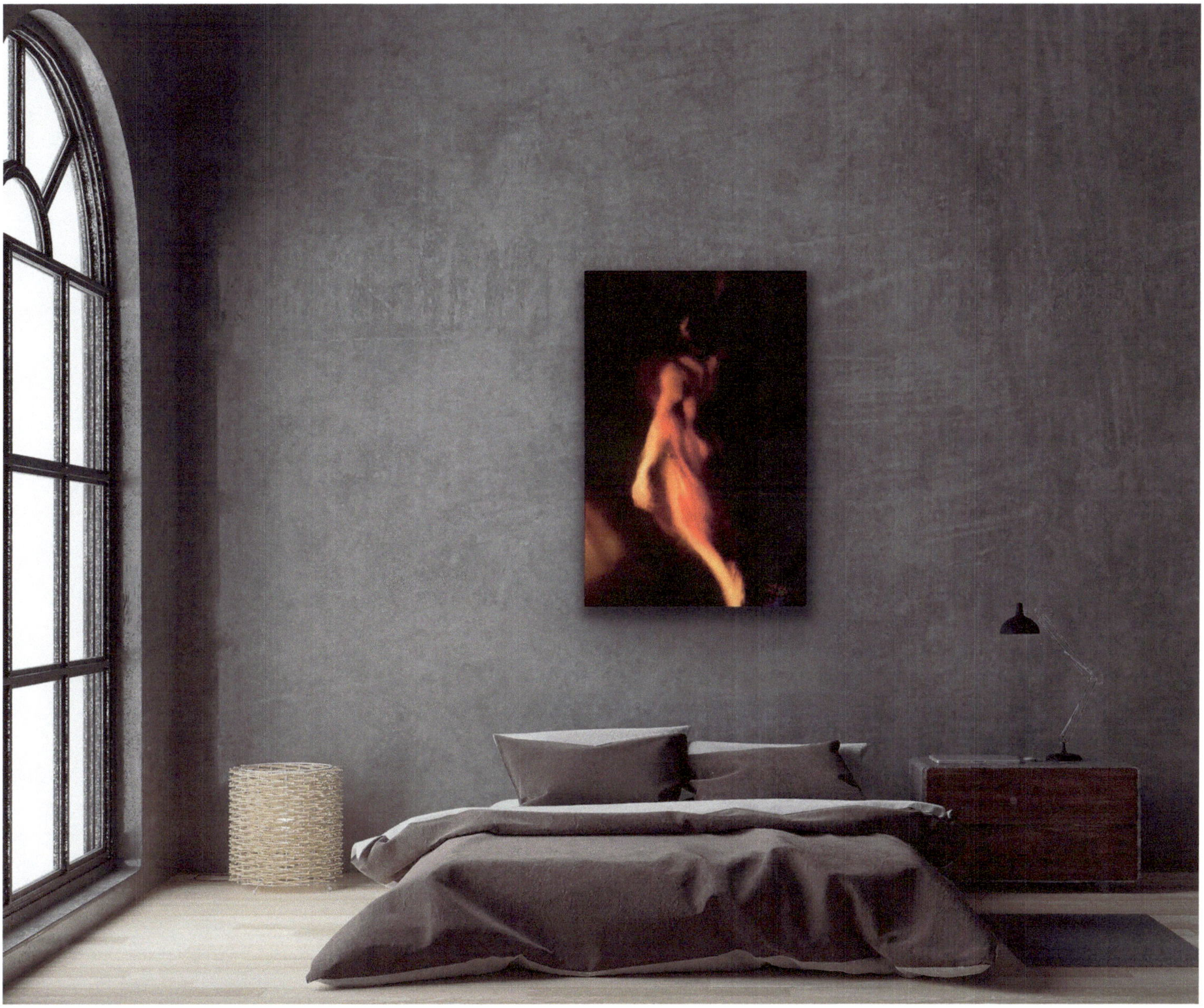

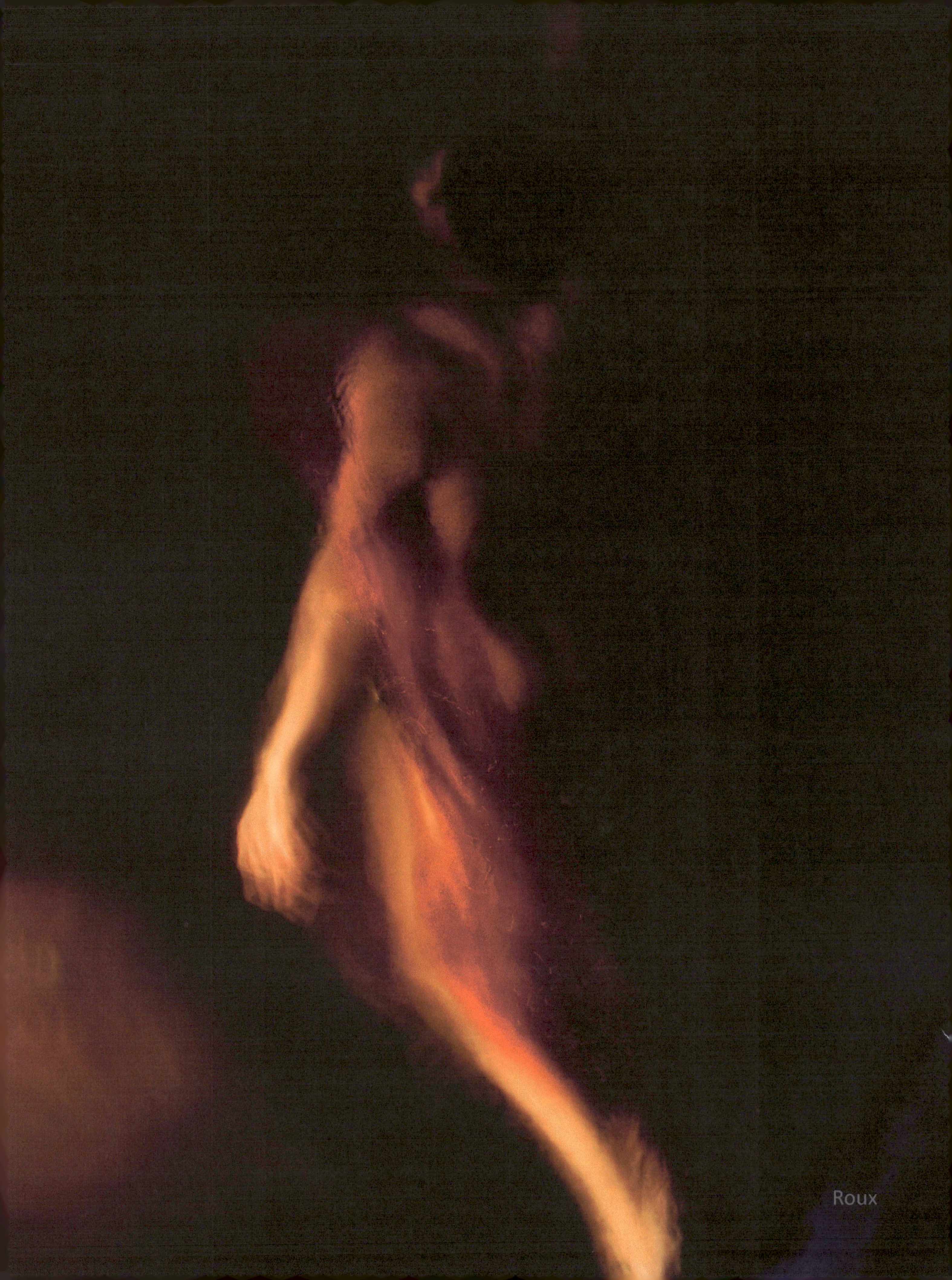

Roux

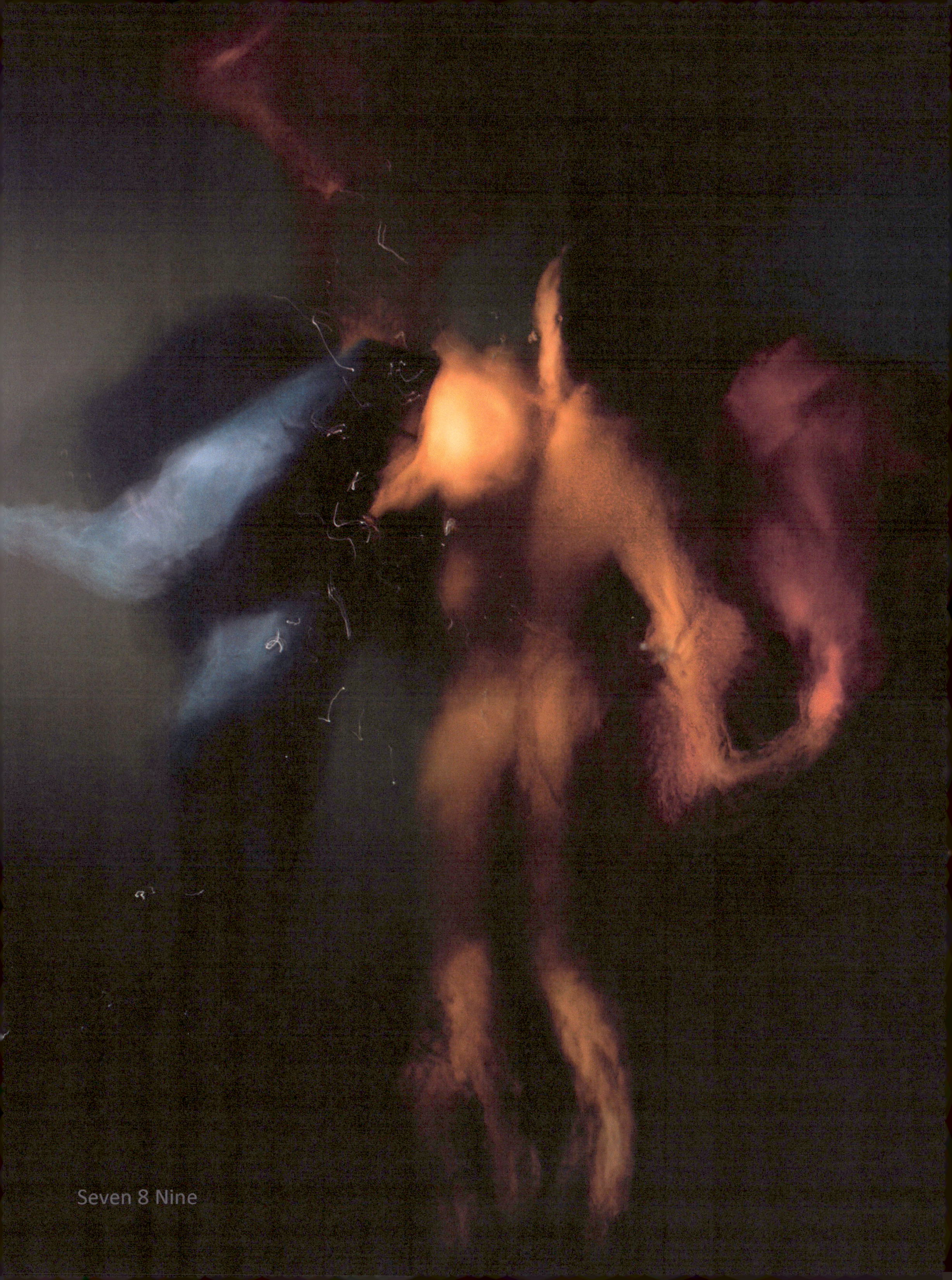

Seven 8 Nine

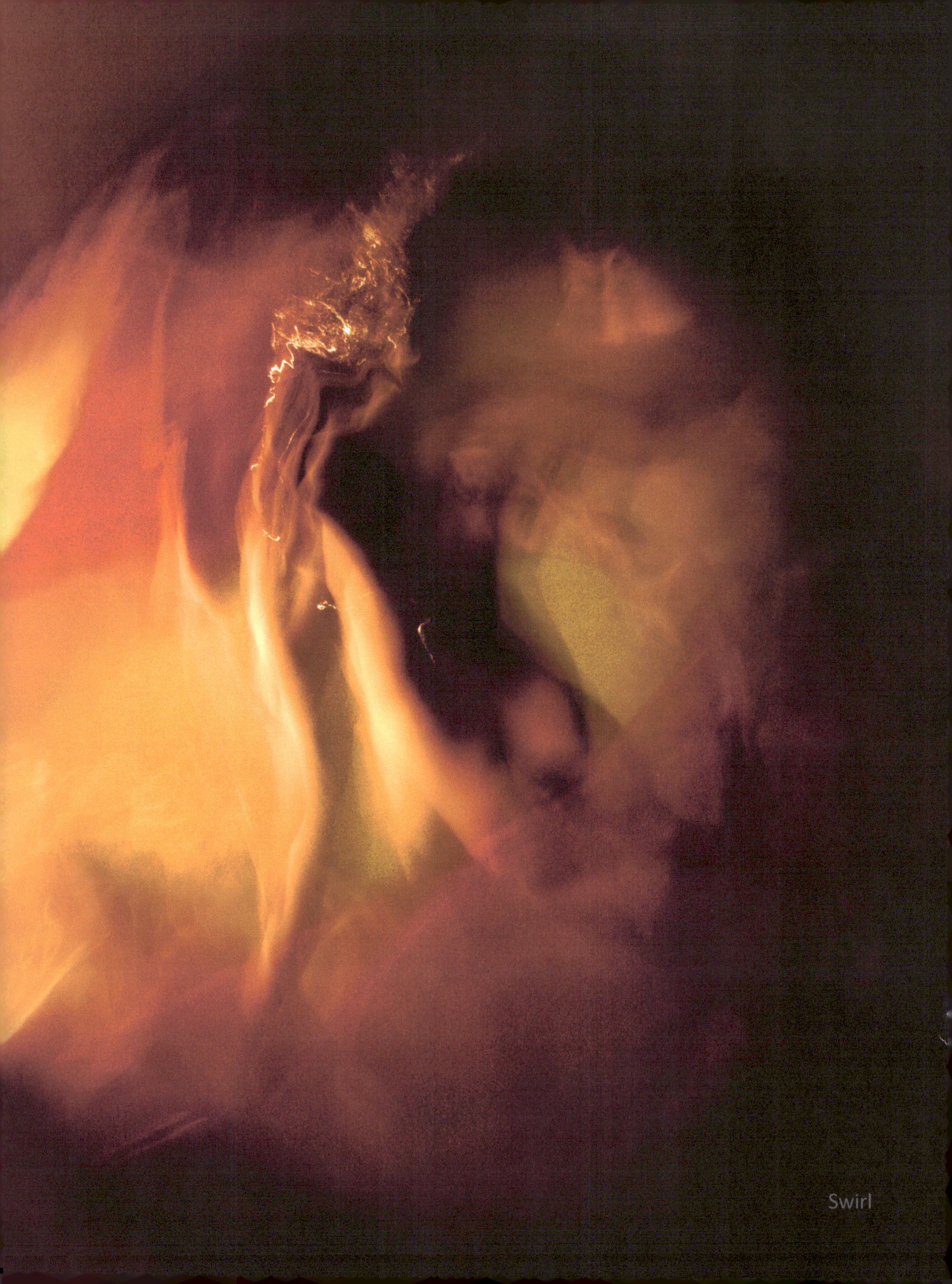

Swirl

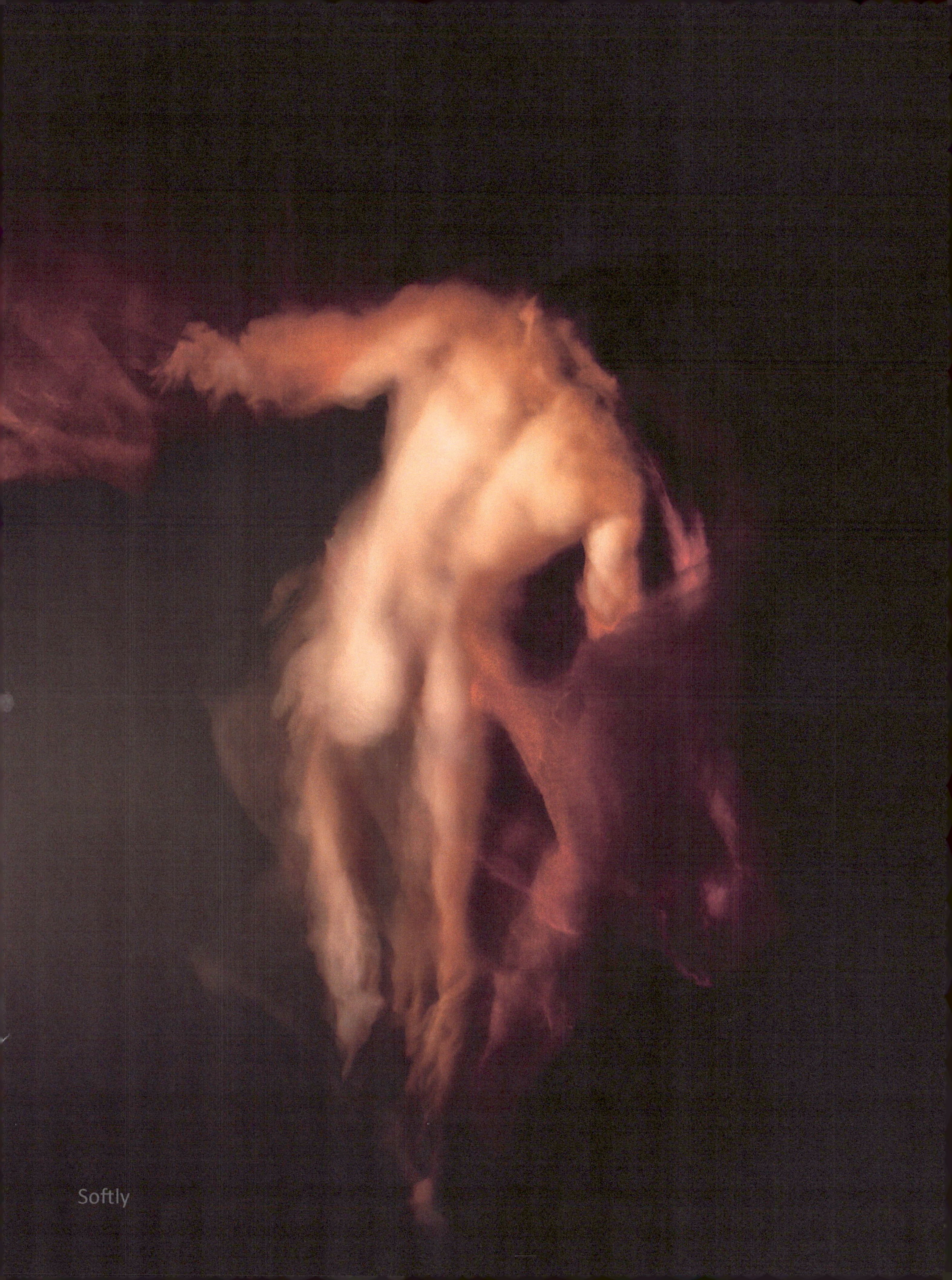

Softly

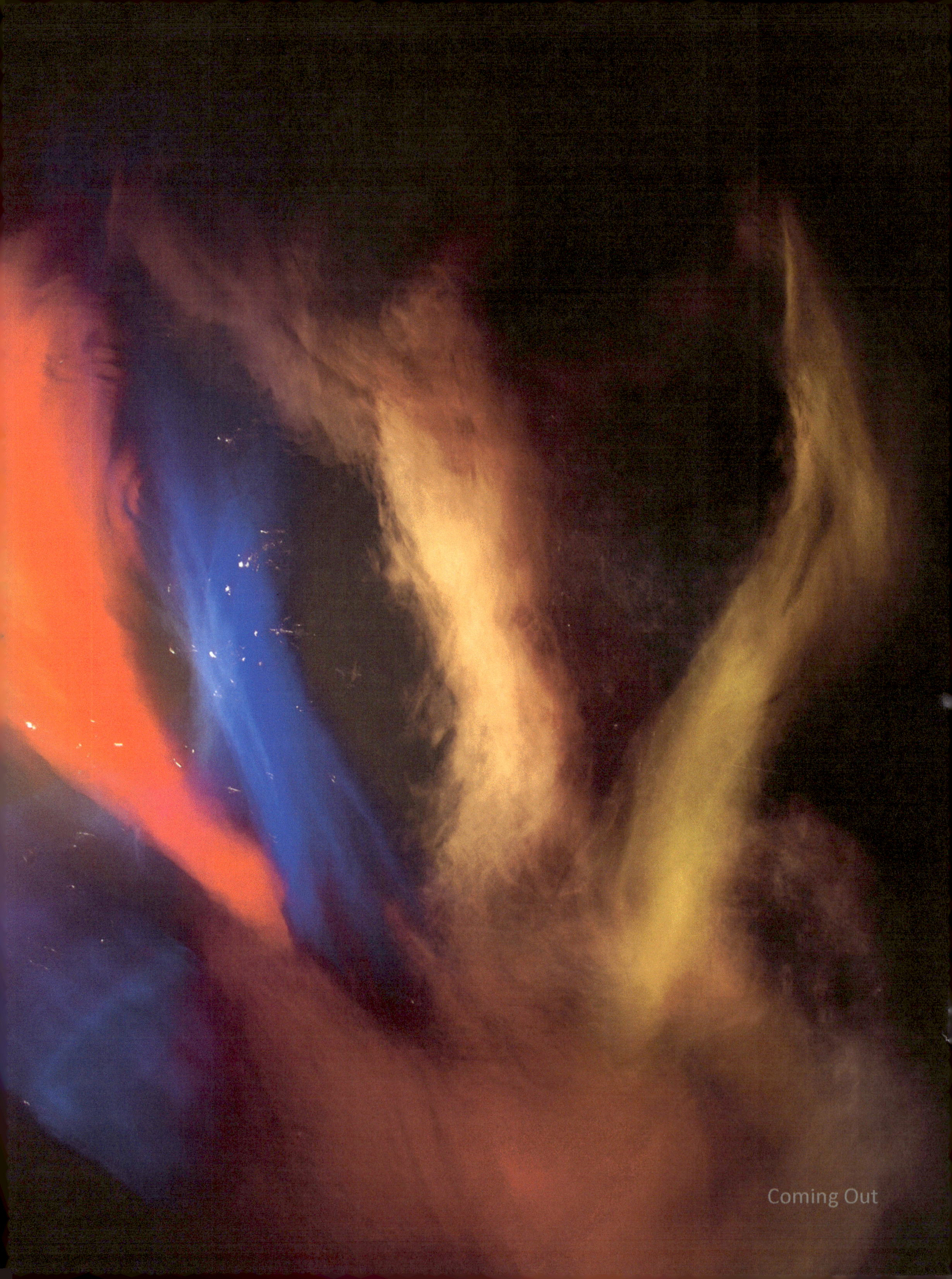

Coming Out

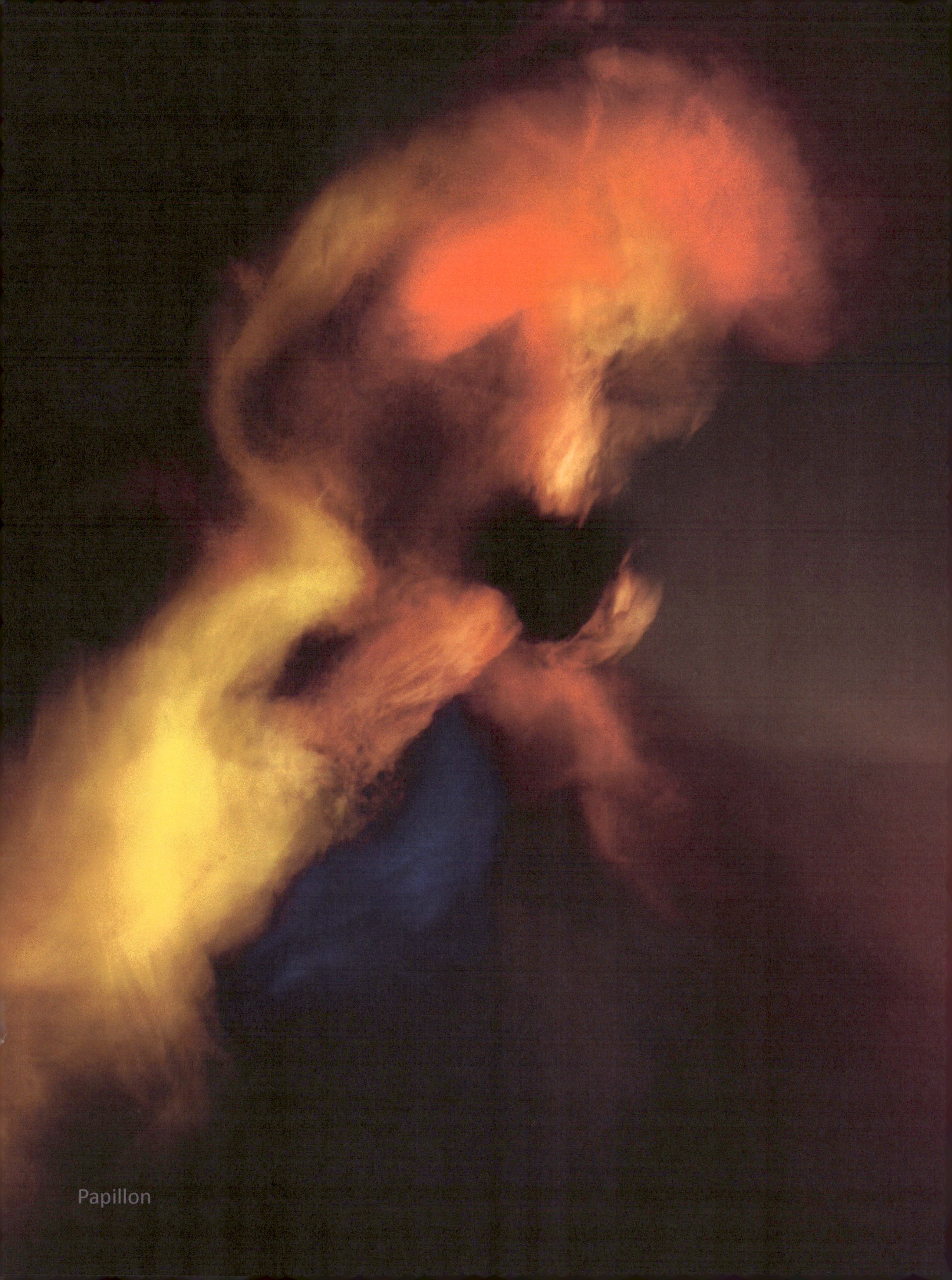

Papillon

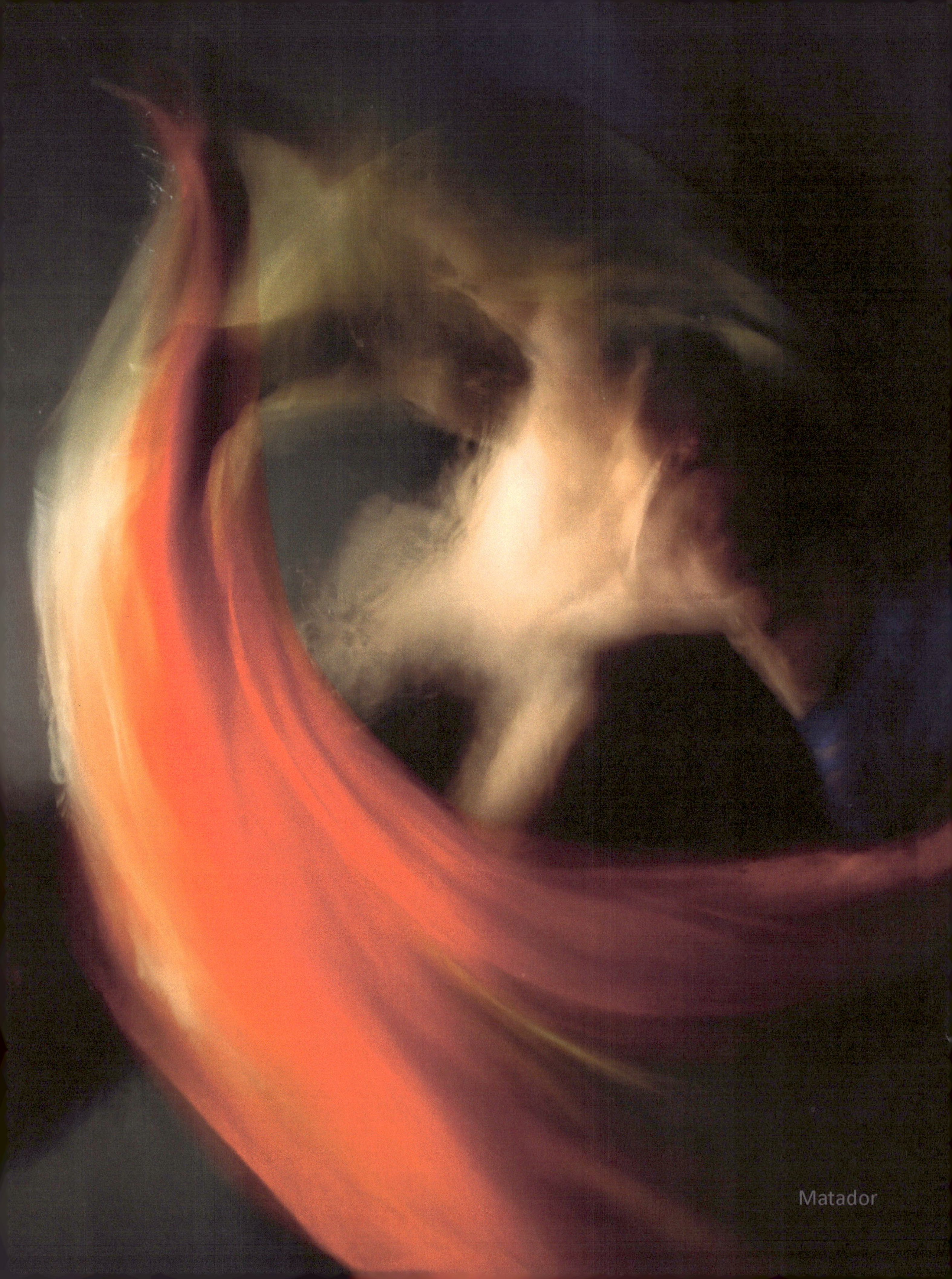

Matador

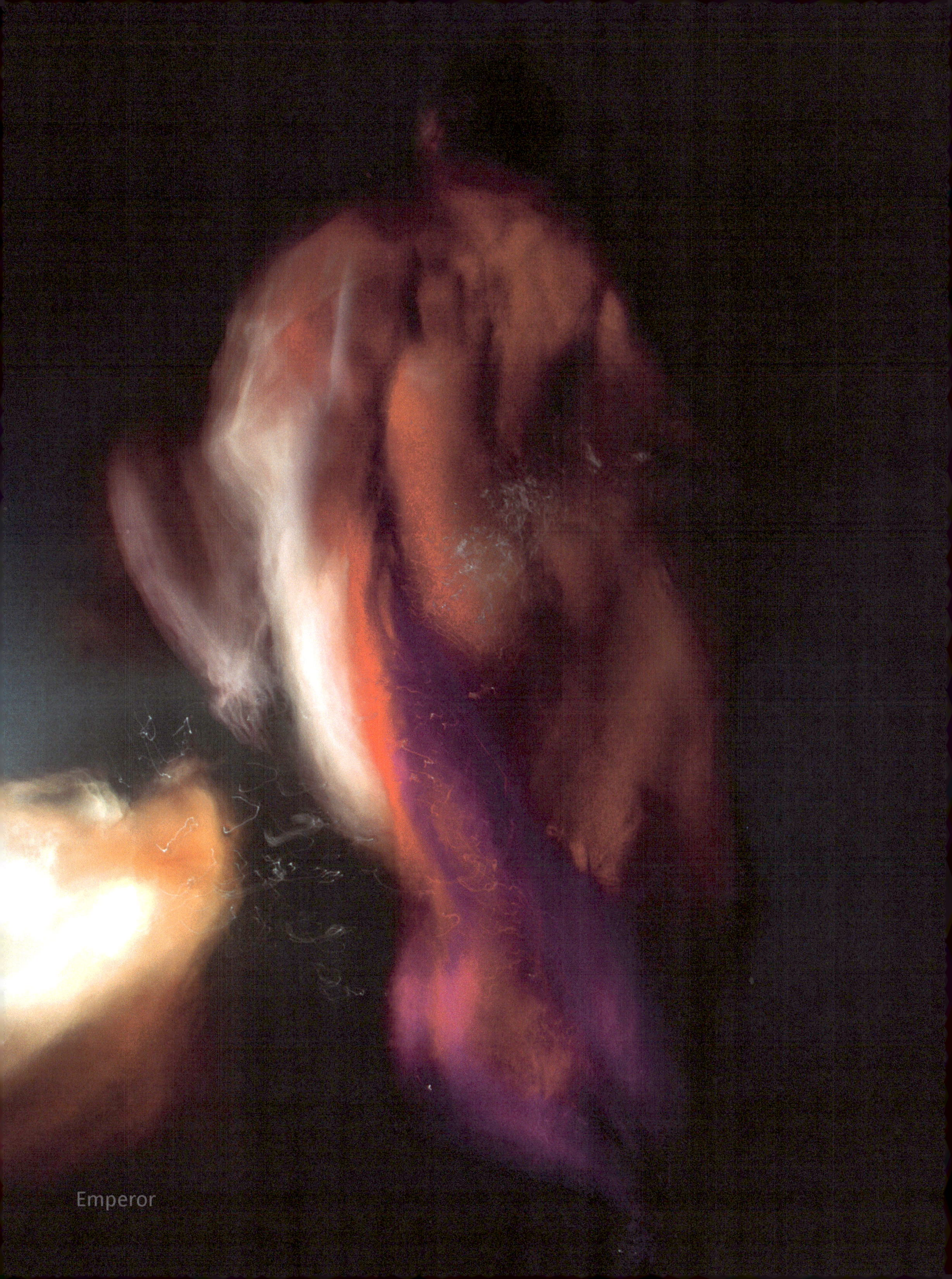

Emperor

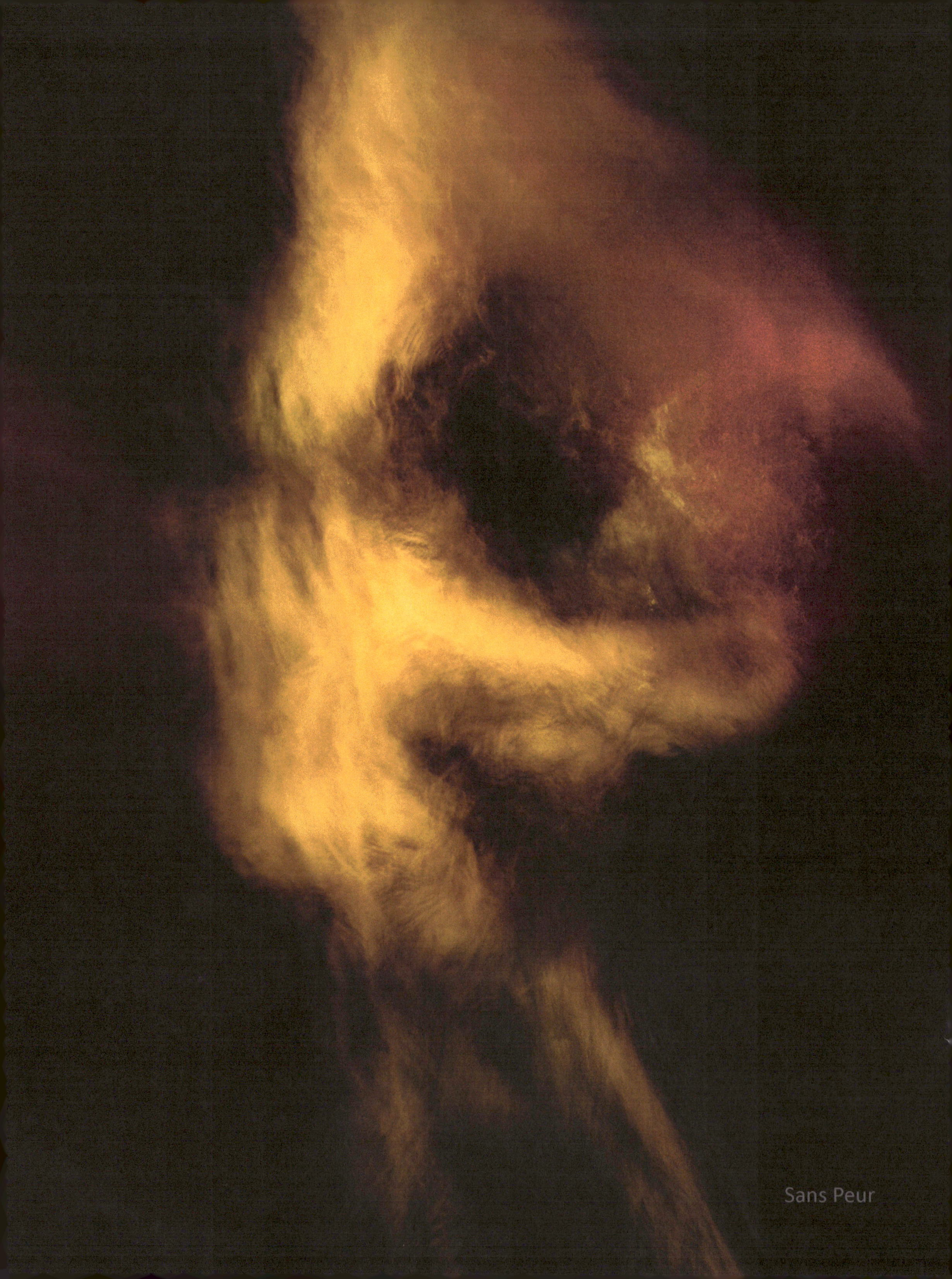

Sans Peur

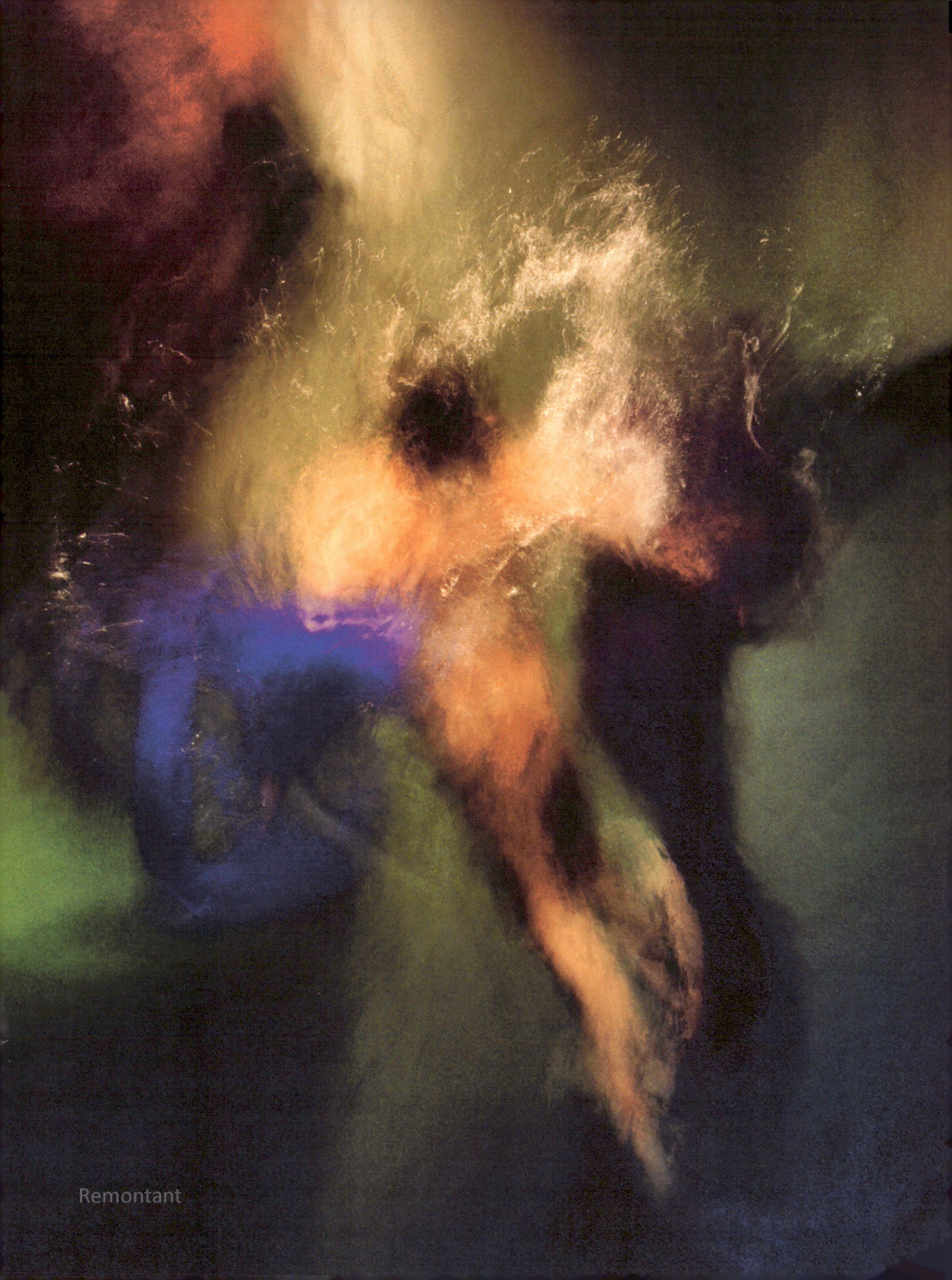

Remontant

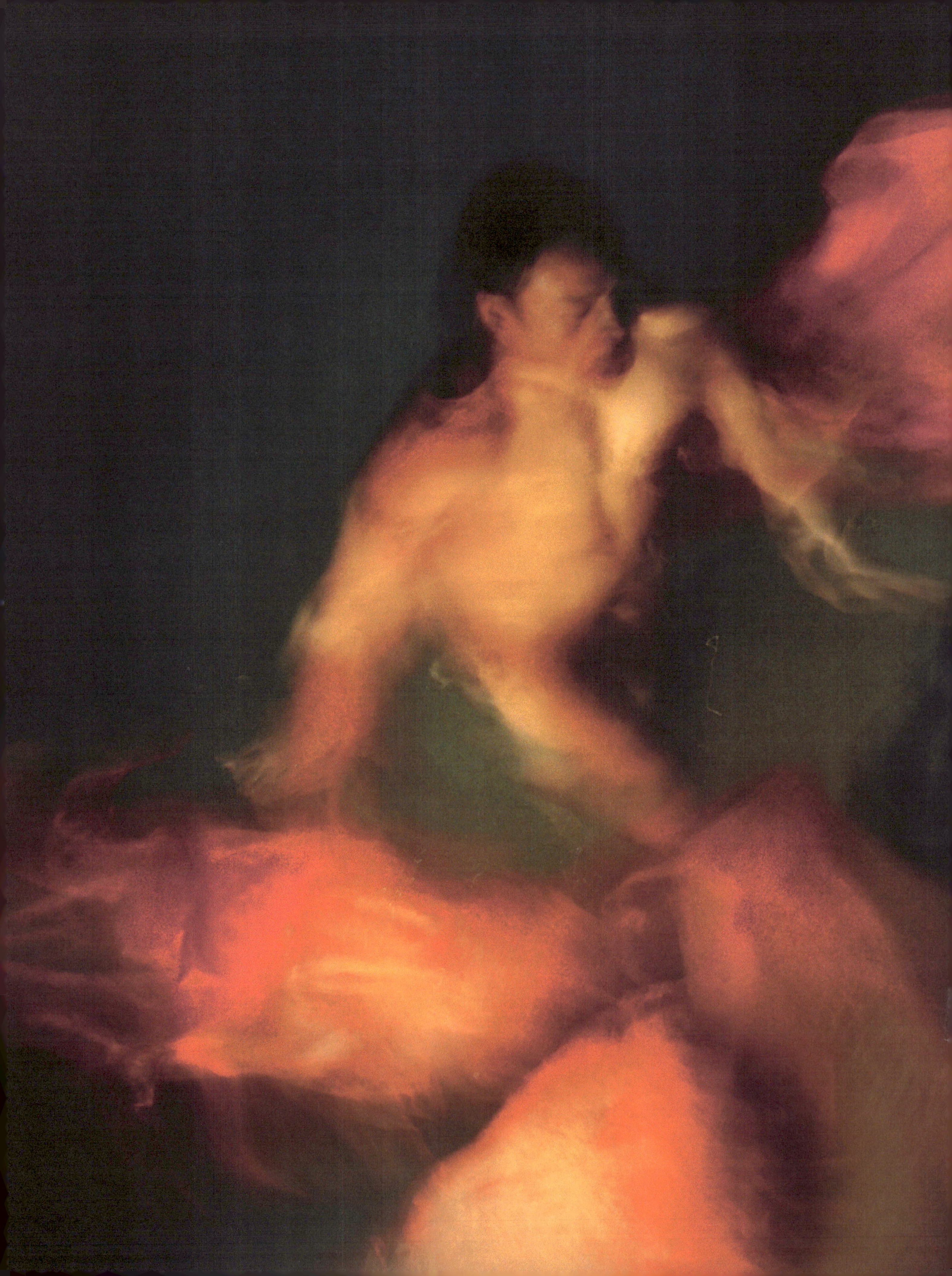

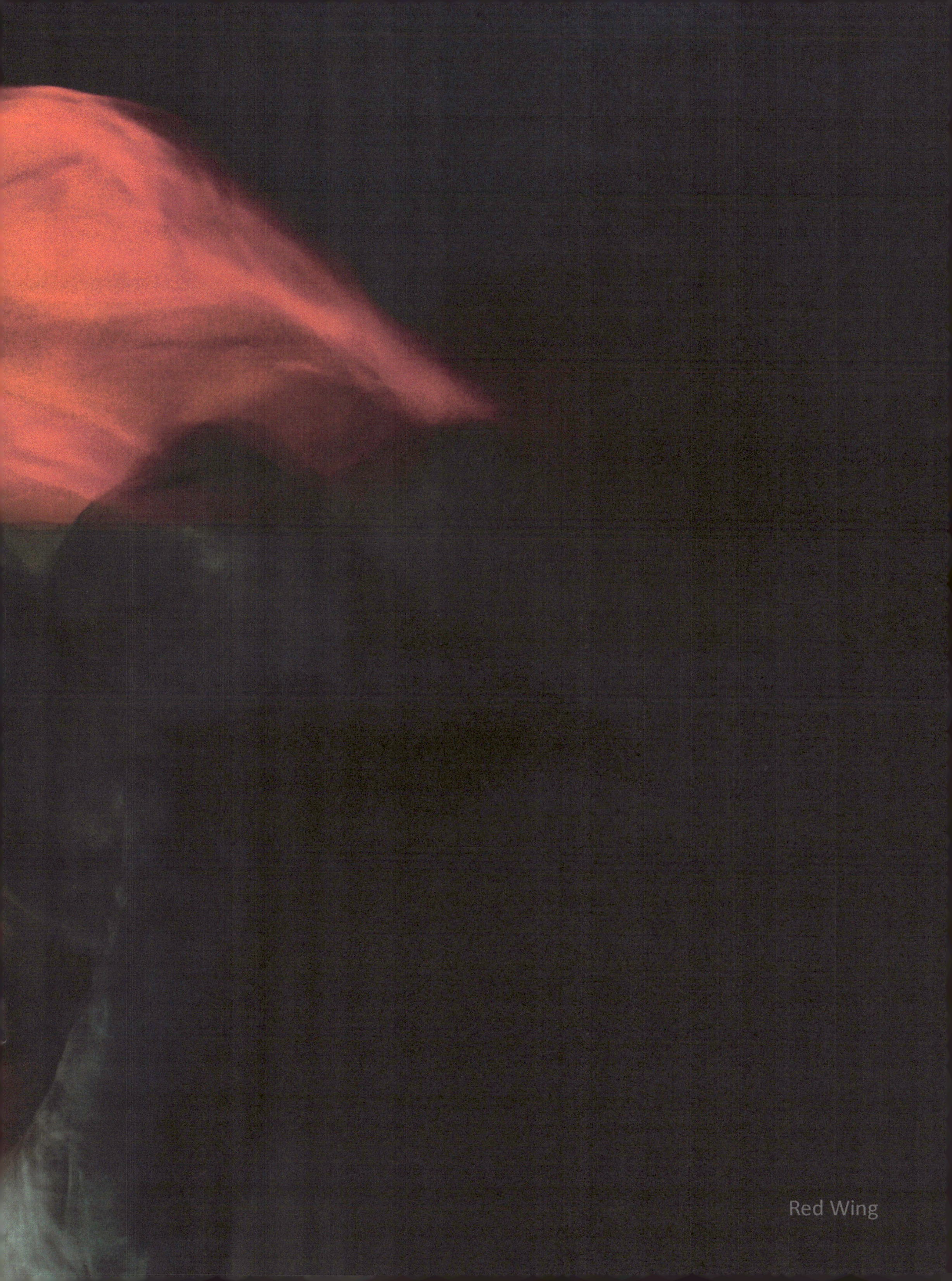

Red Wing

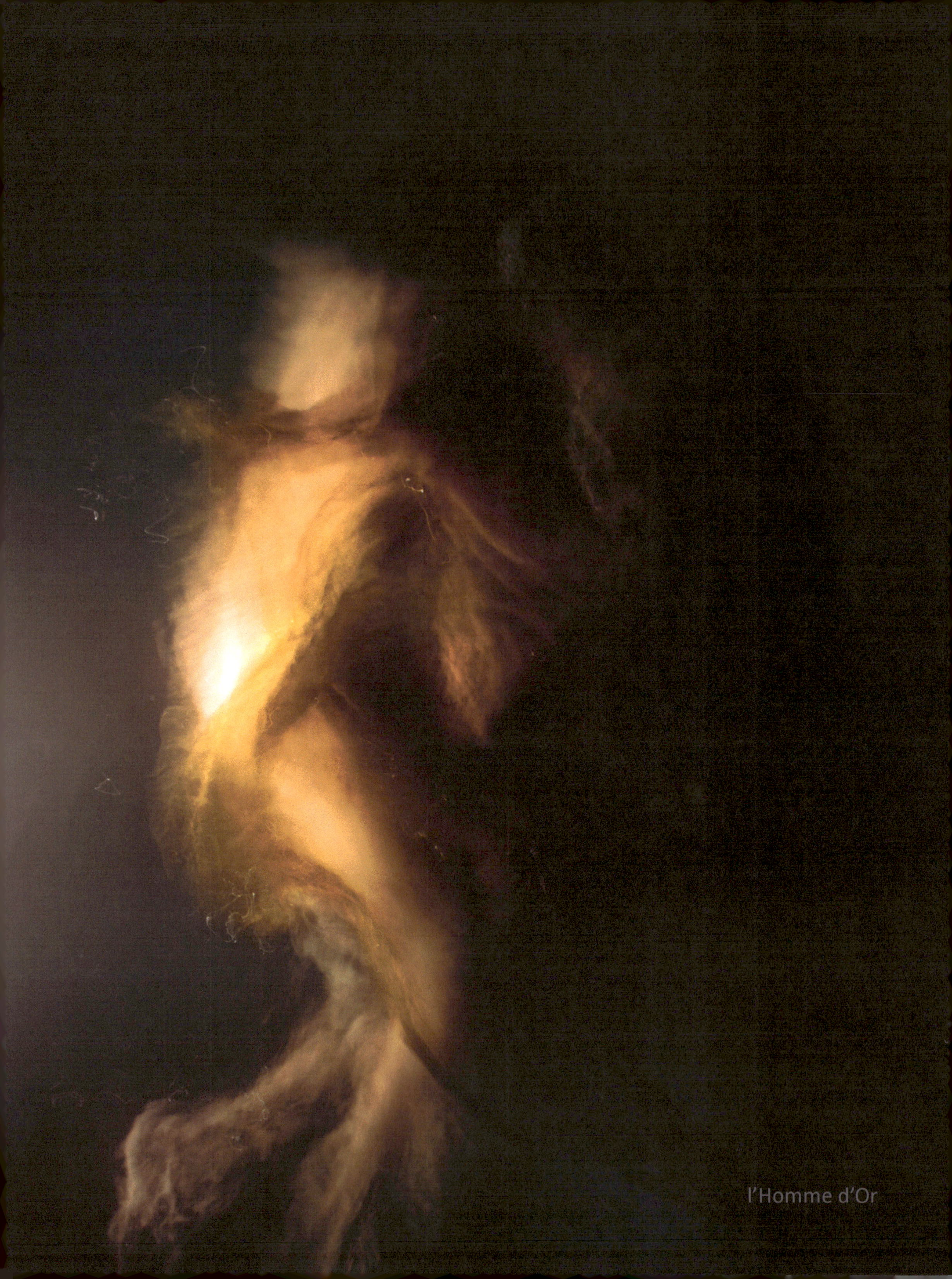
l'Homme d'Or

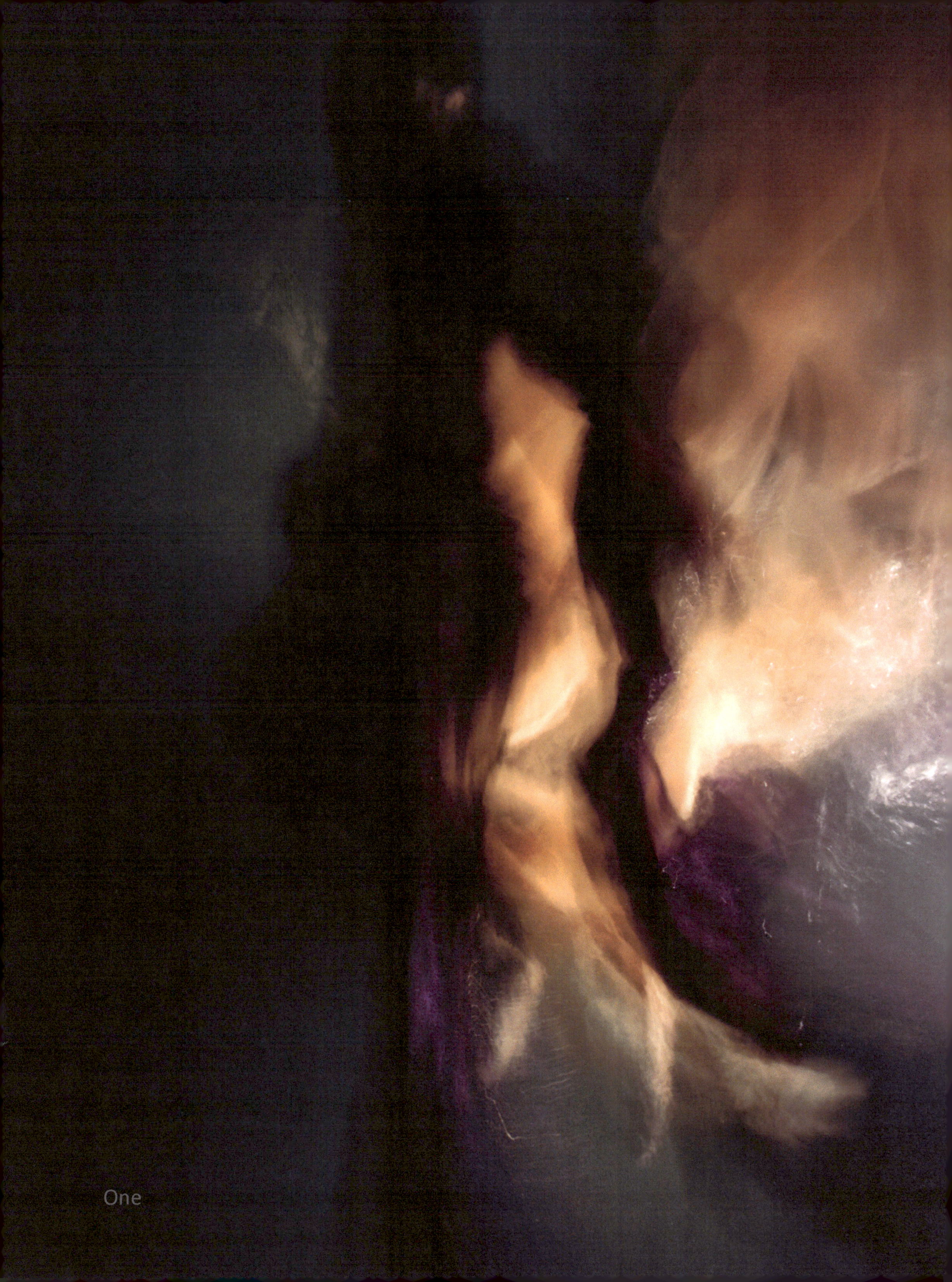

One

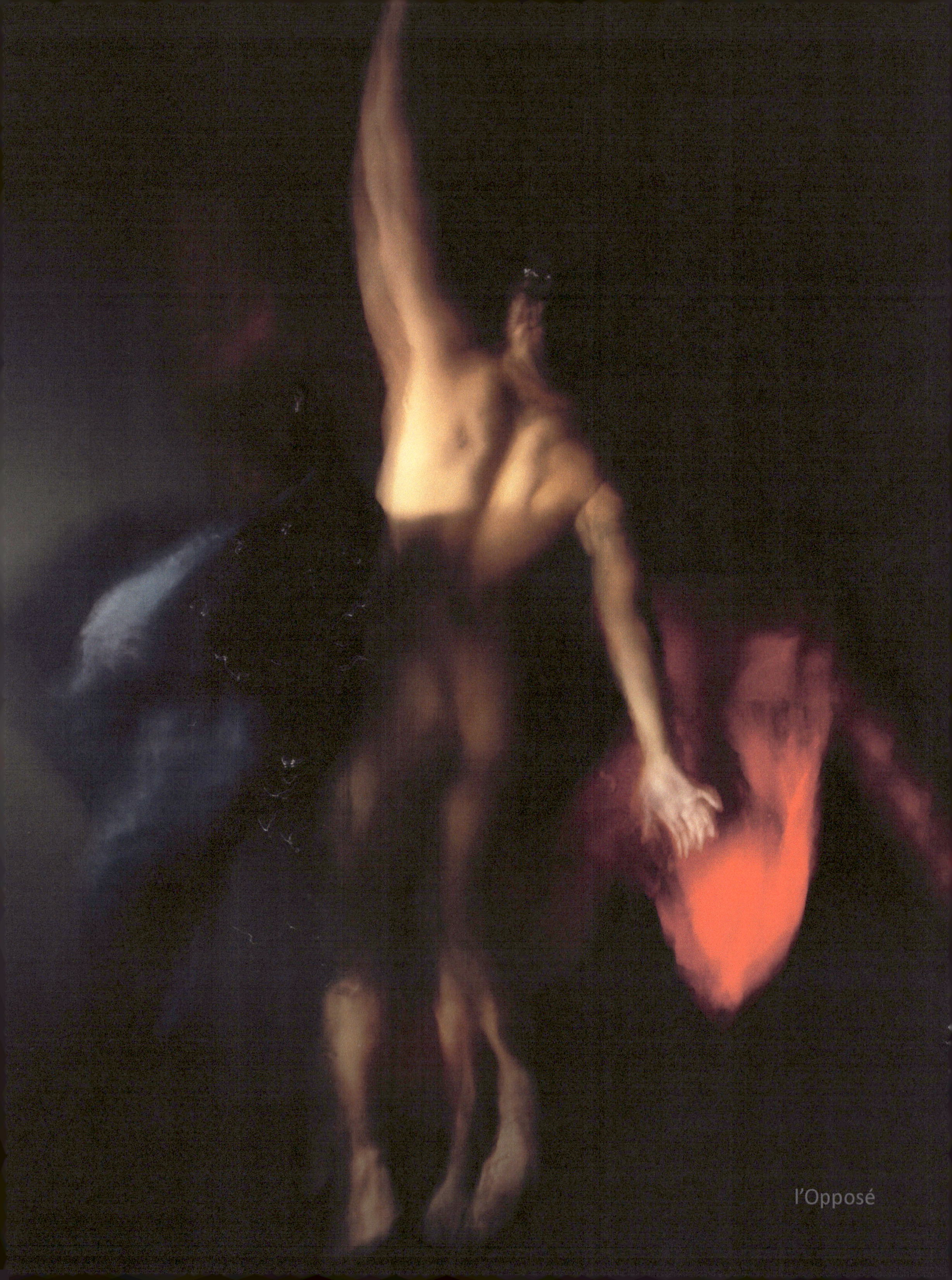
l'Opposé

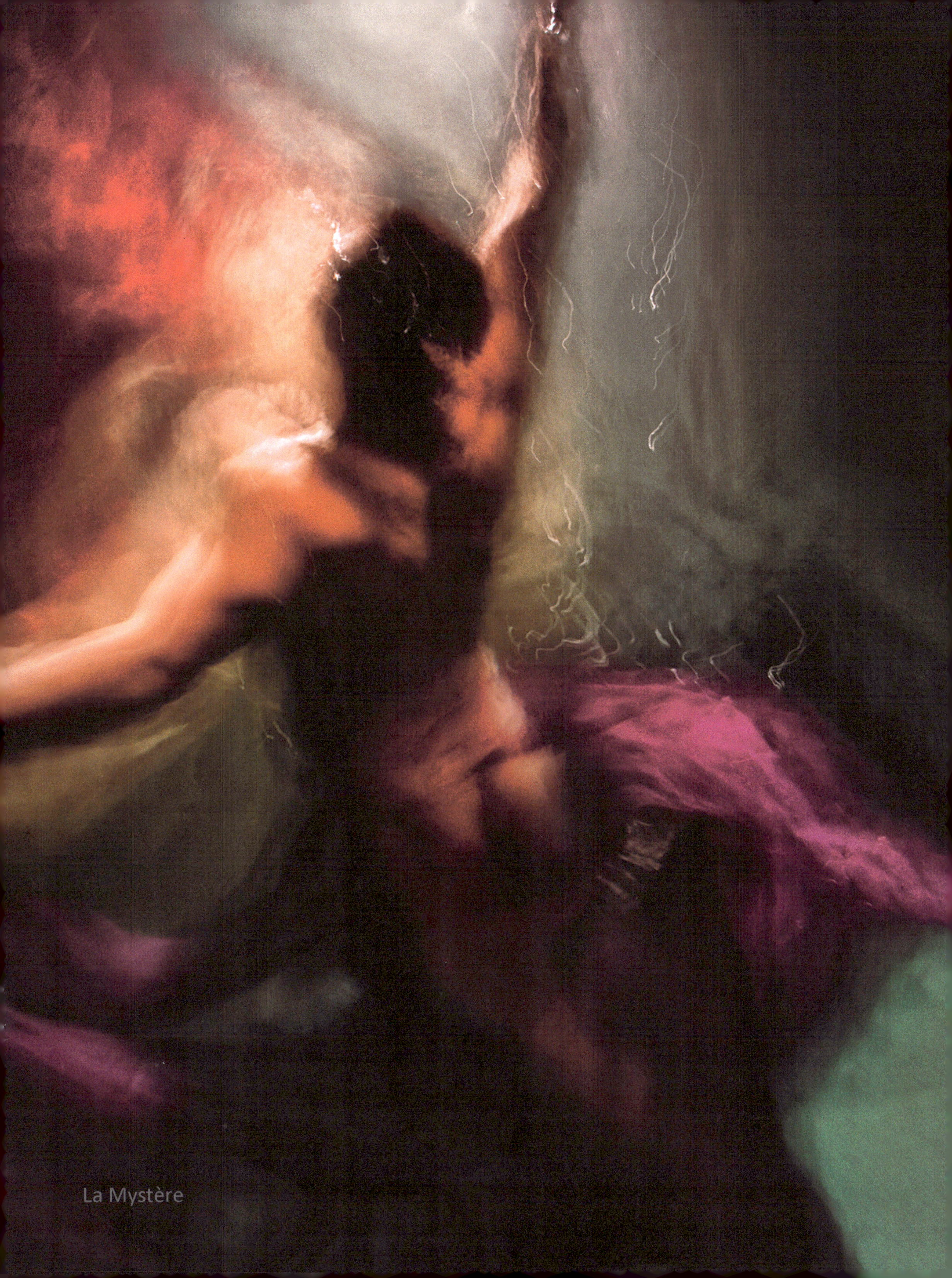

La Mystère

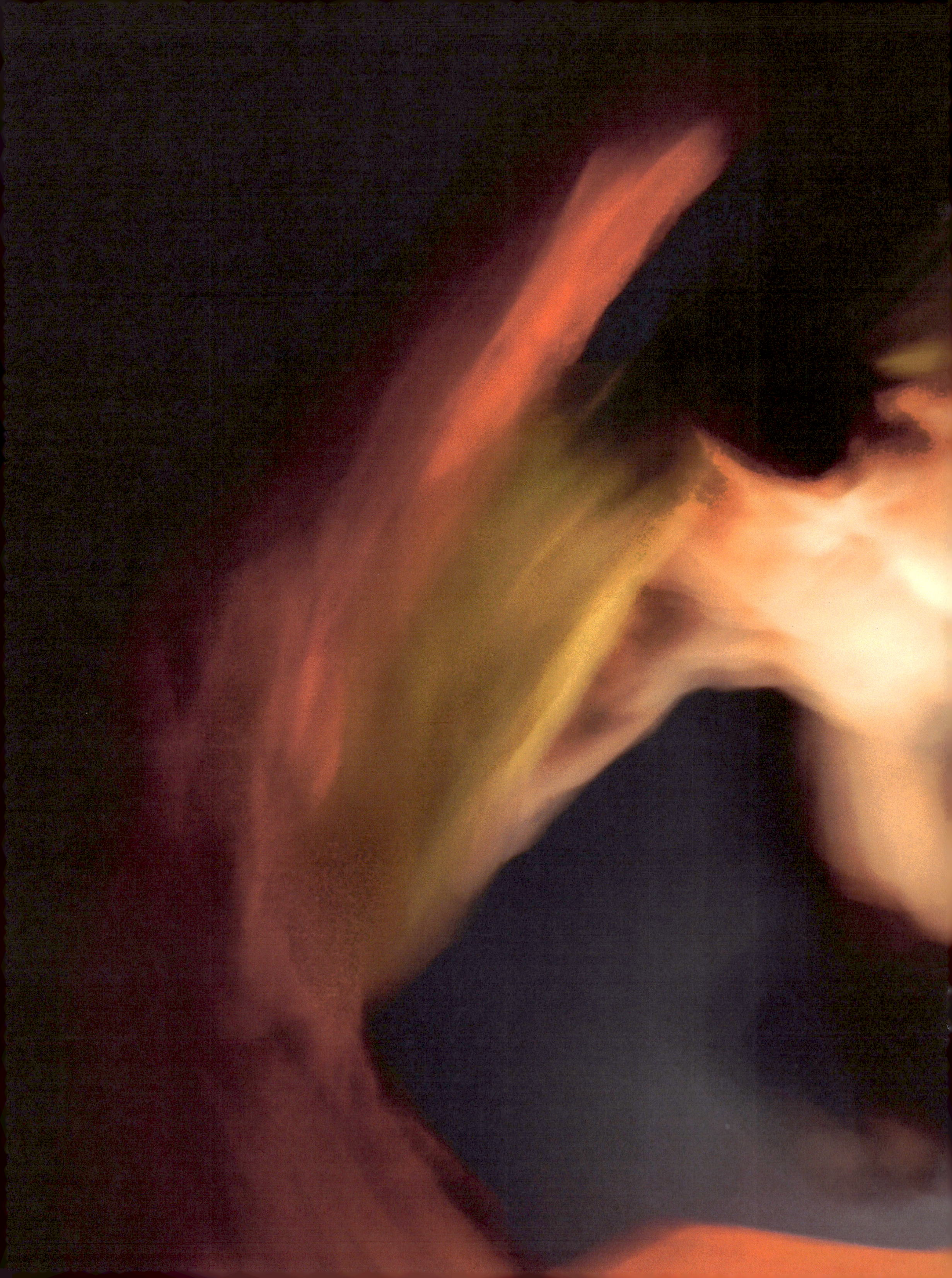

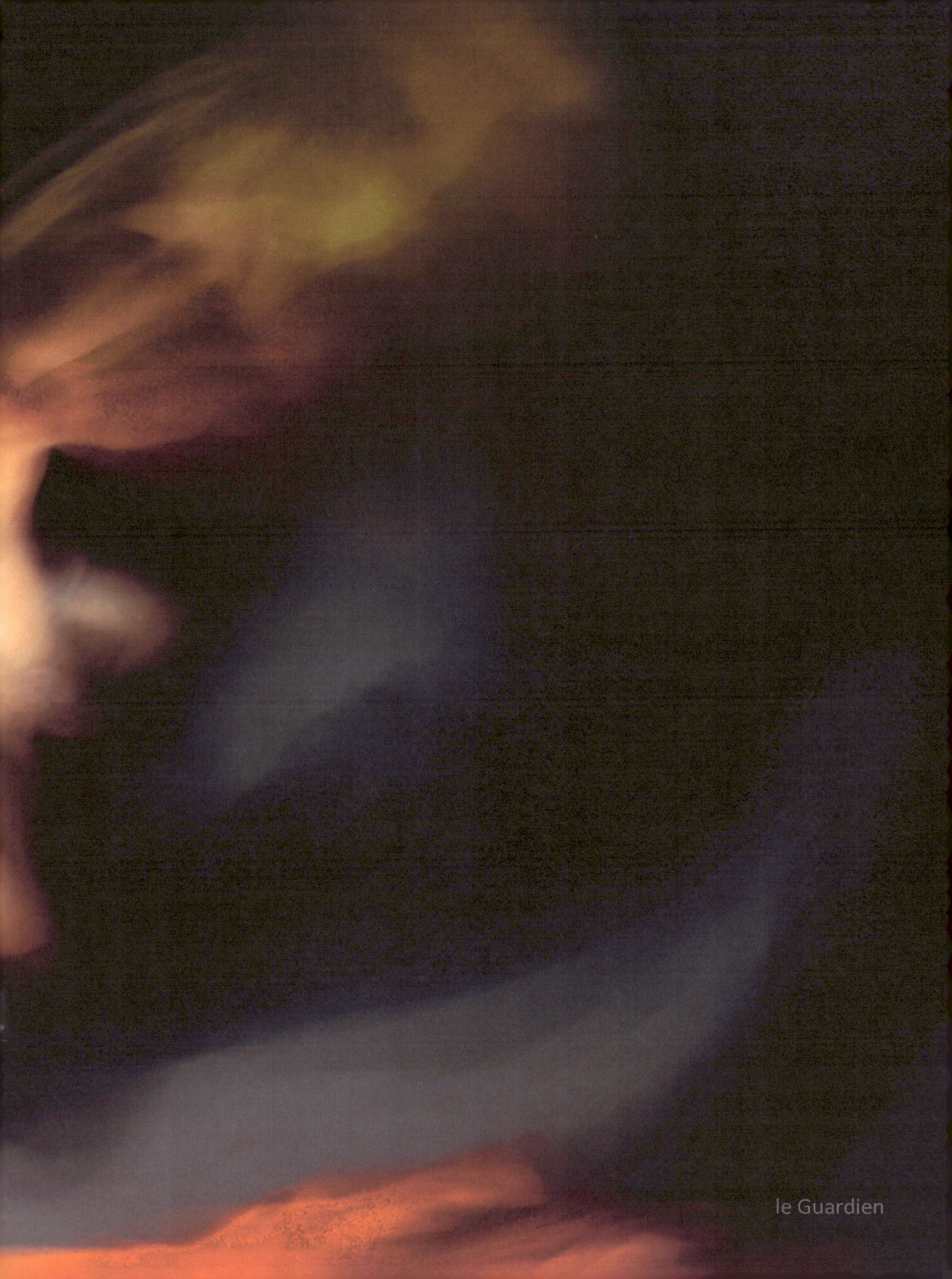

le Guardien

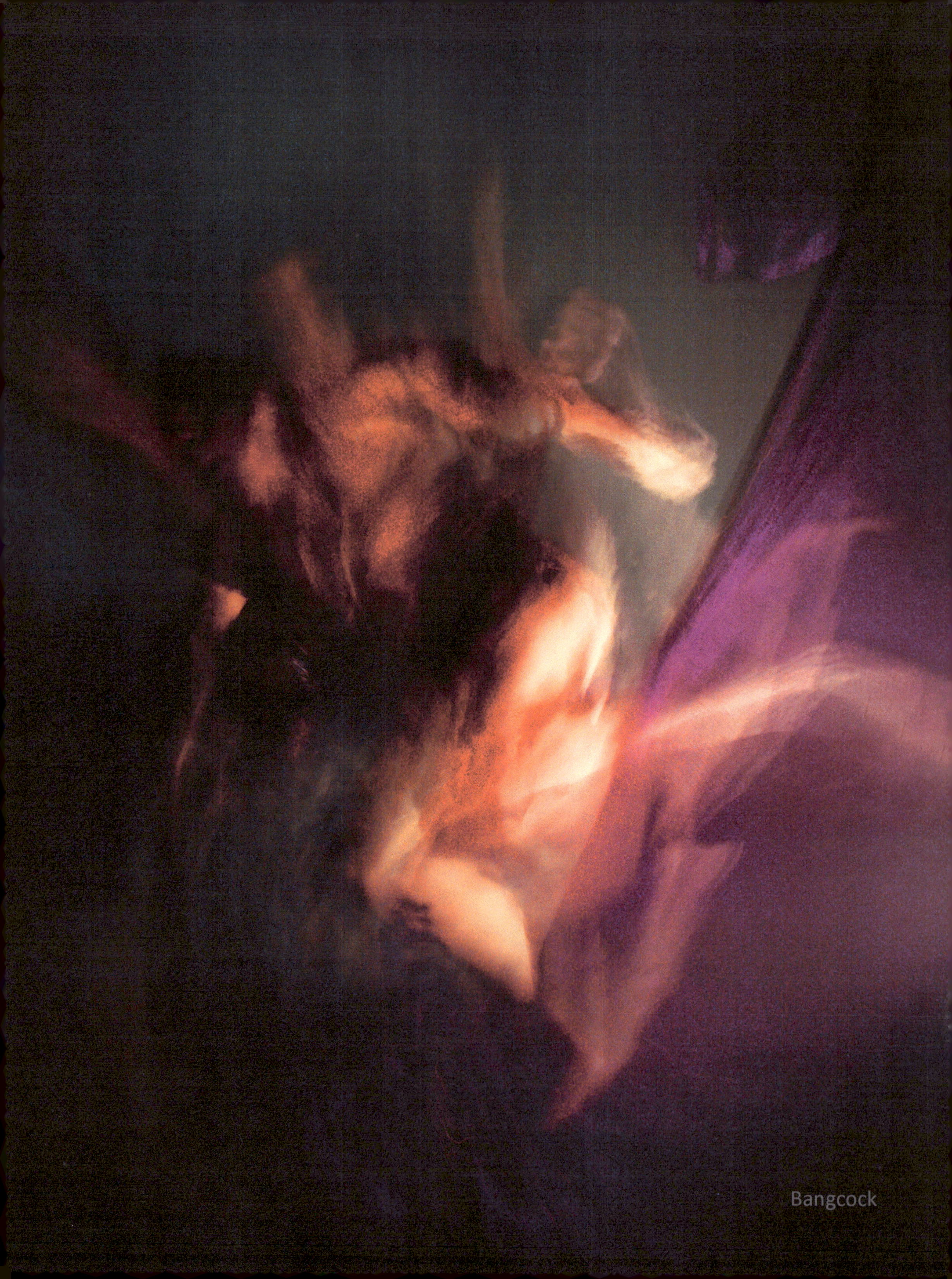

Bangcock

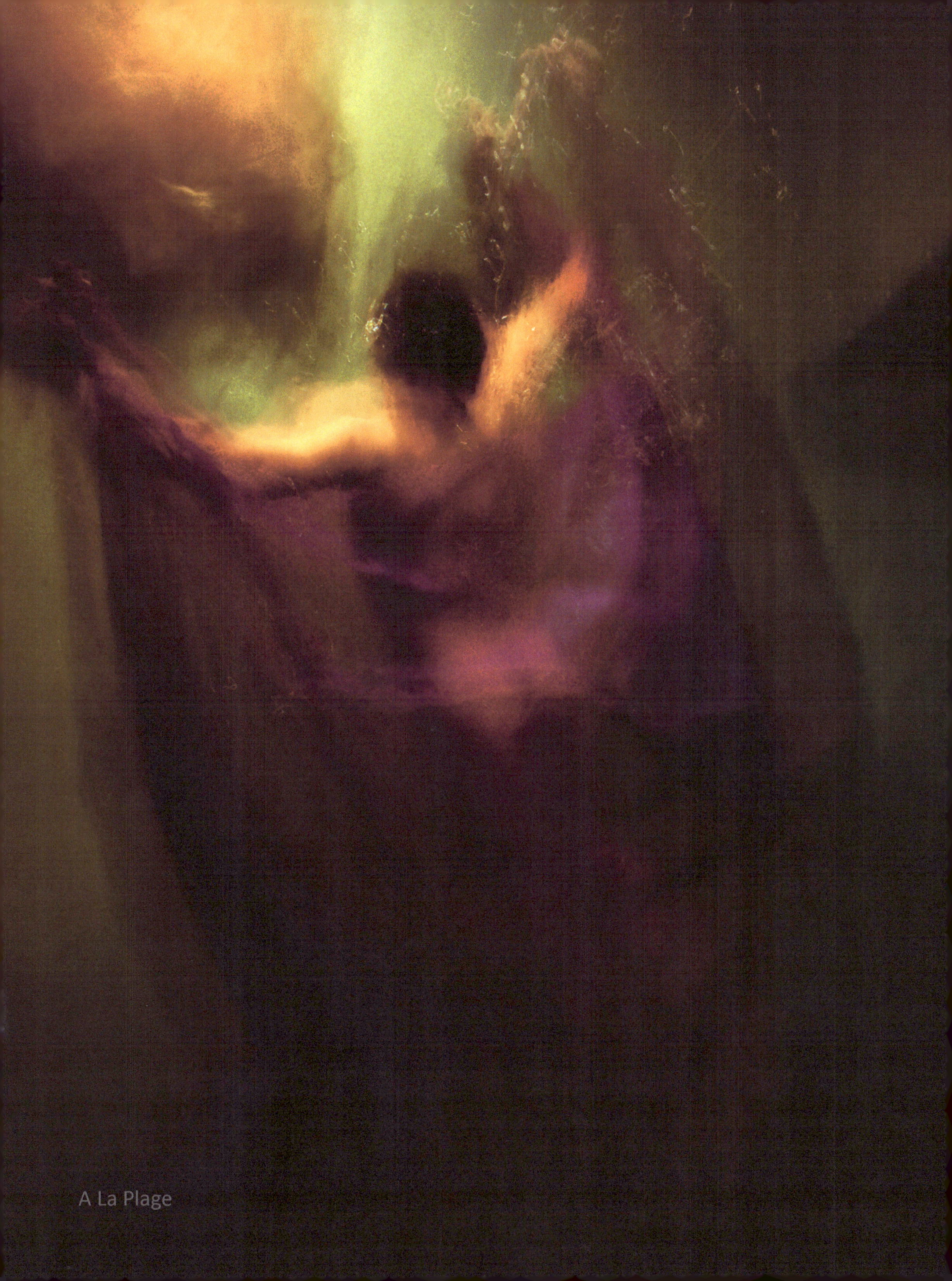

A La Plage

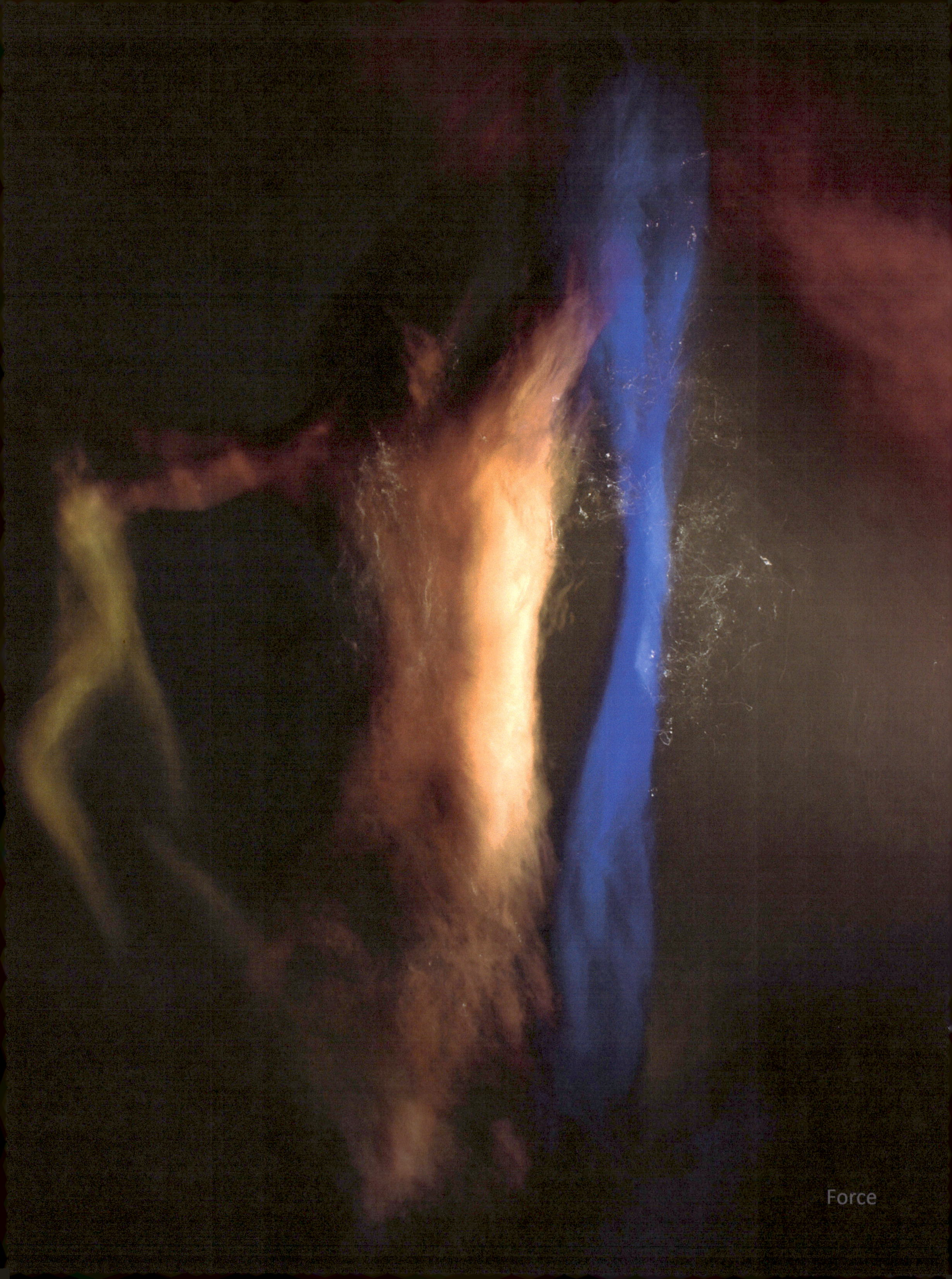

Force

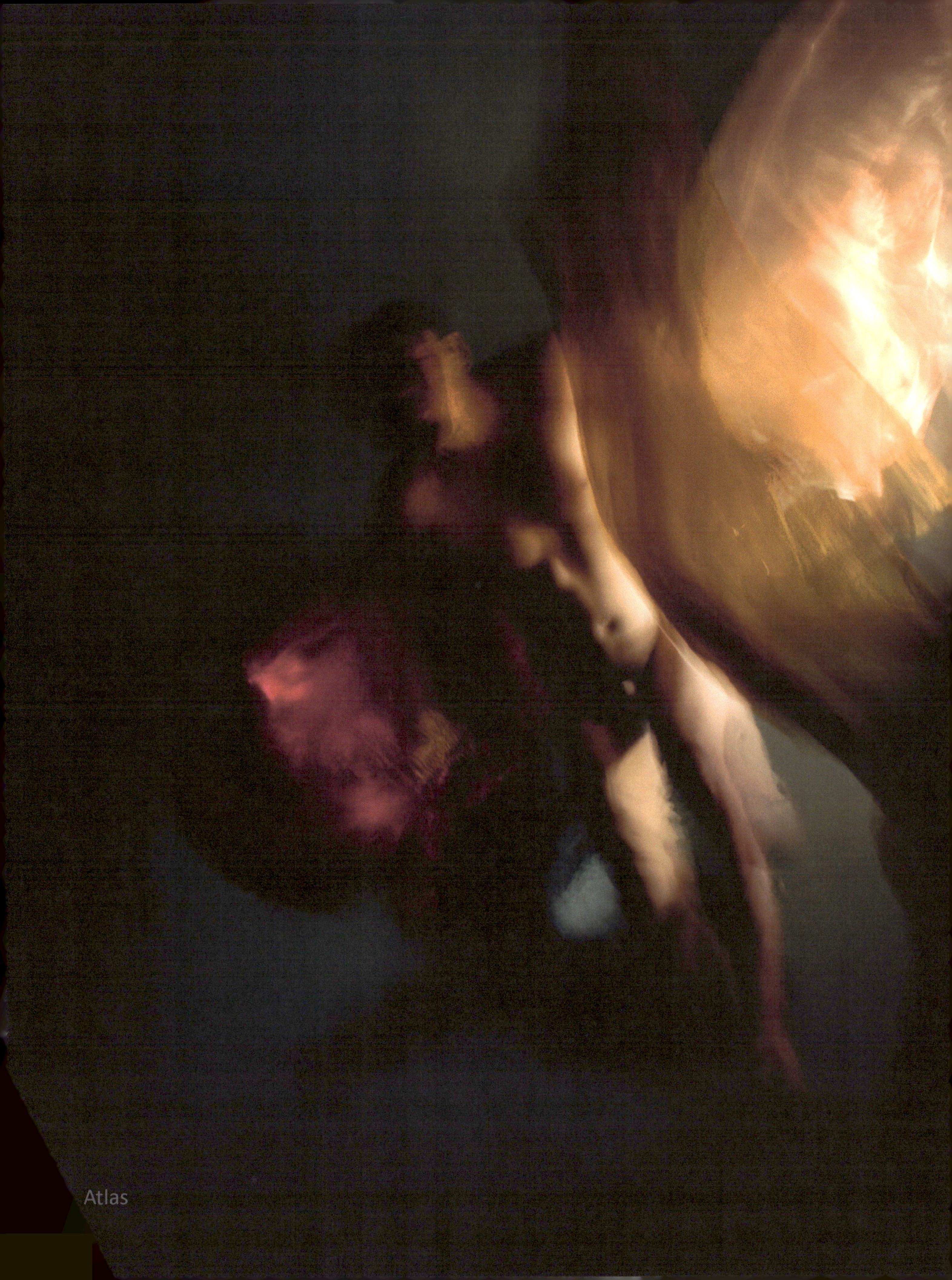

Atlas

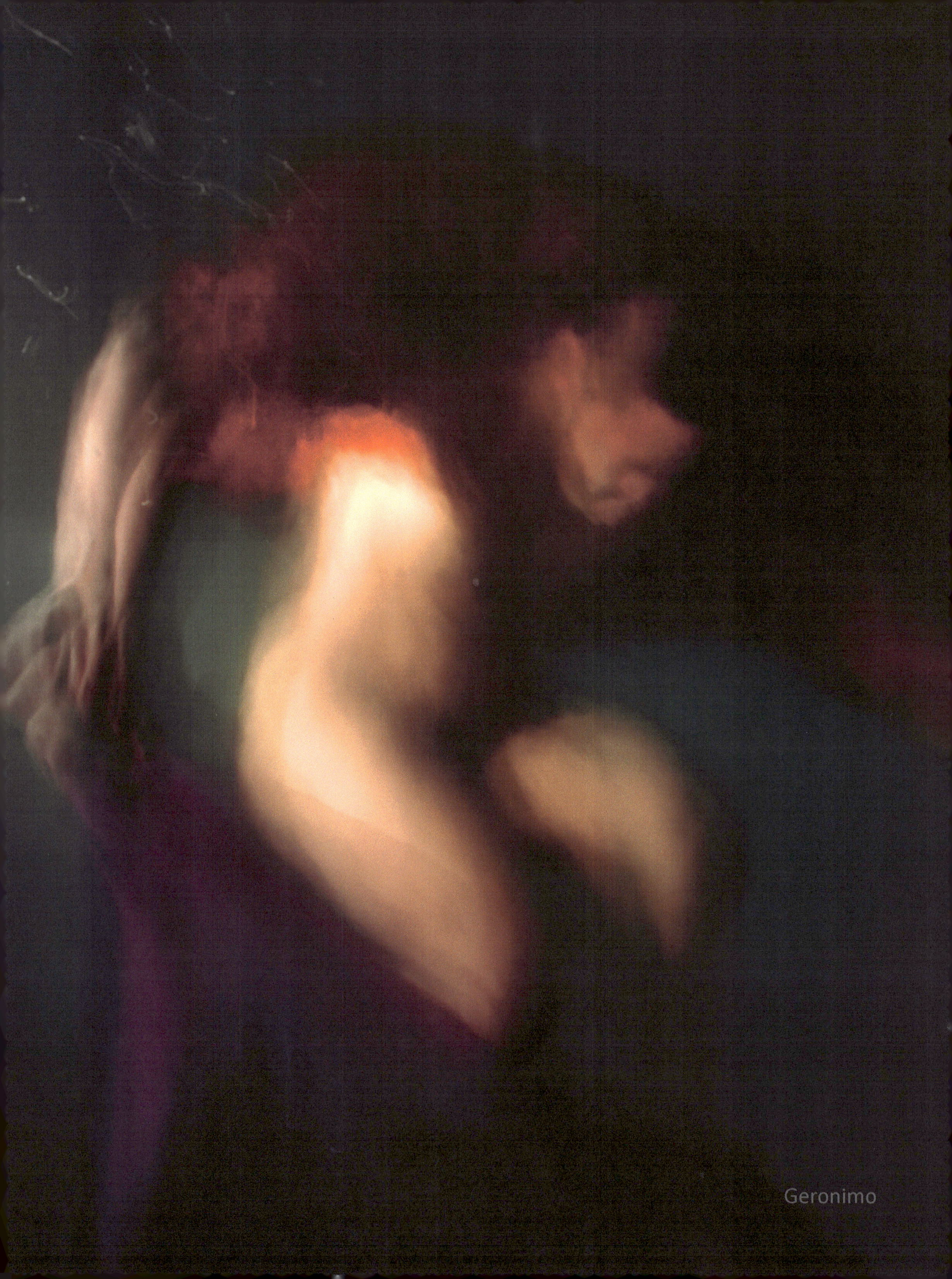
Geronimo

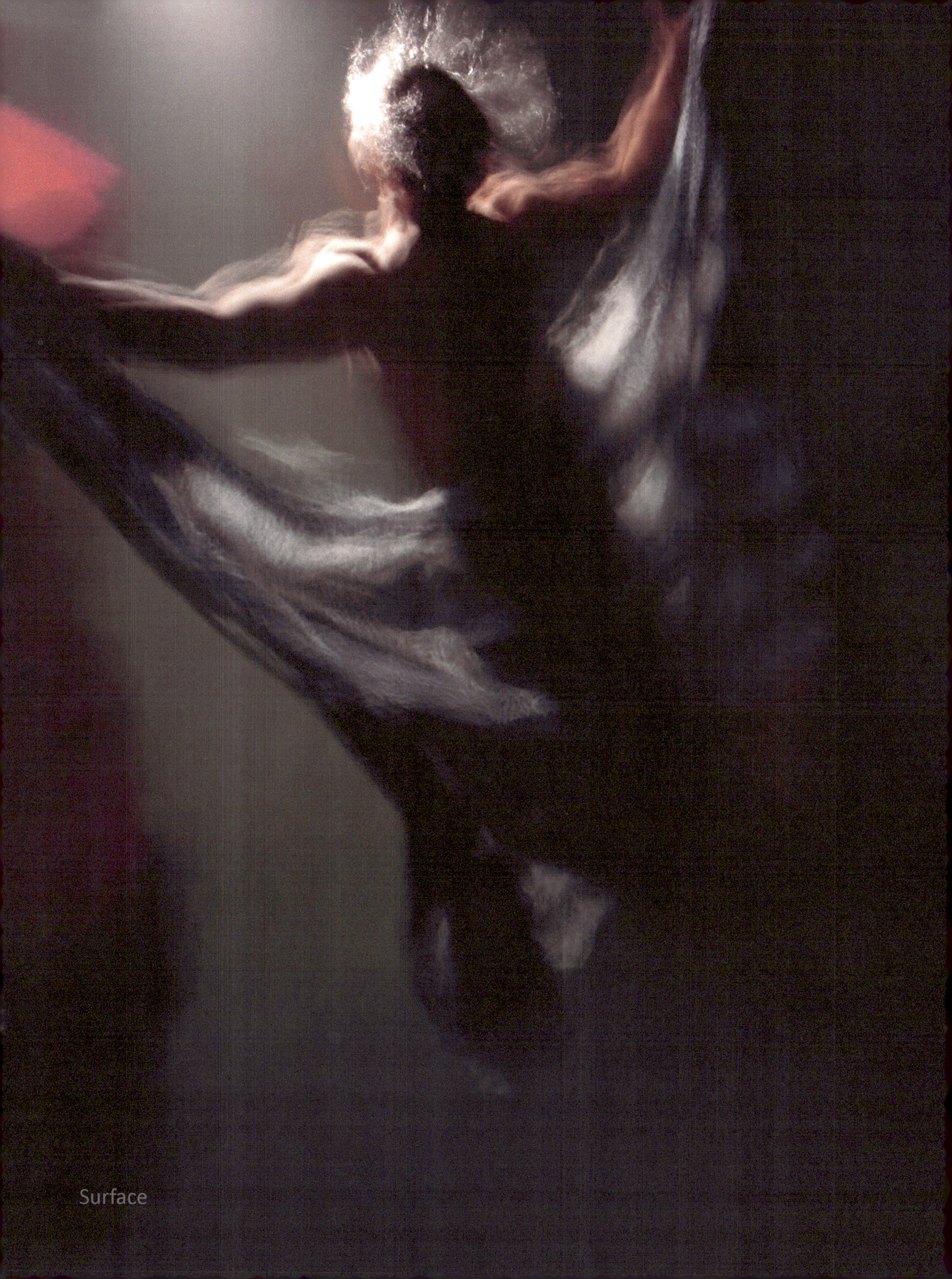

Surface

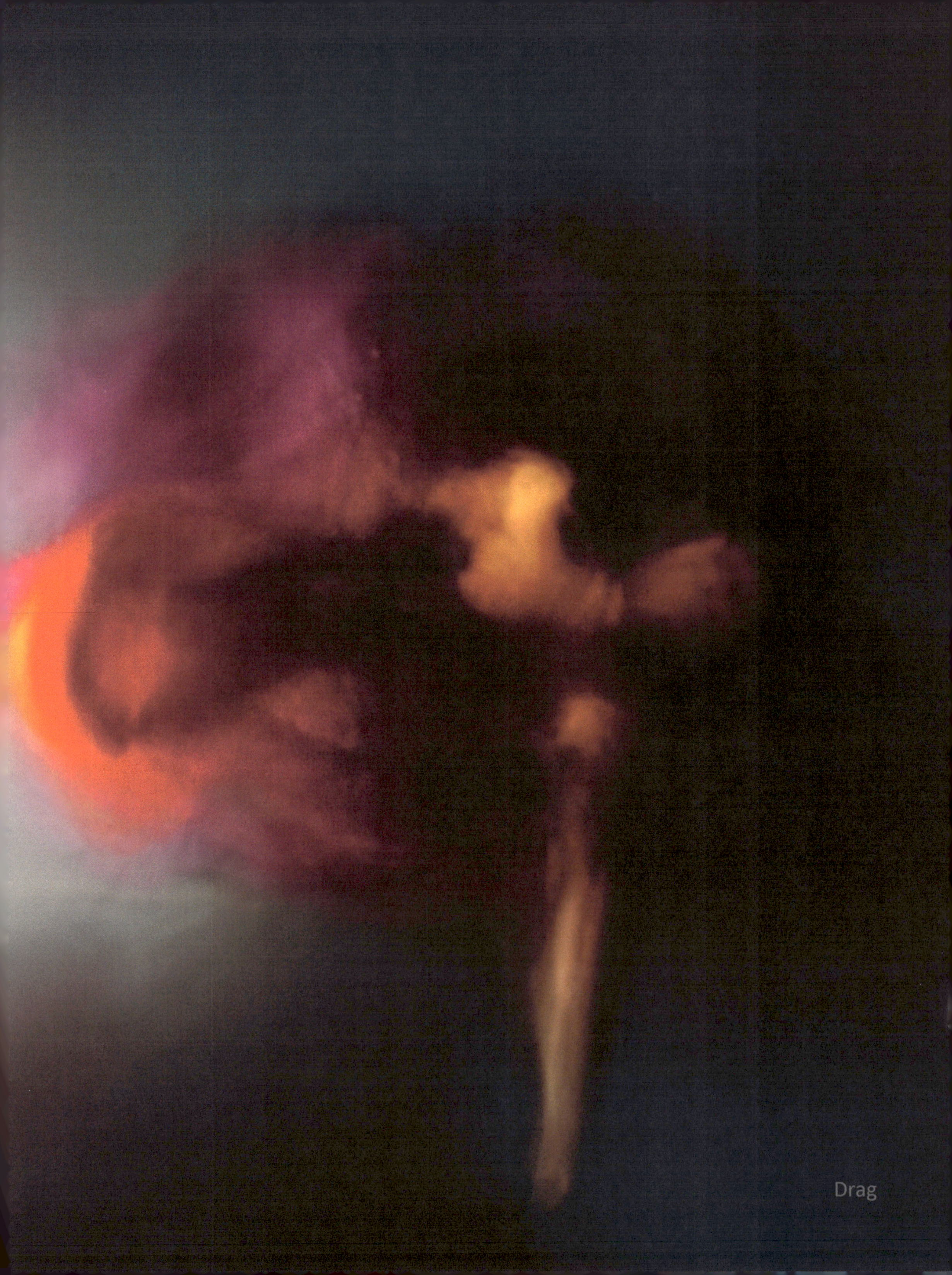

Drag

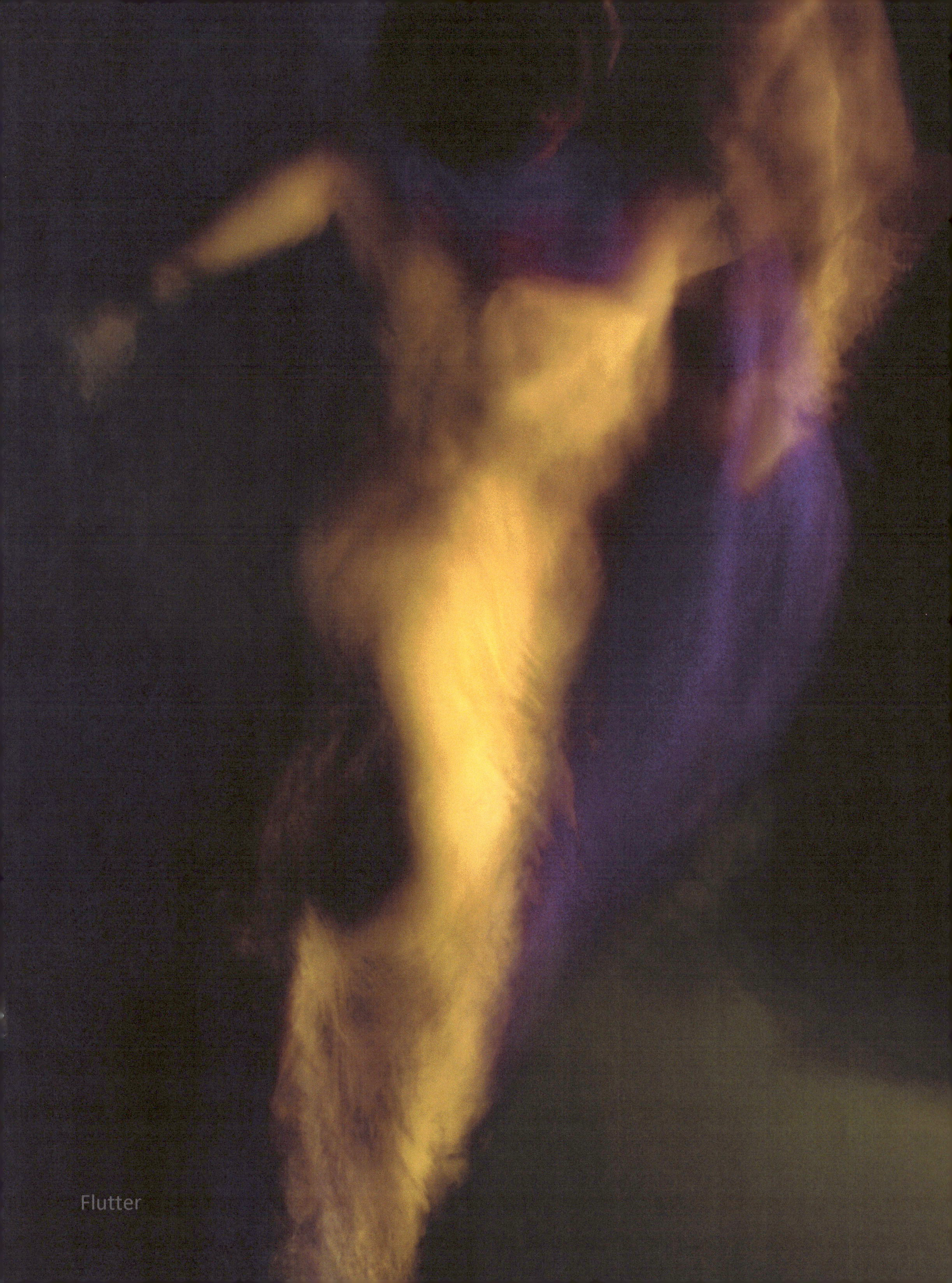

Flutter

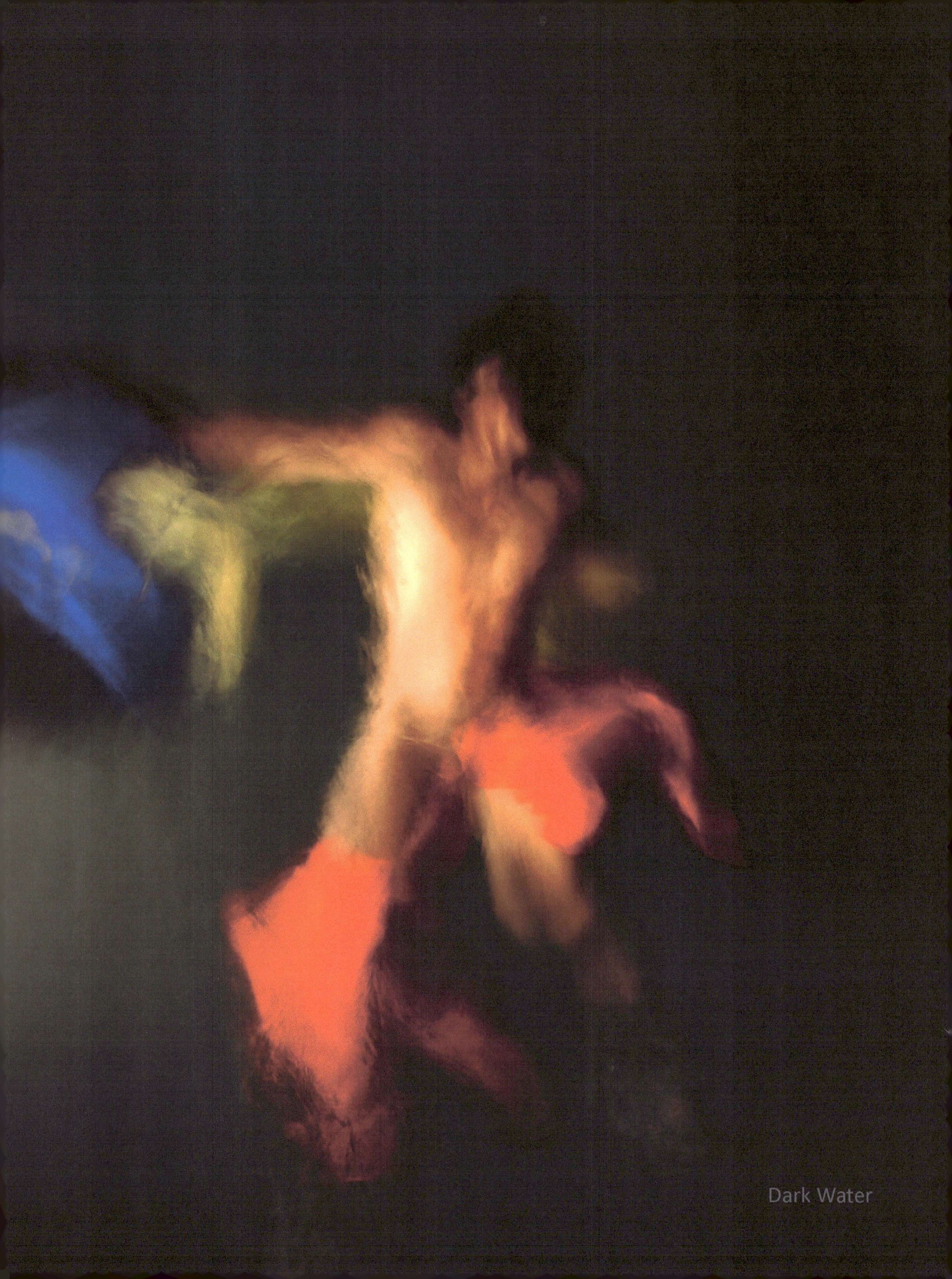

Dark Water

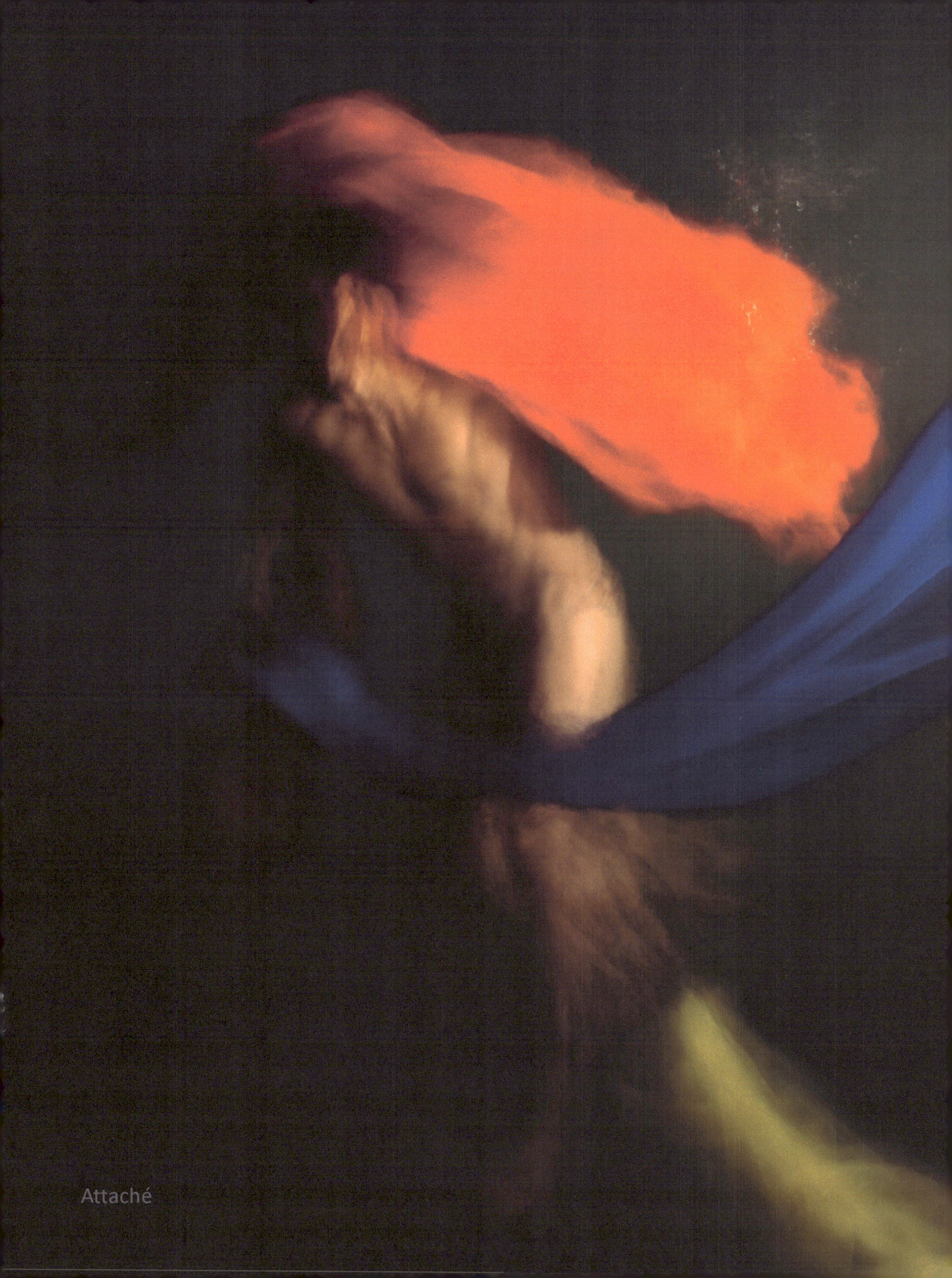

Attaché

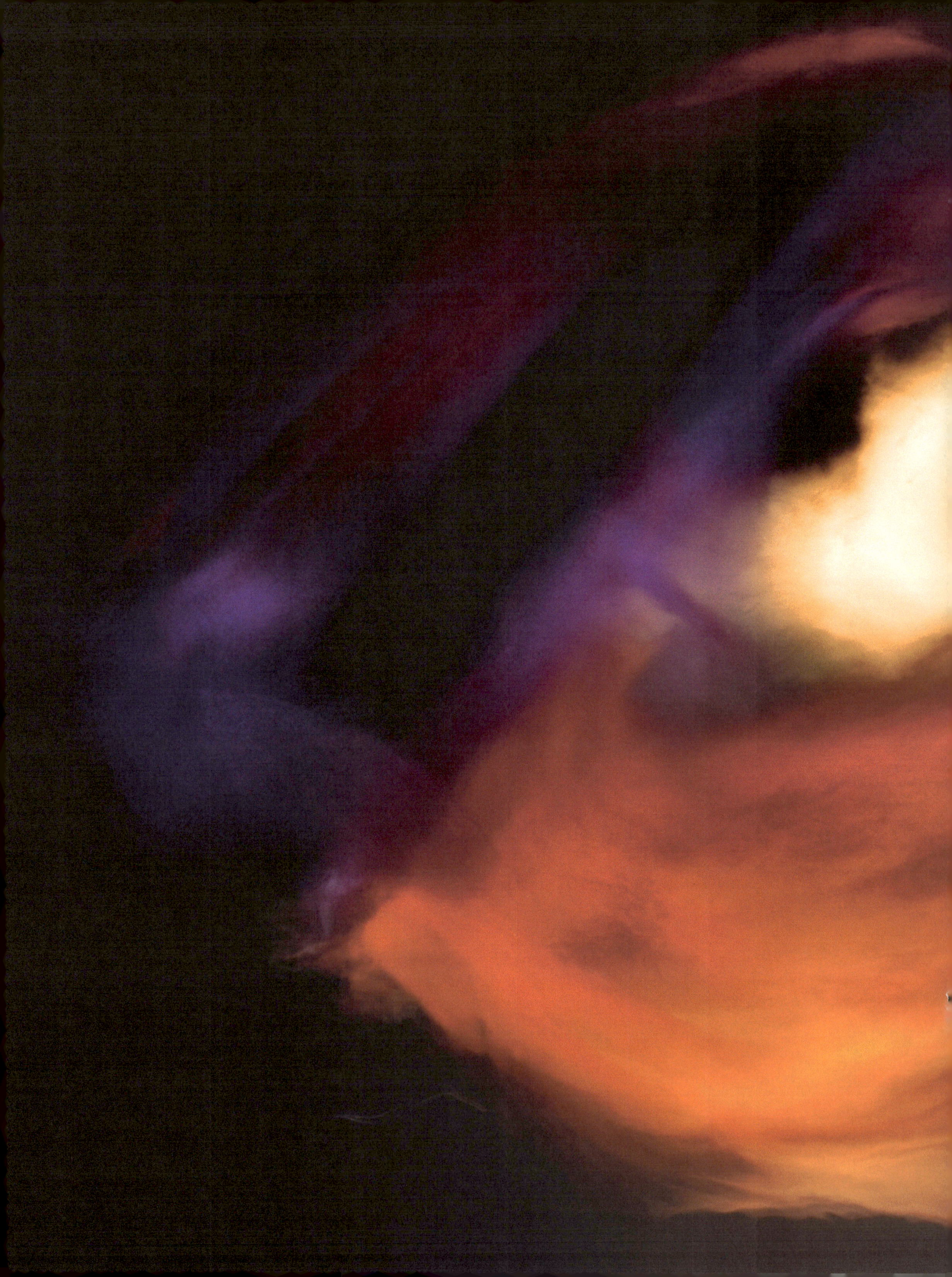

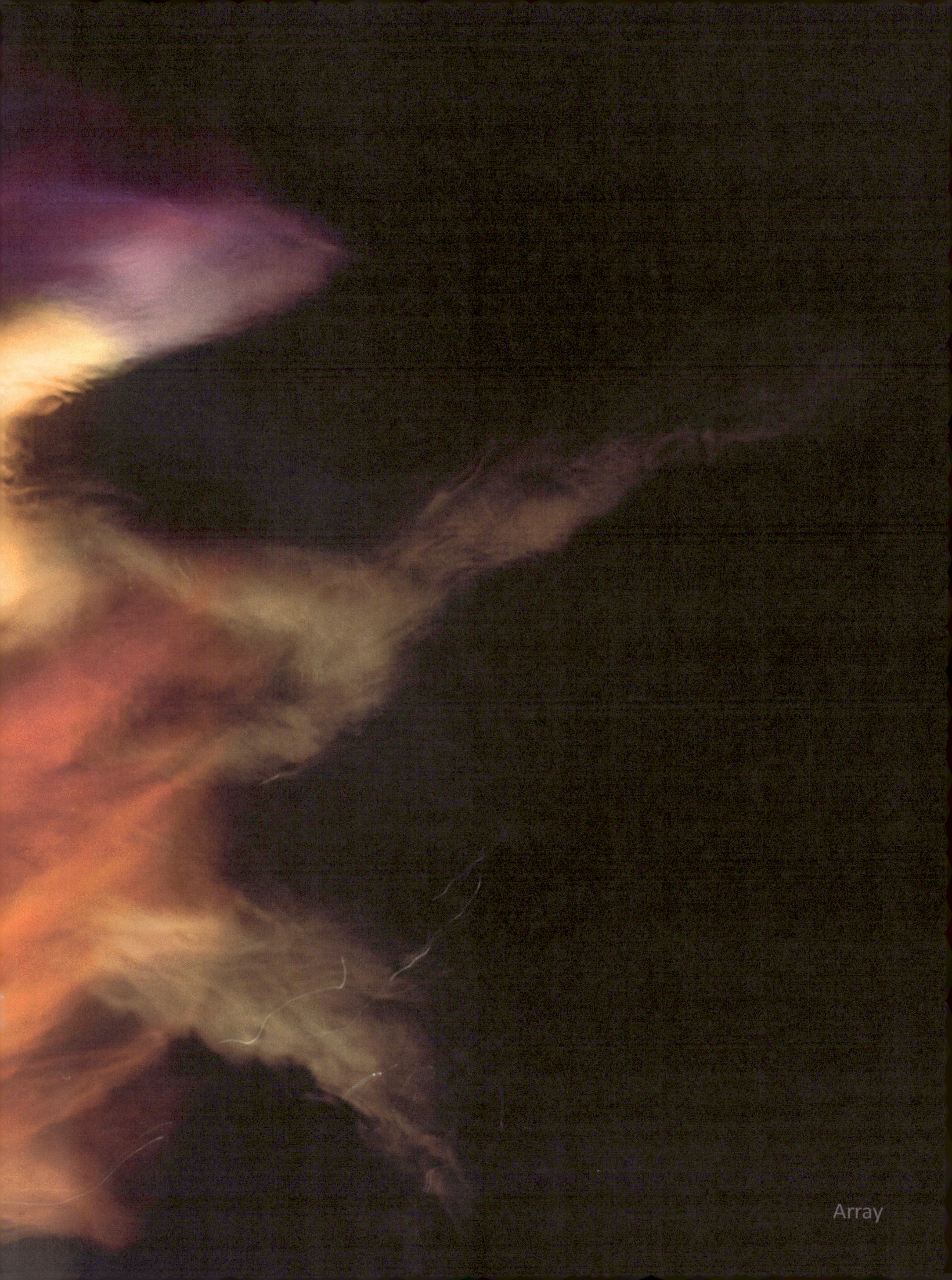

Array

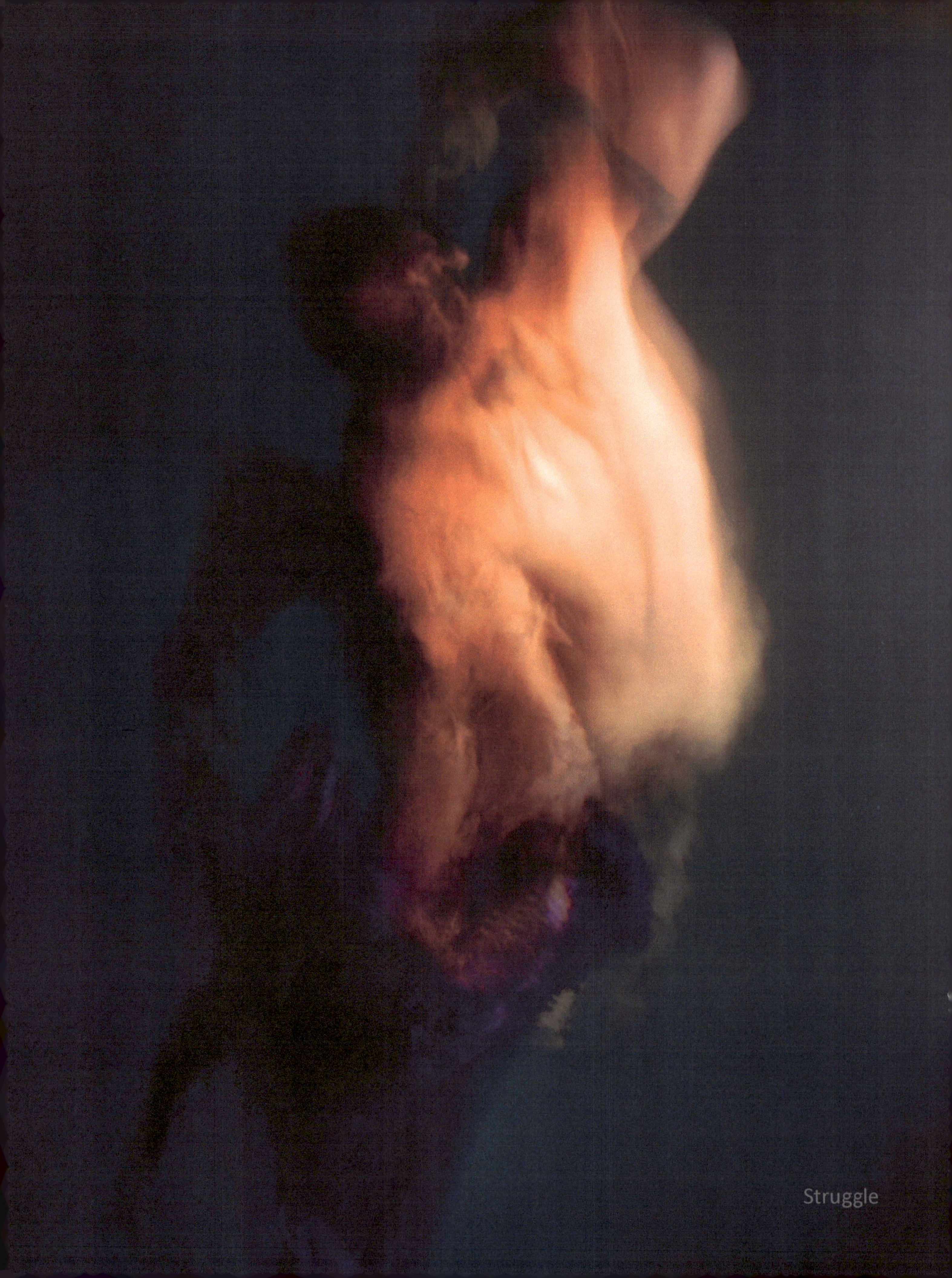

Struggle

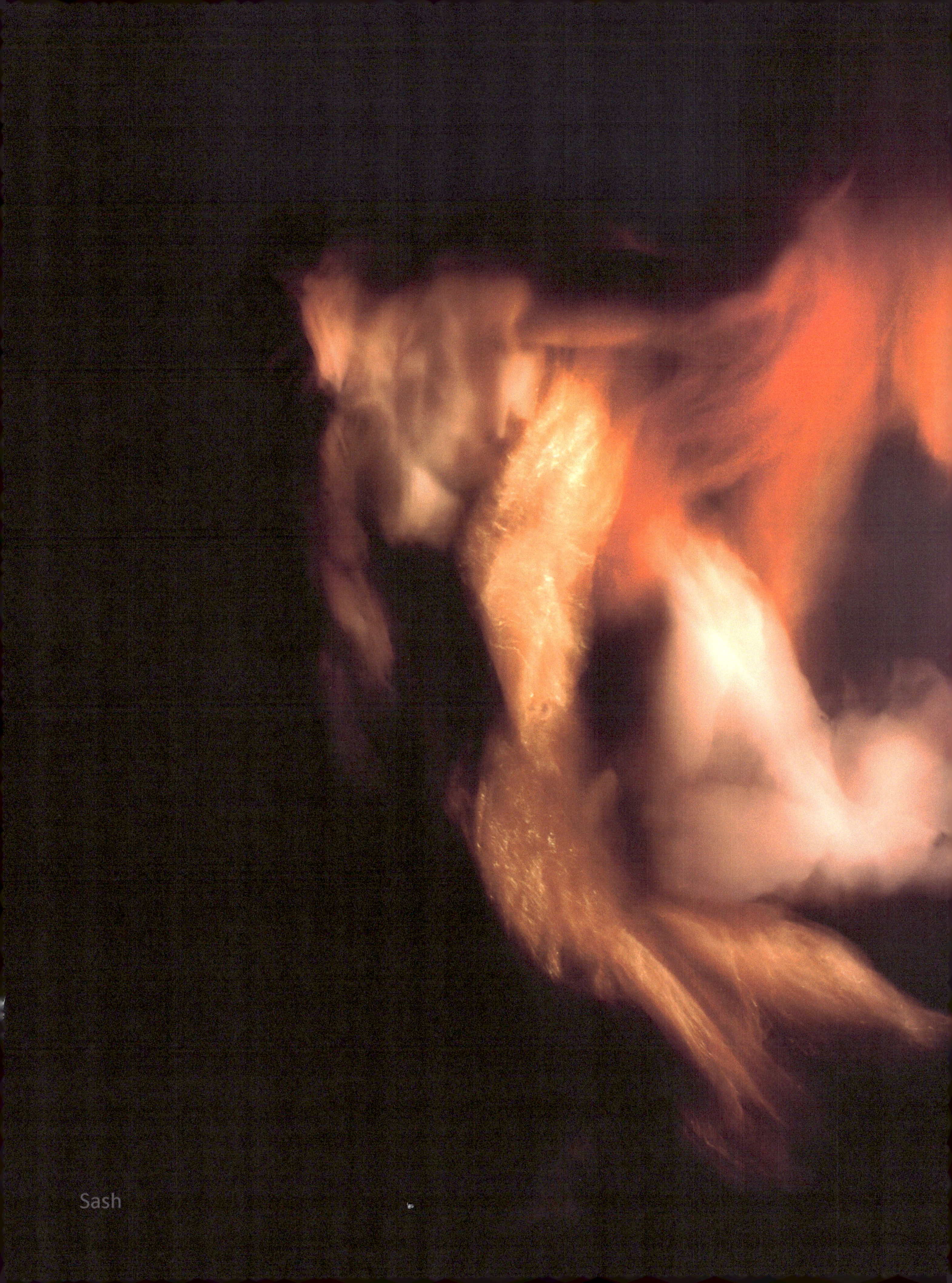

Sash

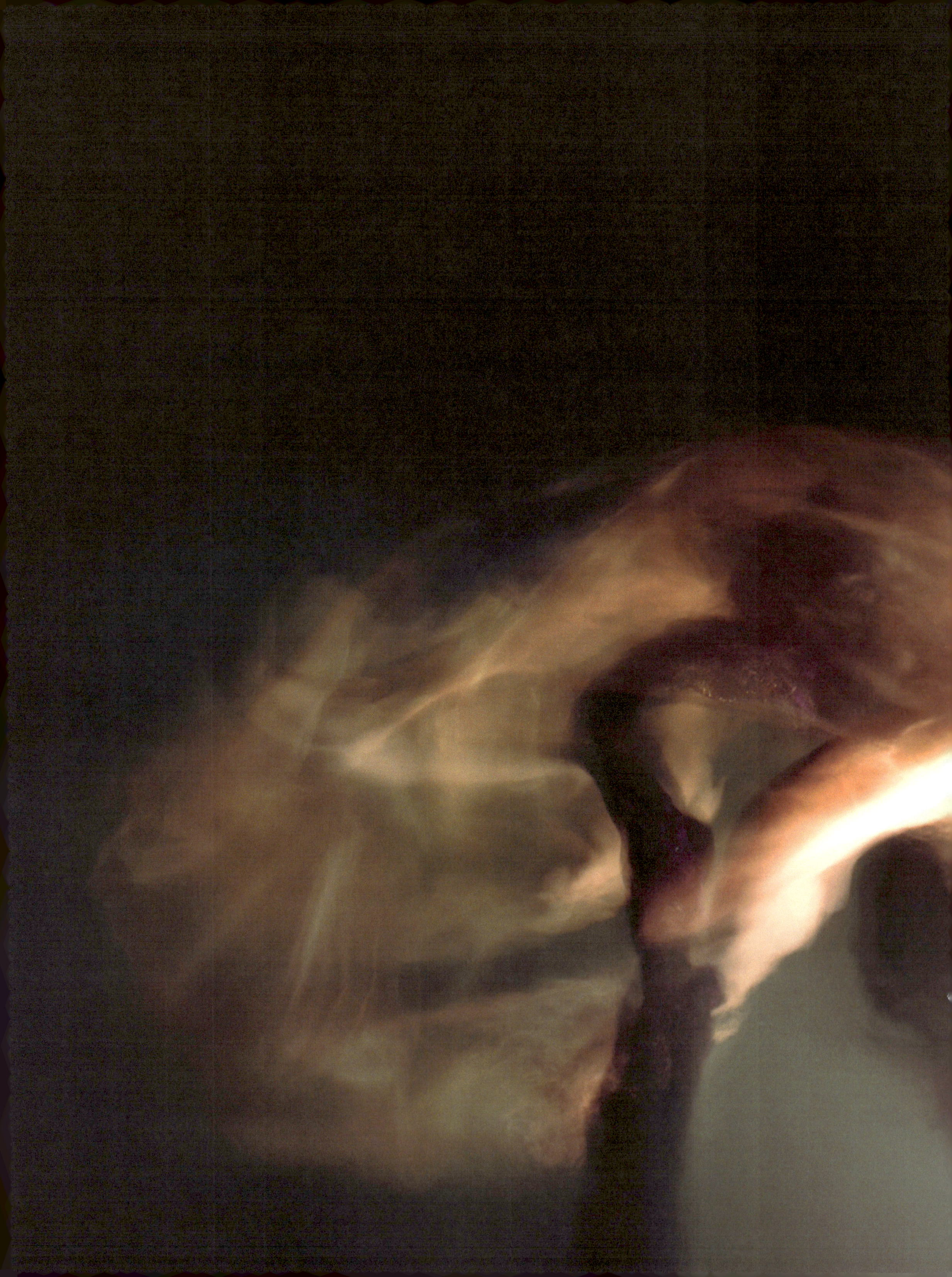

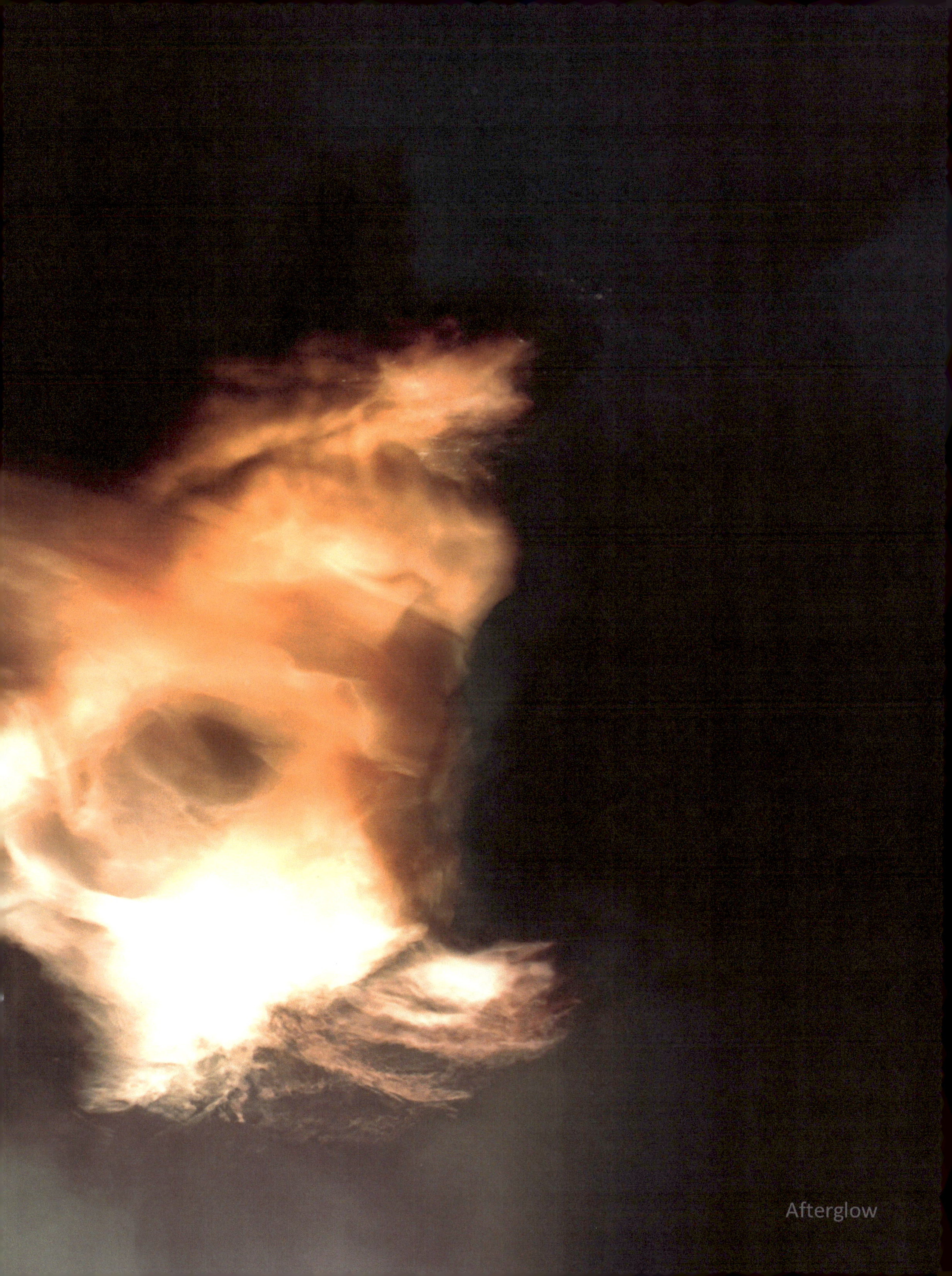

Afterglow

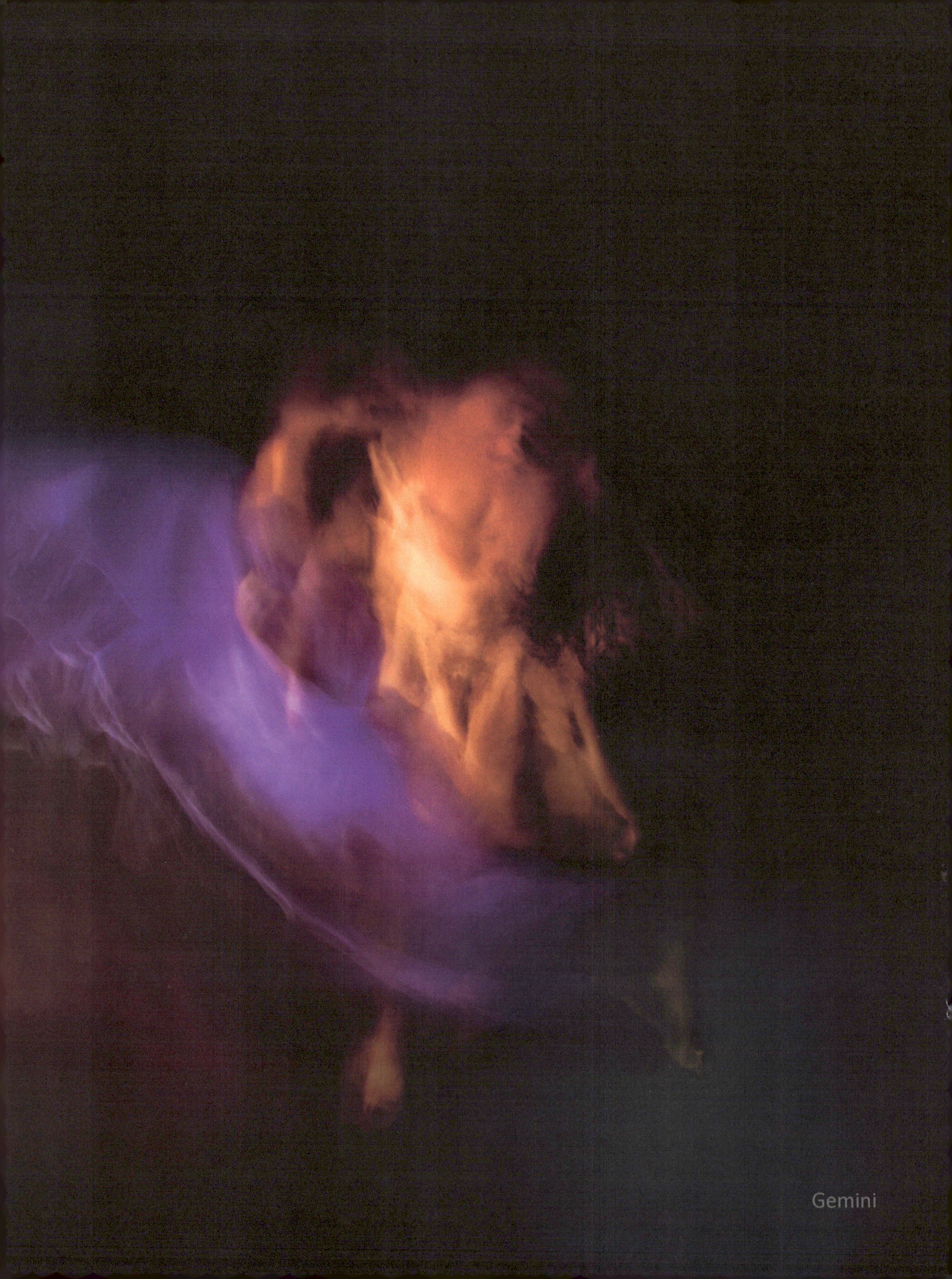

Gemini

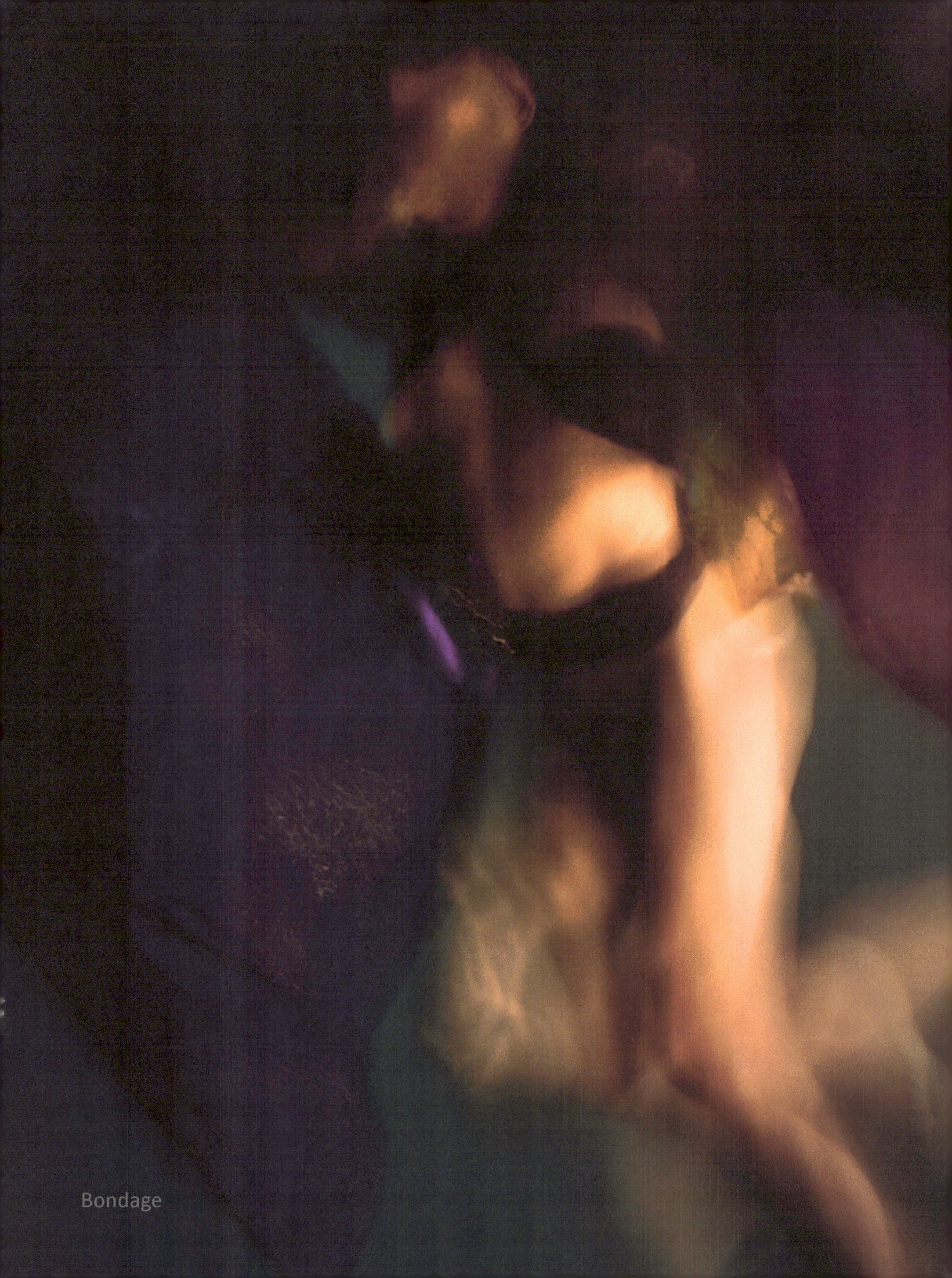

Bondage

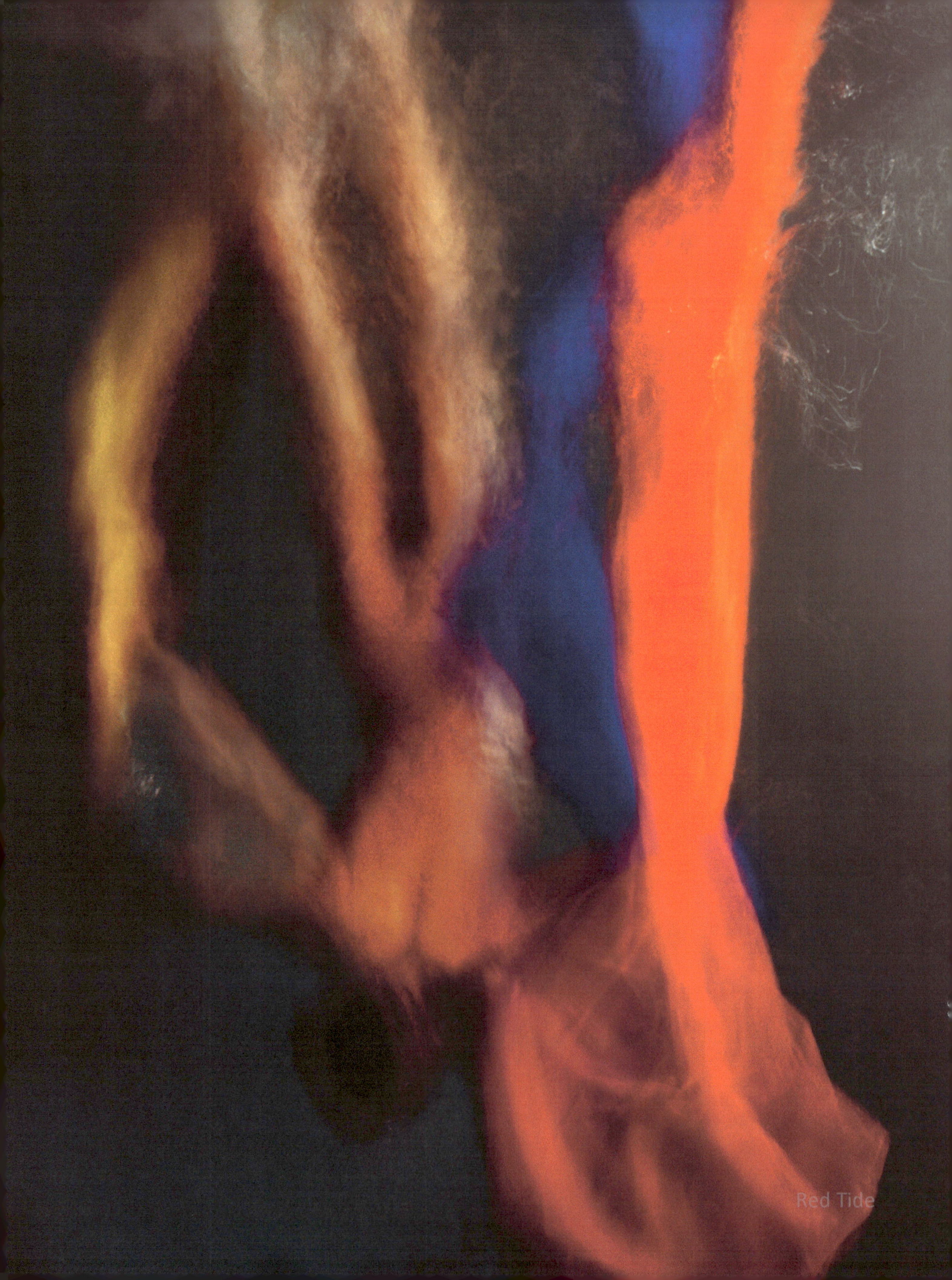

Red Tide

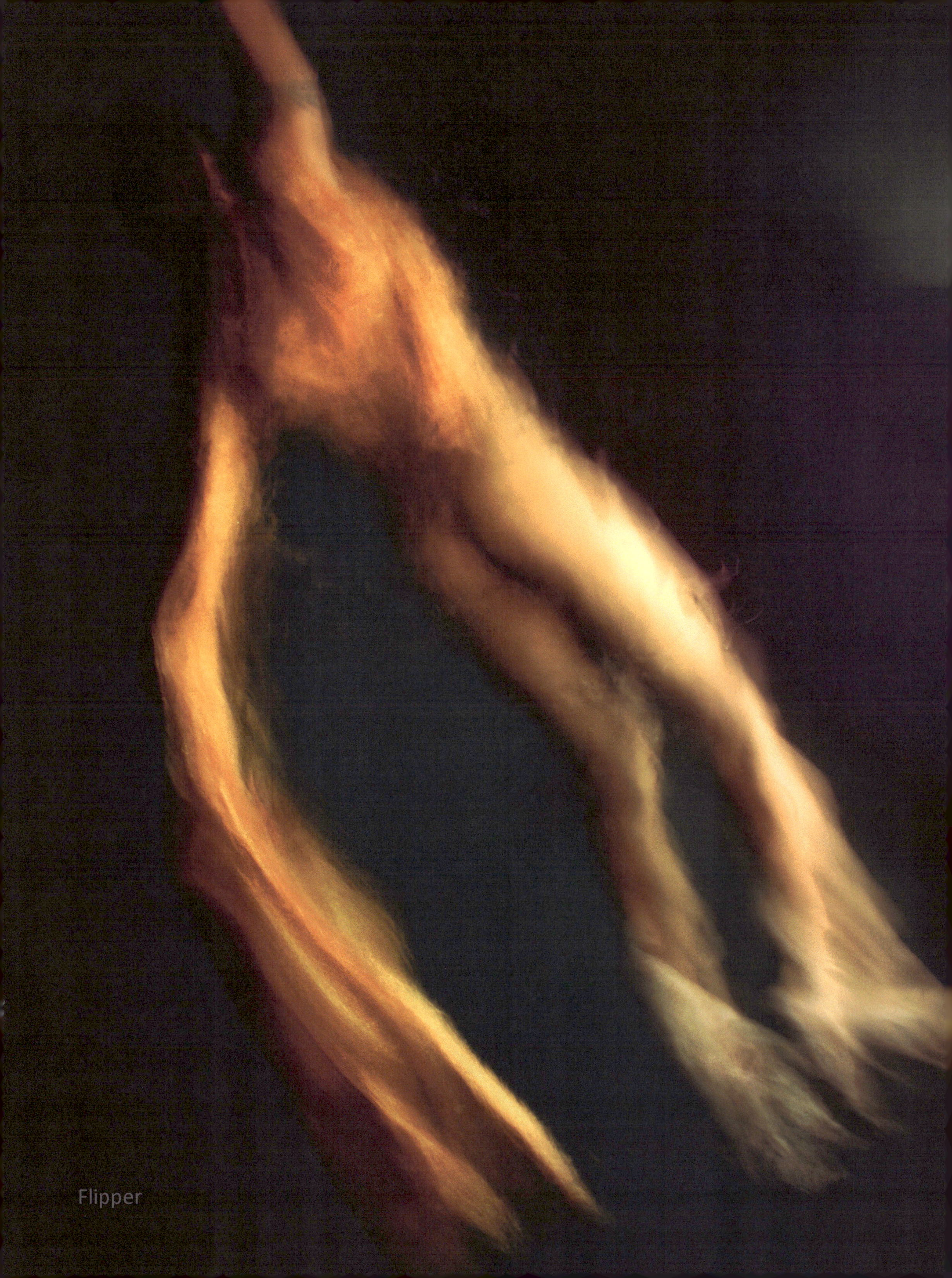

Flipper

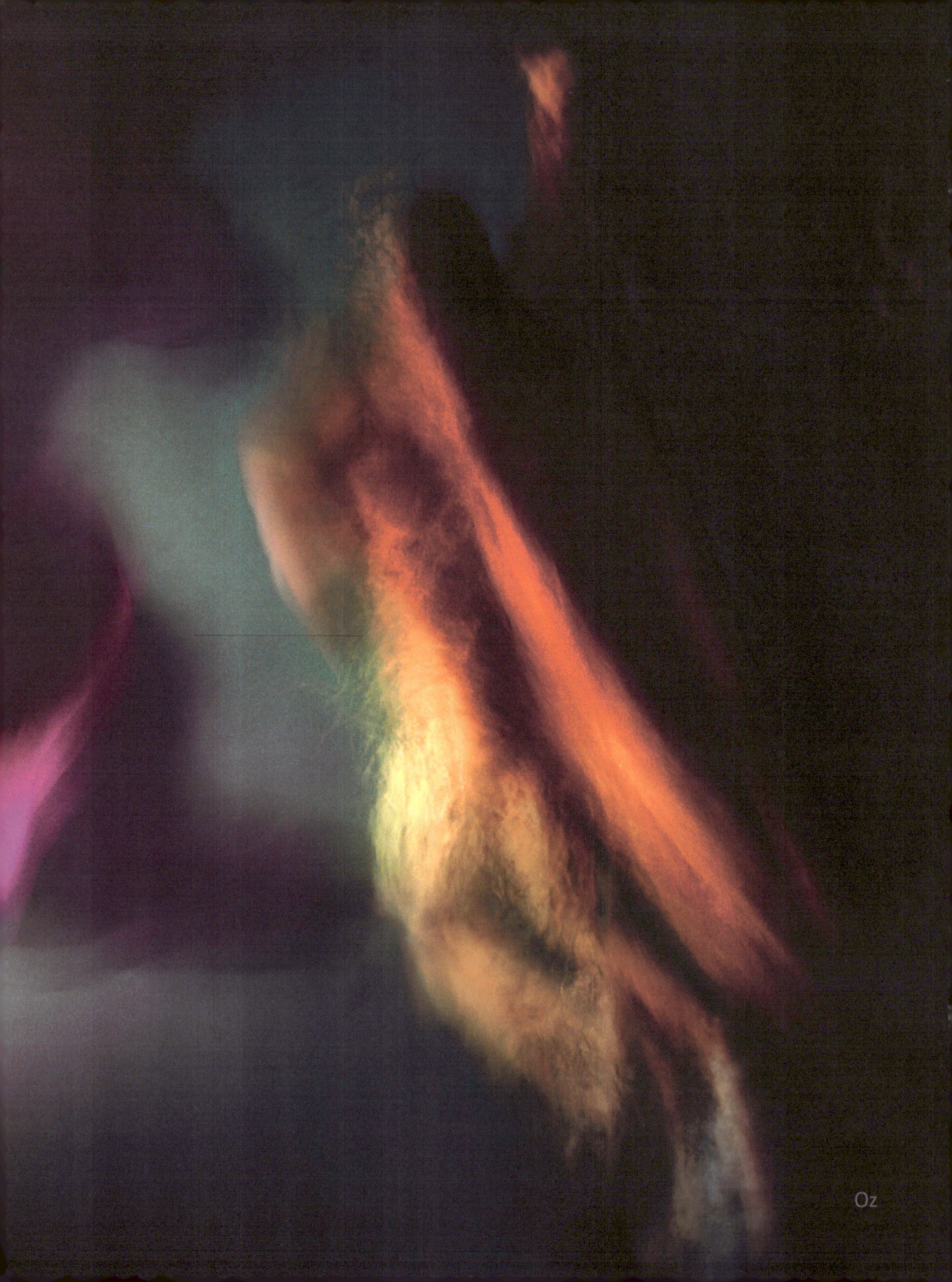

Oz

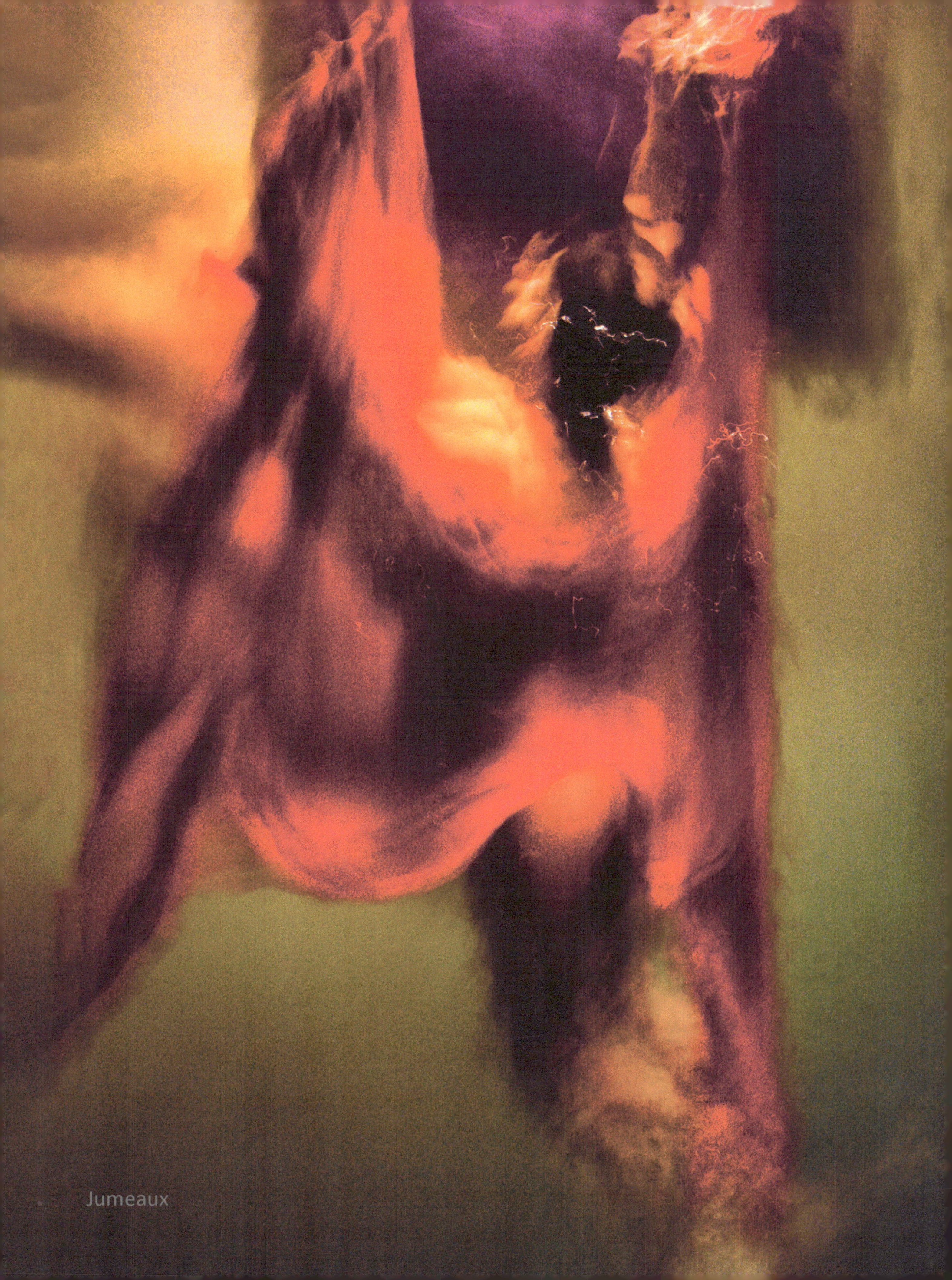

Jumeaux

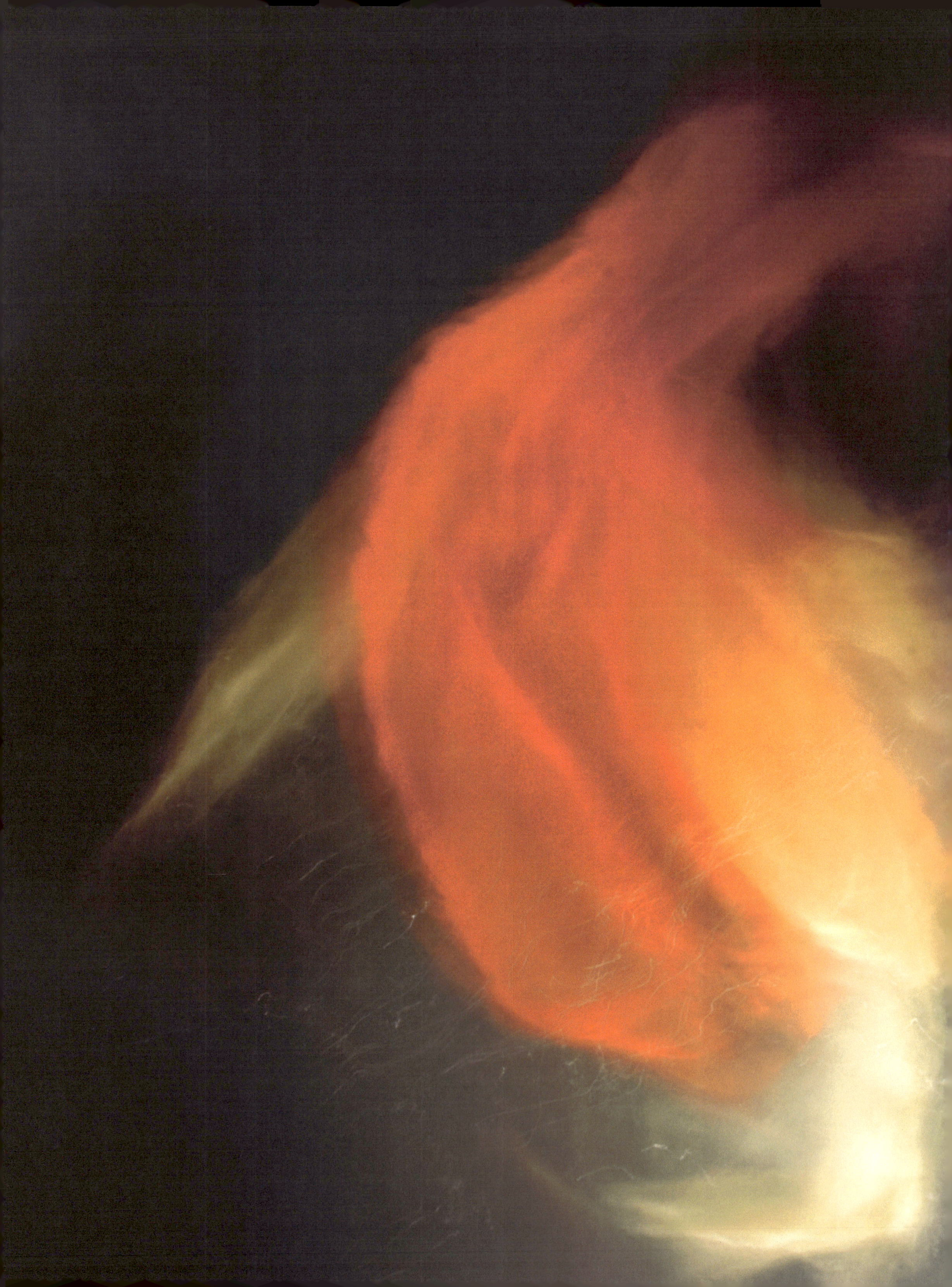

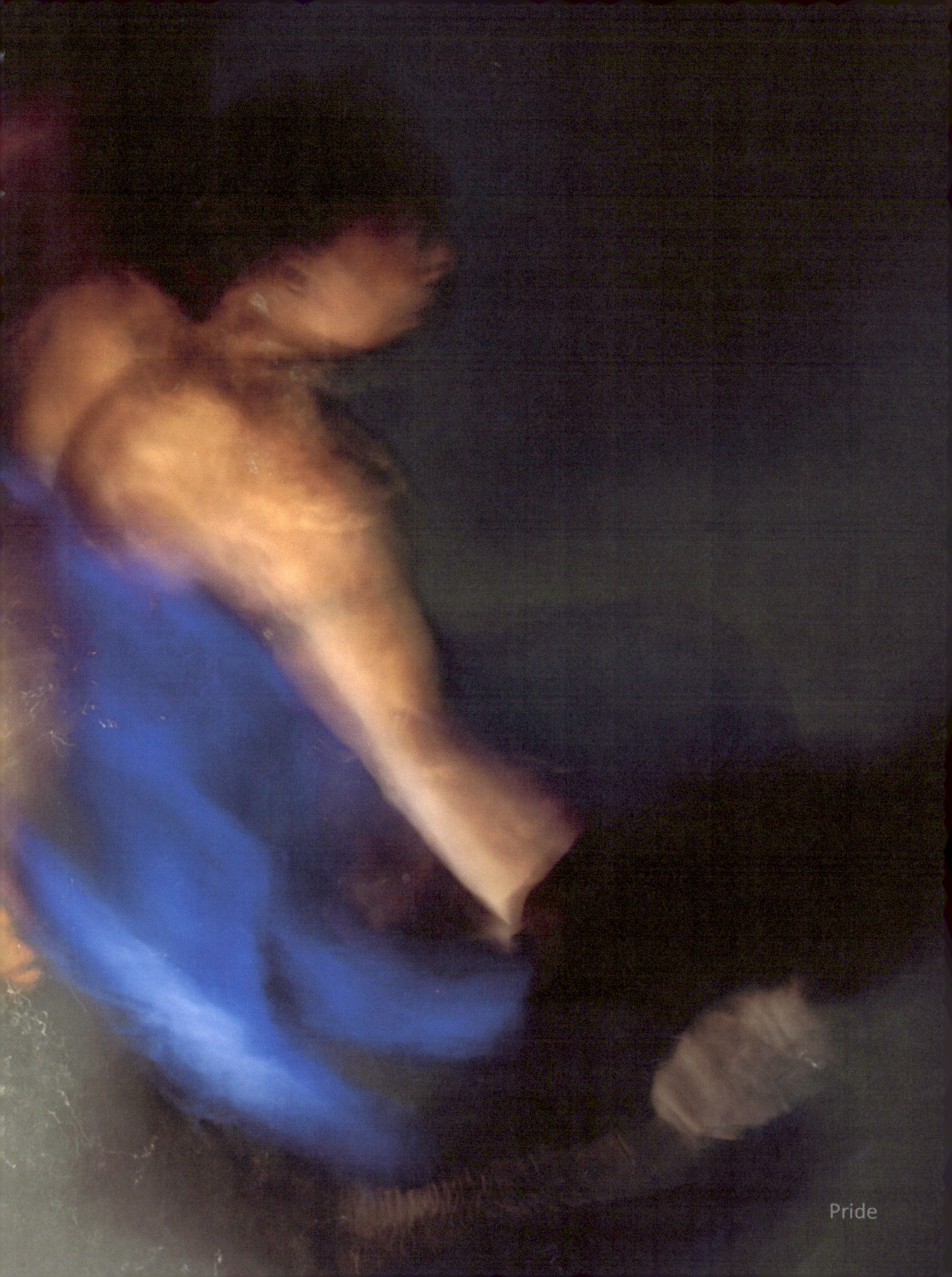

Pride

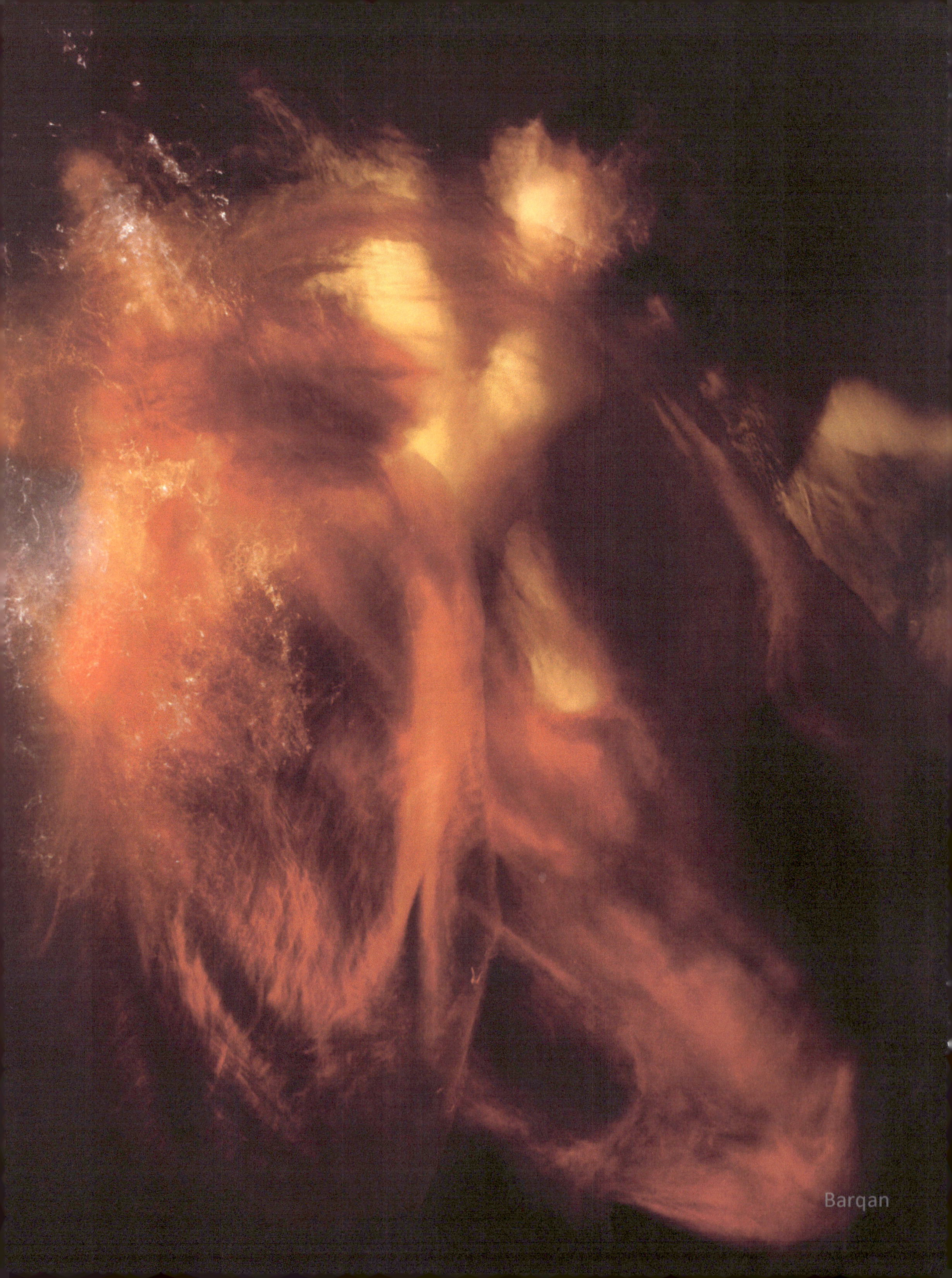
Barqan

About the Artist

Stephen Moody, a renowned artist and master photographer located in Scottsdale, AZ has dedicated his craft to the abstract representation of the human form. Despite his initial foray into Communications and Broadcast Journalism, Moody's passion for creating art proved to be irresistible, drawing him into the world of visual expression.

Driven by his profound love for art and the human form, Moody embarked on a journey that would lead him to create a series of passionate artworks with a spiritual essence. His pieces resonate deeply within the heart, capturing the essence of the human experience and offering a glimpse into the transcendent nature of our existence.

To explore Moody's remarkable artwork, visit his website at https://www.MaleArtForm.com, where you can browse and purchase pieces to adorn your home or business. Experience the unique "Live Preview AR" feature that allows you to envision your favorite artwork hanging on your own walls.

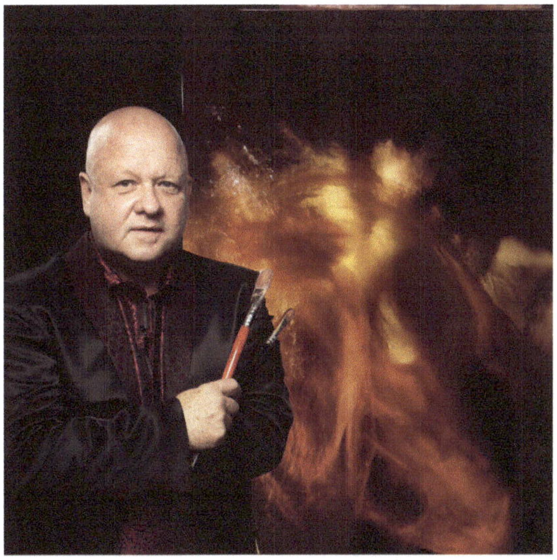

Stay connected with Stephen Moody on social media to keep up with his latest creations and insights. Follow him on Instagram (@stephenmoodyartist), Facebook (@stephenmoodyartist), and Twitter (@smoodyauthor) to witness his ongoing artistic journey and engage with his vibrant community of art enthusiasts.

Lastly, as the author and artist, Stephen Moody expresses his heartfelt gratitude to all readers and art appreciators who have supported his work. If you enjoyed his book and artwork, kindly consider leaving a review on Amazon.com or BarnesandNoble.com as it serves as a catalyst for new readers to discover his captivating creations.

www.ingramcontent.com/pod-product-compliance
Lightning Source LLC
Chambersburg PA
CBHW041457280526
45792CB00004B/1037
9798988469711